IMAGES
of America

HUNTLEY

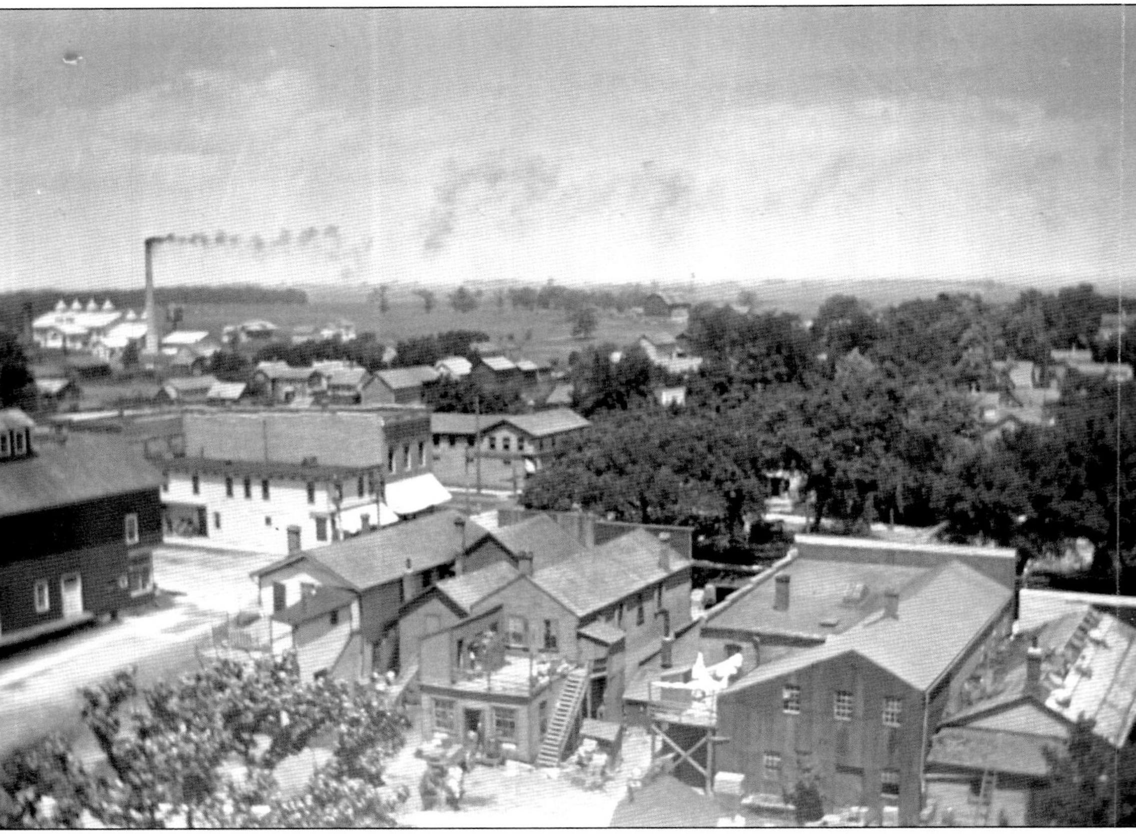

This panoramic view of Huntley is looking slightly to the northwest. Carl Schmalz, who snapped the cover photograph, also took this shot, most likely in the same year, by climbing the town water tower. The backs of the Main Street shops are visible. The trees in the center mark the town square park. At the upper left, the modern, sprawling, Borden's milk factory with its soaring, smoking chimney is in business. (Courtesy of Robert Schmalz.)

On the cover: Town and country meet in this Schmalz family get together sometime around 1915. Huntley-born Carl Schmalz snapped this shot of his father, Otto Schmalz, far right, and his mother, Hattie, far left, visiting relatives on a farm just outside of Huntley. The Schmalz family lived in town where Otto owned a general store. His brother-in-law Will Anderson is pictured in the center. The women are Hattie's sister Minnie (Howe) Bush, left of center, and Otto's sister Agnes (Schmalz) Anderson, right of center. (Courtesy of Robert Schmalz.)

IMAGES
of America

HUNTLEY

Nancy S. Bacheller

ARCADIA
PUBLISHING

ISBN 978-0-7385-6067-0

Published by Arcadia Publishing
Charleston, South Carolina

Printed in the United States of America

Library of Congress Catalog Card Number: 2008939827

For all general information contact Arcadia Publishing at:
Telephone 843-853-2070
Fax 843-853-0044
E-mail sales@arcadiapublishing.com
For customer service and orders:
Toll-Free 1-888-313-2665

Visit us on the Internet at www.arcadiapublishing.com

To Tom, for everything,
and for Brian and Jay

Contents

Acknowledgments		6
Introduction		7
1.	Beginnings	9
2.	Milk and Farming	17
3.	Churches	37
4.	School Days	45
5.	A Mark in the World	57
6.	Historic Square and Aerials	63
7.	Having Fun	77
8.	Life in Huntley	91
9.	Doing Business	107

ACKNOWLEDGMENTS

Before I agreed to take on the project of preparing this book, I knew there was one person whose complete support and approval was absolutely necessary. I told my good friend and noted local historian Mary Beth Manning (a descendant of Huntley founding families), "I can't do it without you." Her contributions to this book have been endless and invaluable. I cannot thank her enough.

In beginning this project, I did not think I would be able to find the 200 historic photographs required for the book. But Huntley people were so incredibly generous, helpful, enthusiastic, and supportive, that I found I far exceeded the required number of photographs. In the end, many pictures did not make it into the book, but all materials that were so generously shared have been added to the Huntley Area Public Library's local history collection.

I gratefully acknowledge the support of the Huntley Area Public Library and its wonderful staff, especially director Virginia Maravilla and reference librarian Scott Lindsey.

Thank you also to Tom and Barbara Conley, who brought me tubs full of old Huntley photographs. Thank you also to Robert Schmalz, Doug Cataldo, Noel and Lillian Hansmann, Bill Byrne and the Kreutzer family, Jake Marino, Dick Michelsen, Vernon and Shirley Drendel, Jim Drendel, Earl "Pete" Kalsow, Sue Melby, Rita McMahon and the Village of Huntley, Helen Marlowe, Carol and Wayne Donahue, Ralph Drafall, Doris Marsh, Gene and Norma Lindsey, Thom Palmer and the Huntley Park District, Steve Grechis, Ann and Tim Essig, Theresa Darby, Donna and Tom Kalsow, Lonni Oldham, McHenry County Historical Society, Mary Ellen Moerke, School District 158, Rev. Charles Kittel and Trinity Lutheran Church, Sue Paulsen, William Leggee, Margene Mobley, Barbara Hemmer Ernesti, Margaret and Joseph Manning, Linda Moore, Jim Weltzien, Vi Williams, Jaye Powers, Don Peasley, and, especially, Tom Bacheller.

This book is by no means the complete and definitive history of Huntley. If anyone has additional historical information or photographs, they are urged to contact the Huntley Area Public Library.

Introduction

It was milk that made Huntley grow big and strong. Milk made Huntley prosper.

When the Native Americans vacated the northern Illinois area following the Black Hawk War, white immigrants from the east took up residence. The new settlers traveled for weeks by wagon, often bringing with them broods of children and several of their best dairy cows. They purchased their sections of land from the federal government and took up farming.

From the 1830s to the 1850s, the main purpose of the farms was for subsistence for the families, but the fertile soils of the northern Illinois area proved to be a boon to the farmers. A surplus of farm products developed, and entrepreneurs found a way to bring these products to market. Creameries, cheese factories, and milk processing and condensing plants were built around the area. The arrival of the Chicago and North Western Railway line into Huntley in 1851 brought the farmers a means to ship their excess milk, eggs, butter, cattle, and other farm surplus into the big city and beyond.

The newly emerging village of Huntley prospered and grew as a result. Feed and seed supply stores, hotels, general stores, blacksmiths, wagon makers, livery stables, and numerous other businesses began to emerge to support the local farmers and their growing milk trade.

The July 21, 1894, edition of the *Huntley News* reported, "Farmers in the district surrounding Huntley produce more milk to the square mile than any other area in the world." The same article reported on one particularly successful enterprise, noting, "The Huntley cheese factory owned by Messrs. Weltzien and Cornell is the largest in capacity and output of any in existence." It further stated, "The average receipts of the creamery are not less than ten tons of milk for every day in the year." It was these early successful businessmen and farmers who built the town of Huntley.

Thomas Stillwell Huntley already was a wealthy man when he arrived in the area from New York in 1846 with his wife and three children. He purchased several hundred acres of land, including 80 acres along what was to be the railroad line. He maintained his many farms, but donated and platted what was to become a village. He set aside land for churches and a cemetery, sold other lots for businesses and homes, and opened a general store.

With the growing milk trade came continued prosperity for Huntley. From the late 1850s through the 1920s, the village was a growing, bustling community center with an active, thriving downtown square.

The town, known first as Huntley Grove or Huntley Station, incorporated in 1872 as the Village of Huntley. John Cummings, the son of one of the area's earliest settlers, was named village president.

In 1839, the first religious services in the area were held in the home of early settler Prescott Whittemore. He and his wife, Lucy Geer Whittemore, had arrived in the area in 1838 with their brood of 10 children. Their family was among the first to hold local offices, to run a local hotel, and to name the township Grafton in honor of their New Hampshire home.

More organized religious congregations developed over the years. Three churches were established in the village: Lutheran, Catholic, and Congregational. All three were built on property donated by Huntley, a deeply religious man. He was a founder and active member of the First Congregational Church.

As the town grew, so did the need for educational facilities. The first school was established in a log cabin to the west of the future town in 1842. The first teacher was Cynthia Thompson. In 1860, a school was established along east Main Street, then later moved to Church Street to make way for a newer, more modern brick building. That school, built in 1875 to the east of the Congregational church, and the various one-room rural schools that dotted the countryside served Huntley-area children for many years.

In January 1920, nine rural school districts voted to combine with the Huntley town school to form McHenry County's first consolidated school district. Busses brought rural students into town for education. The large brick edifice that already had been expanded in 1909 no longer could house all students from elementary through high school. A new high school was built in 1924 east of the earlier school. That building was in use until 1955. During the late 1800s and early 1900s, as more students funneled into the town school, the community continued to grow.

In the 1920s, trucking made it possible to ship whole milk to larger, more modern factories near Chicago where pasteurization was available, and Huntley's local milk plants began to close. Farming and dairy production continued to be the area's main industry.

When Grafton Township was founded in 1850, the area population was recorded at 440. By 1870, the township population had grown to 1,359. The U.S. Census Bureau recorded Huntley's town population in 1880 at 505 and in 1910 as 773. But by 1920, the population had begun to decline. As elsewhere in the country, trade and social activities suffered during the Depression years of the 1930s. A cultural highlight for Huntley residents at that time was the weekly free movies in the town square park, as businesses attempted to draw customers into town.

With the milk factories closed, many residents took jobs in other communities, especially the watch factory in Elgin.

When what previously had been only a local dirt road known as Vine Street was paved and extended in 1936, Huntley residents could travel to Woodstock and beyond along Route 47.

With the milk factories closing, other manufacturers took over use of the plant facilities. After prohibition ended in 1933, beer was produced at the former Jelke milk factory. Bel Boy, Indian Maid, and Copperhead beer were brewed at the site on south Church Street that most recently housed Catty Corporation.

The Route 47 facility now occupied by Union Special was once Borden's milk plant, a much-noted landmark and the jewel in the crown of the Huntley milking industry. After the milk factory closed, the facility became a furniture factory and later the William Fencil Gasket Company.

When World War II broke out, William Fencil brought more industry to Huntley with its fuze plant division. That facility was built on a farm just to the southeast of the village limits. For three years during the 1940s, the company made detonator caps for weapons for use in the war. The company provided jobs for hundreds of local and McHenry County residents.

Dean's Milk Company brought jobs to Huntley after the war when its new plant opened in 1946. Union Special, a maker of industrial sewing machines, took over the old Borden plant in 1948 and became the largest employer in the area. With Dean Foods and Union Special, the Huntley community again began to thrive, and the population slowly started to increase.

However, the population never exceeded 2,000 residents until the 1990s. It was then that the area's longtime farmers found they could make more money selling their valuable land than they could farming it, and once again the village of Huntley began to grow.

More than 100 years later, the land that produced an excess of milk now produces an abundance of homes. With Del Webb's Sun City and other new subdivisions, Huntley has grown to be a thriving 21st century community.

One

Beginnings

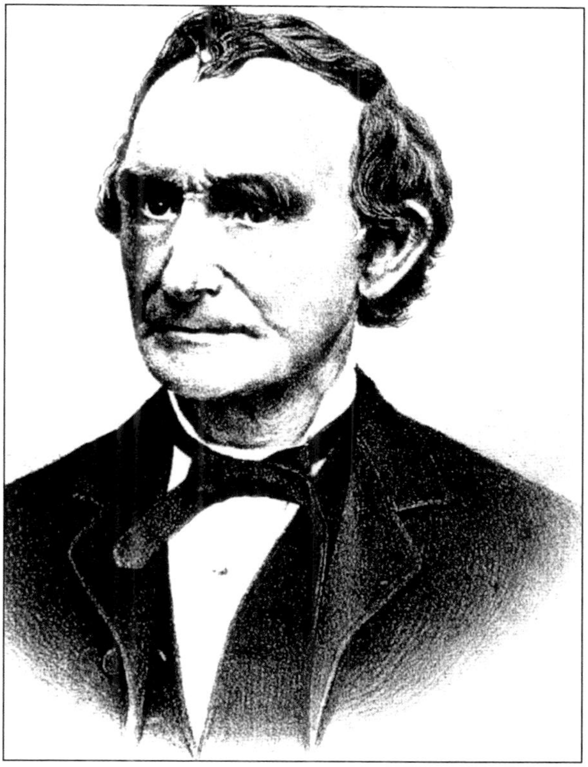

The village of Huntley is named for Thomas Stillwell Huntley. Born March 27, 1807, in Cortland County, New York, Huntley married Eliza Fox in 1830. They had three children: Charles, Harriet, and William. The Huntleys arrived to northern Illinois in 1846, eventually purchasing 80 acres along what was to be the Chicago and North Western Railway line. From that 80 acres, Huntley generously provided a site for the train station, a small general store, businesses, and homes, and he earmarked three sites for churches and set aside land for a central town park. (Courtesy of Huntley Area Public Library.)

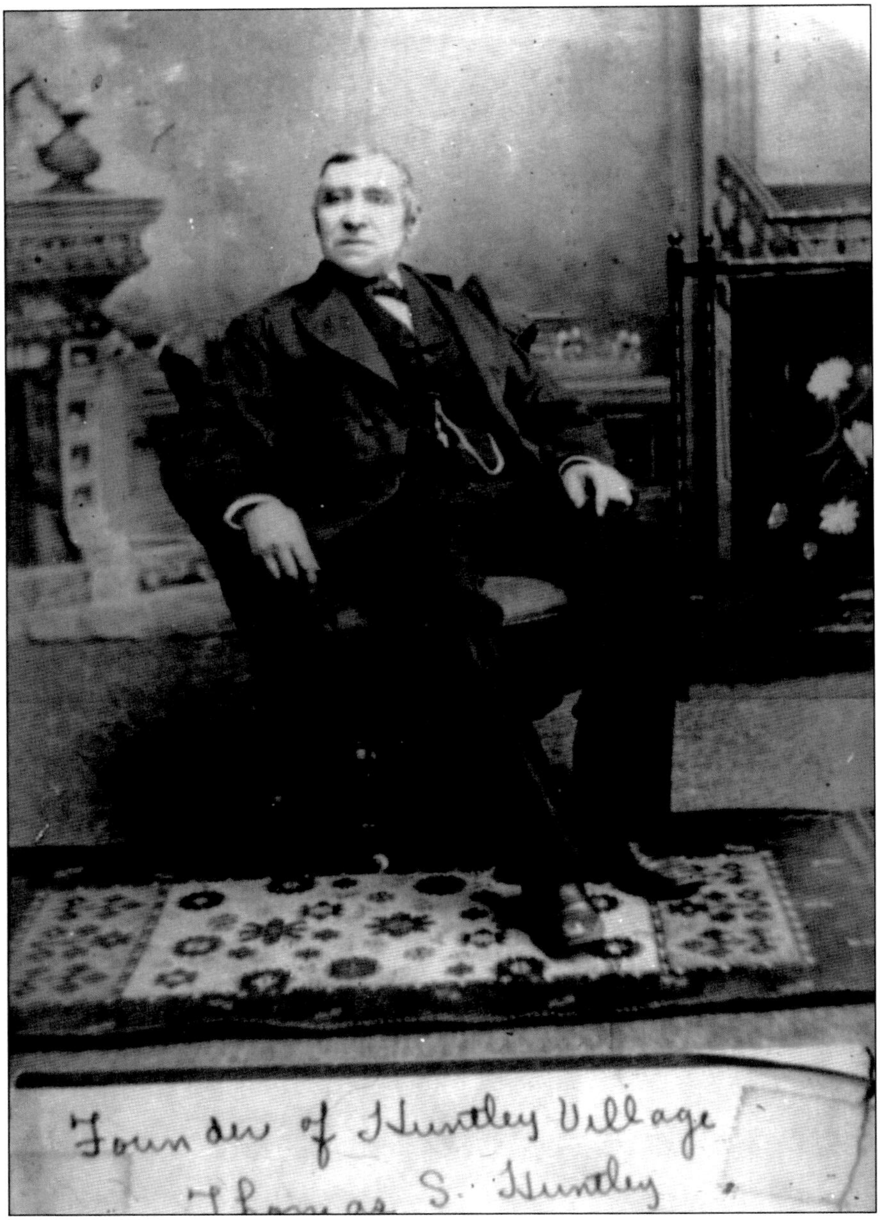

This undated photograph of Thomas Stillwell Huntley shows the village's namesake in his later life. He was a much loved, well-respected citizen for whom the town was named Huntley Station, also known as Huntley Grove, and, later, simply Huntley in his honor. Although public spirited, he held only one elected office, that of the first supervisor of Grafton Township in 1850. Huntley outlived most of his family. His wife Eliza died in 1873 and all three of their children predeceased him. In 1876, Huntley married Emma Brinkerhoff. At the time, he was 69 years old and she was 34. Their son Thomas Jr. was born in 1878. Emma died in 1882, leaving the 75-year-old Huntley to raise their nearly four-year-old son. Huntley died on May 21, 1894, at the age of 87. His obituary stated that his "kindness and generosity will always be remembered so long as the history of this town remains." (Courtesy of Huntley Area Public Library.)

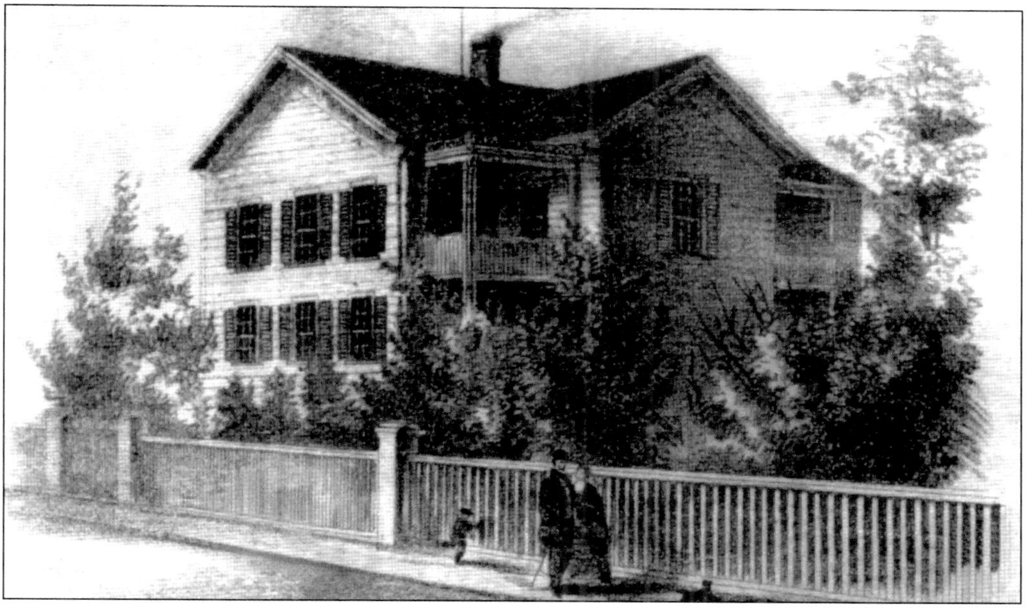

This early illustration shows the federal-style home Huntley built in 1856 at the southeast corner of Woodstock and Third Streets. Huntley was a wealthy landowner who bought and sold property and made loans to others in the years before a bank was opened in town. McHenry County tax records for 1851 indicate Huntley's land holdings had reached 880 acres by that time. (Courtesy of Tom and Barb Conley.)

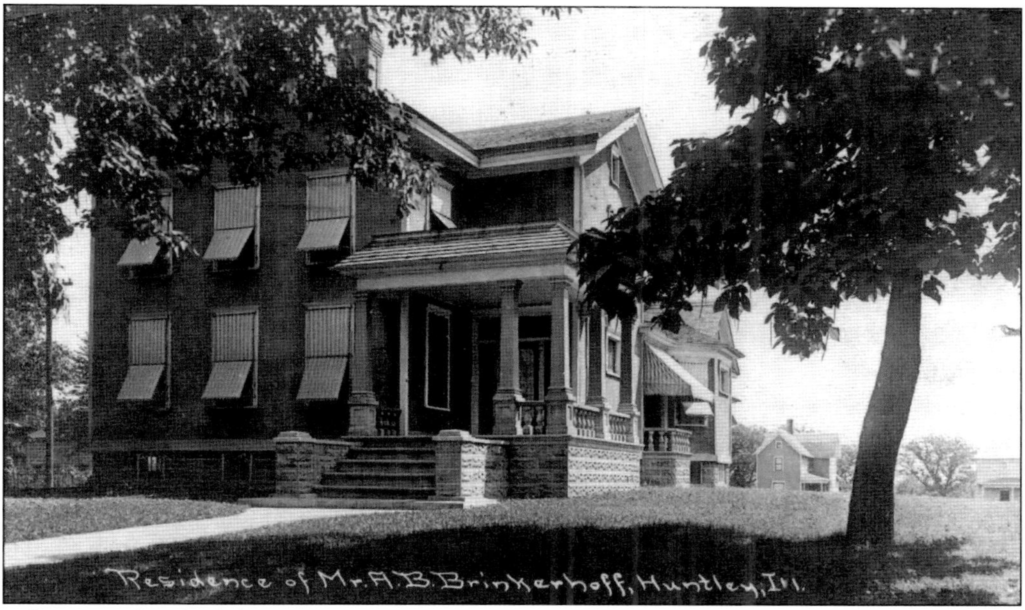

When Huntley died, his son Thomas Jr. was just 15 years old. Huntley willed the Woodstock Street house to his late wife Emma's brother Abram Brinkerhoff, who was to care for young Thomas Jr. This photograph shows the changes the Brinkerhoffs made to the home in 1906, including doubling the size and removing the clapboard, shutters, and corbels and applying the then very popular stucco material. (Courtesy of Tom and Barb Conley.)

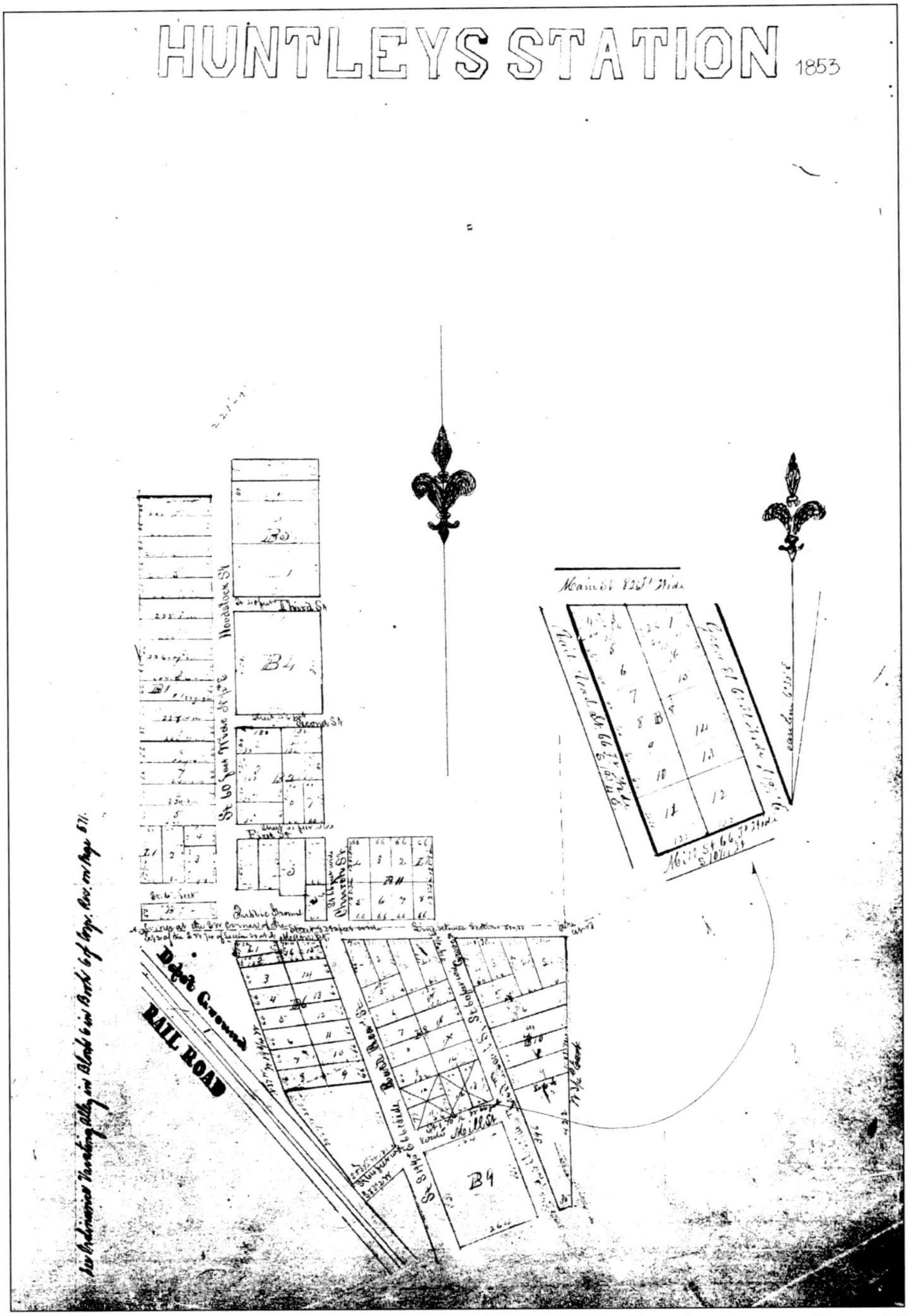

The village of Huntley was known first as Huntley Grove or Huntley Station. From 1851 to 1853, Thomas Stillwell Huntley deeded many parcels of his property to serve various purposes in the town. He donated land for churches, public grounds, and the railroad depot and sold lots for homes and businesses. This plat shows the streets with their names designated as well as indications as to how wide each street was to be. Most of this old section of town still exists today as it was platted by Huntley in the early 1850s.

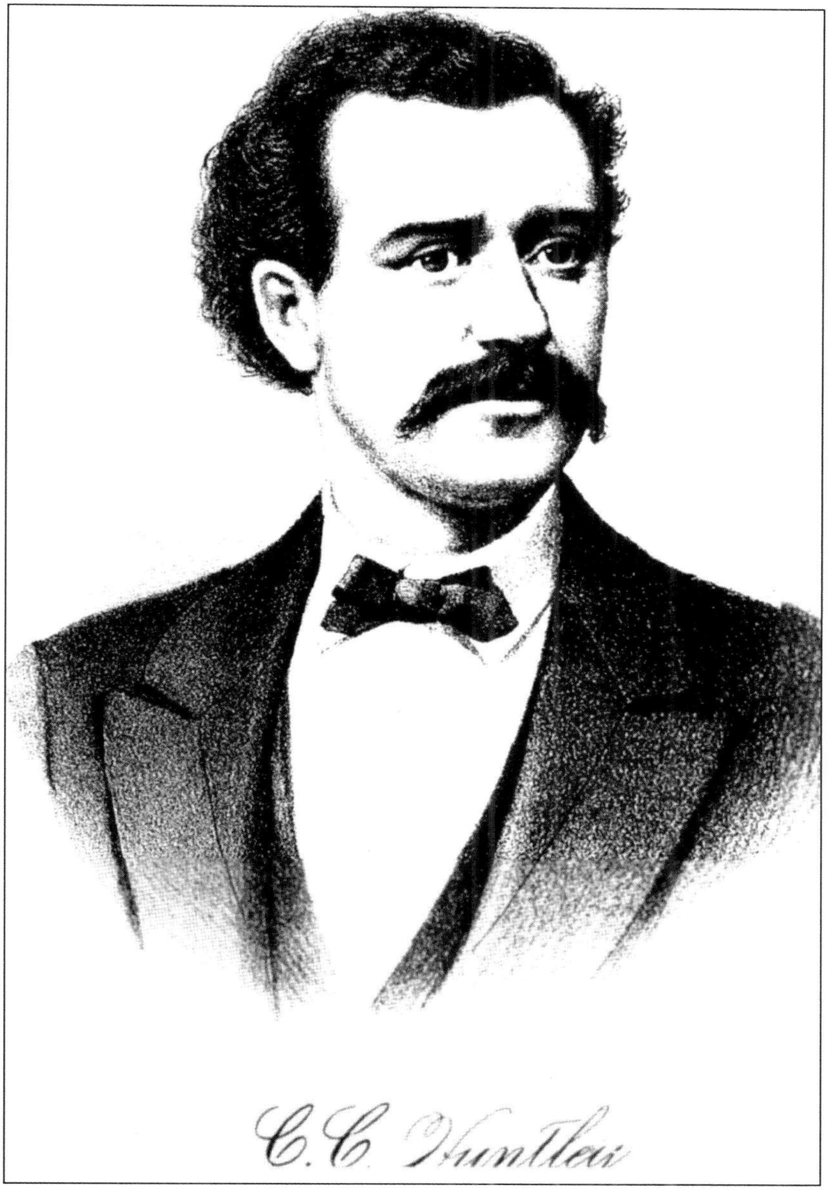

Charles Clarence Huntley (1834–1883), the son of Thomas Stillwell Huntley and Eliza Fox, came to Illinois with his family when he was 12 years old. He was among the first from the area to enlist when the Civil War broke out, serving as a lieutenant and, later, a captain in the 16th Illinois Cavalry. His troops were captured after a long battle at Strawberry Plains, Virginia, and he spent the remainder of the war in southern prisoner of war camps, including the notorious Andersonville Prison in Georgia. After the war, he established passenger stagecoach and mail routes through Oregon and California and the territories of Utah, Idaho, and Washington. The Wells Fargo Company eventually purchased the routes to add to their existing routes. Charles was a wealthy man when paralysis, brought on by exposure and starvation during his prisoner of war years, caused him to return home to Huntley, where he died at age 49. (Courtesy of Huntley Area Public Library.)

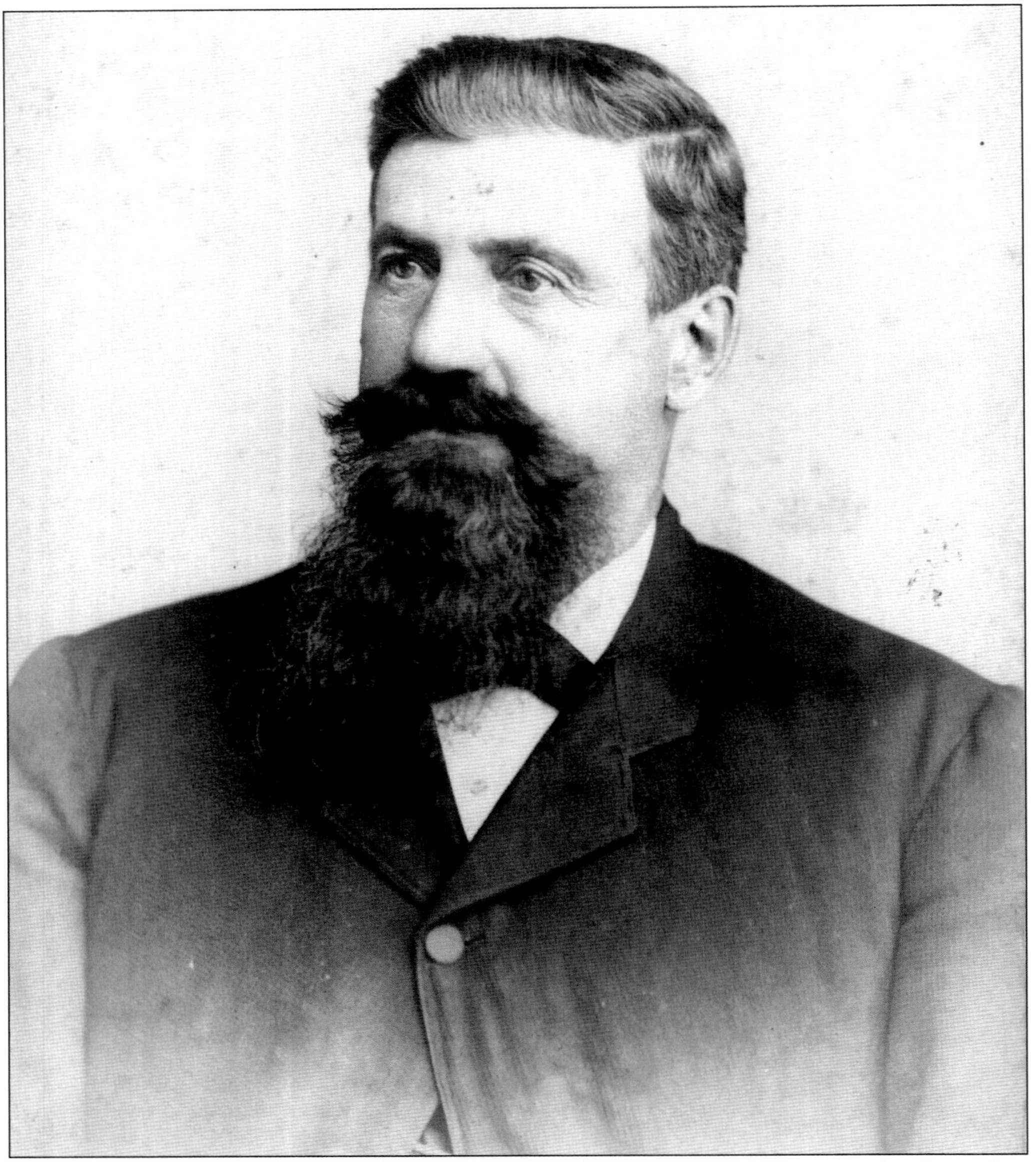

Huntley's first village president, John S. Cummings (1830–1912), was the son of early settlers Guy and Eleanor Cummings, who arrived in the area about 1838. Their family, consisting of 13 children, settled on 200 acres of land along what is now west Main Street and built the farmstead today known as the Huntley Park District's Sun Valley Farm. John S. Cummings served as Huntley's town constable before he was 21 years old, then left the position to follow the gold rush to California in 1852. He returned to Huntley in 1857 and purchased half of his father's farm. John was a member of the lively Huntley Brass Band from 1859 until he and most of its other members left to serve in the Civil War. He enlisted as a musician with the volunteer Seventh Illinois Regiment Band. When Huntley incorporated as a village in 1872, he was its first president. When the Huntley Library and Literary Association was organized in 1880, he was its first president. In 1885, he was Grafton Township assessor. (Courtesy of Huntley Area Public Library.)

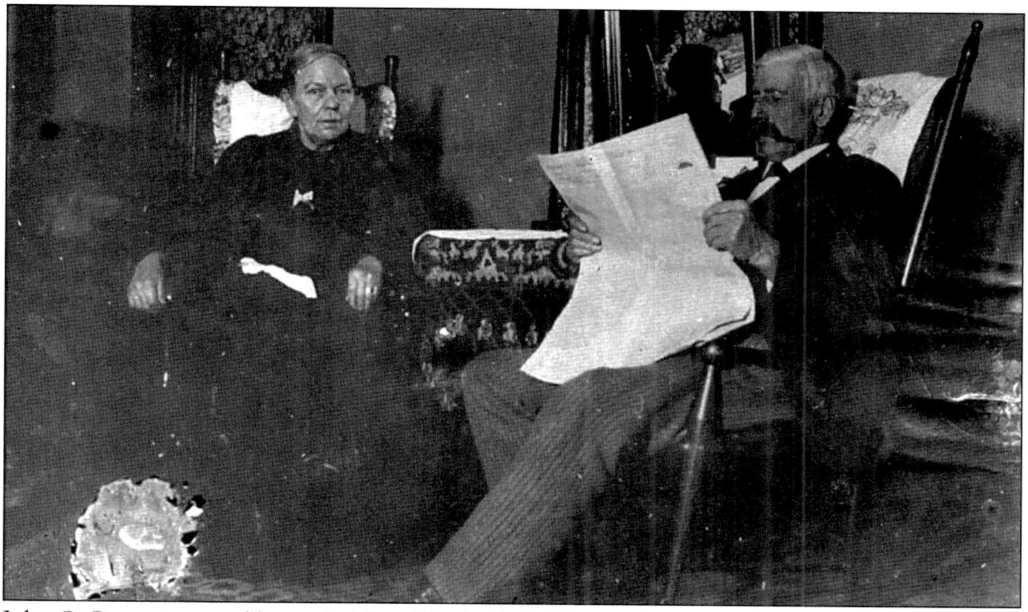

John S. Cummings and his wife, Mary Elizabeth Baldwin, relax in their Woodstock Street home in this photograph from an 1898 album. As Huntley's first village president, he was a successful businessman, selling agricultural implements and real estate. He was a very public spirited man who was said to have held every office in town from constable to supervisor and was also McHenry County coroner for one term. (Courtesy of Tom and Barb Conley.)

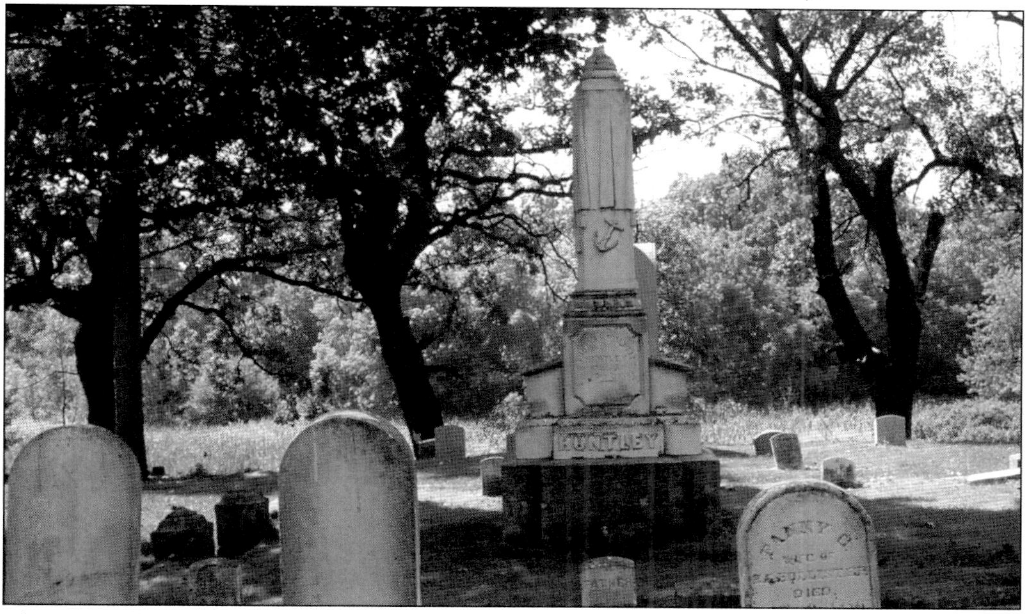

Thomas Stillwell Huntley, his children Charles, Harriet, and William, and his two wives, Eliza and Emma Annette, are buried in the family plot in the Huntley Cemetery on Dean Street. Huntley donated the land for the cemetery where his young son William, who died at age 14 in December 1852, was among the first to be buried. Other founding families, including the Cummings, also are buried in the cemetery. (Courtesy of Gene and Norma Lindsey.)

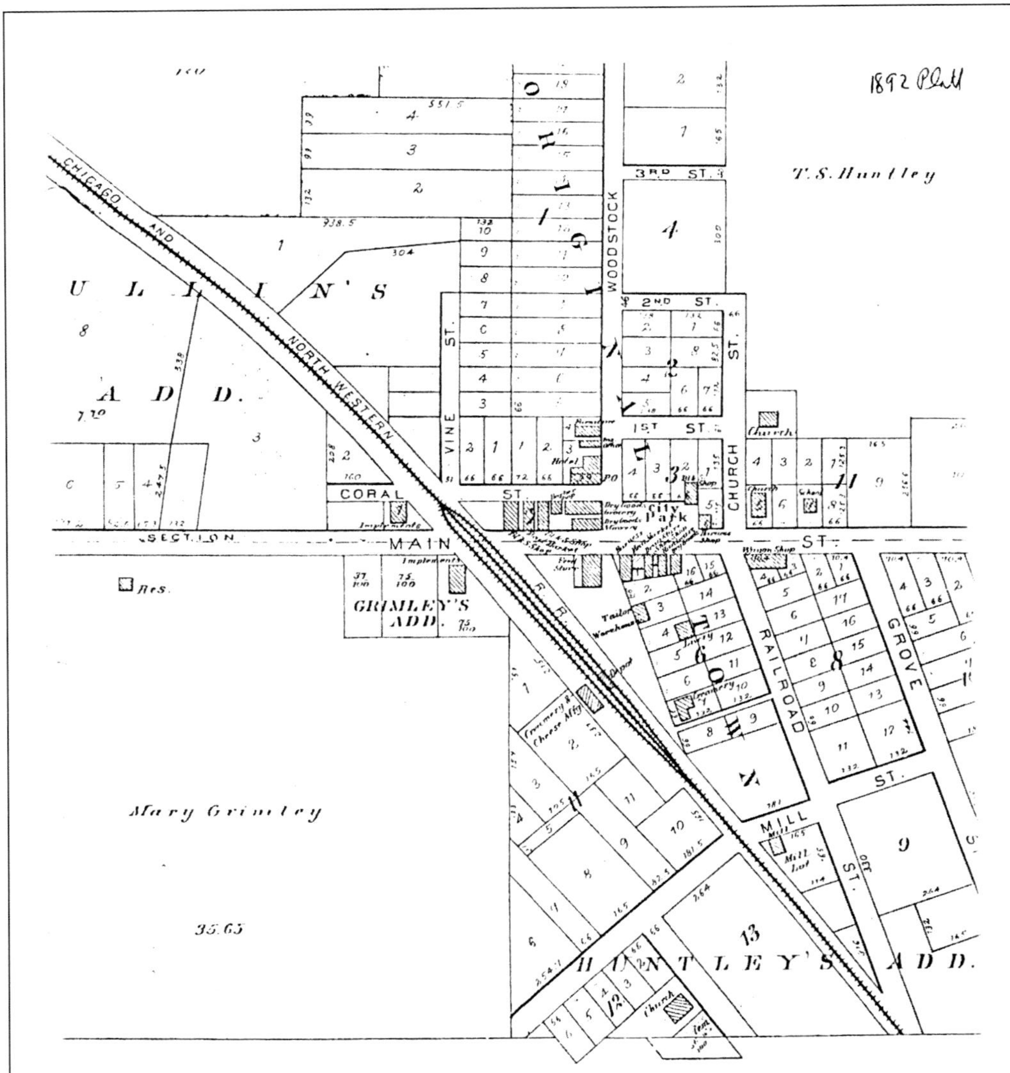

This 1892 plat map shows Huntley's growth in the years since it was first laid out in the early 1850s. New home and business lots were opened to the west of the railroad tracks. St. Mary Catholic Church is indicated to the far south of town next to the town cemetery. Both pieces of property were donated by Thomas Stillwell Huntley. The name of the road marked Railroad Street later was changed to Church Street to reflect the southern extension of that road, and the extension of Woodstock Street south of Main Street became known as Railroad Street. This better reflected the location of the street that paralleled the train tracks. The types of businesses in operation as well as the locations of the three churches and the school all are indicated on the map.

Two

MILK AND FARMING

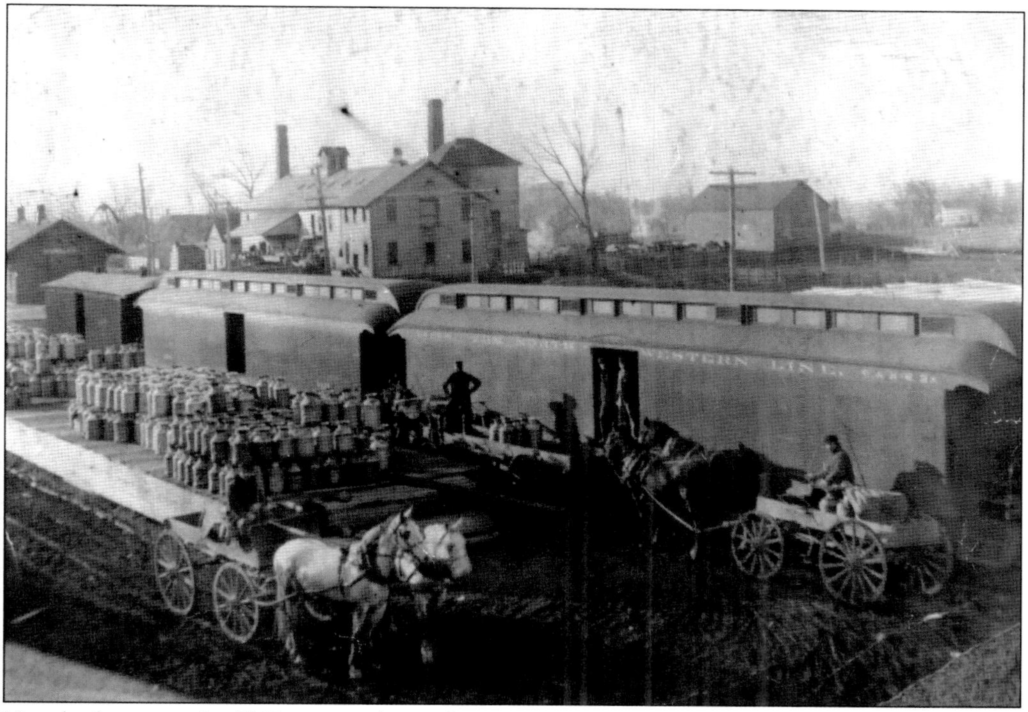

Huntley began in the 1840s primarily as a farming community. Families worked the land for their own subsistence. Good times made a surplus of farm products available, and farmers were able to produce enough milk to supply local creameries and to send to other milk plants in Chicago. The numerous milk cans waiting on the platform to be loaded on to the train show just how much excess milk Huntley farmers could supply each day. The large building in the background is one of the major local milk factories, owned by the Cornell brothers. This photograph, taken in March 1907, likely was one of the last of the factory at that location. The building burned to the ground on May 7, 1907. (Courtesy of Tom and Barb Conley.)

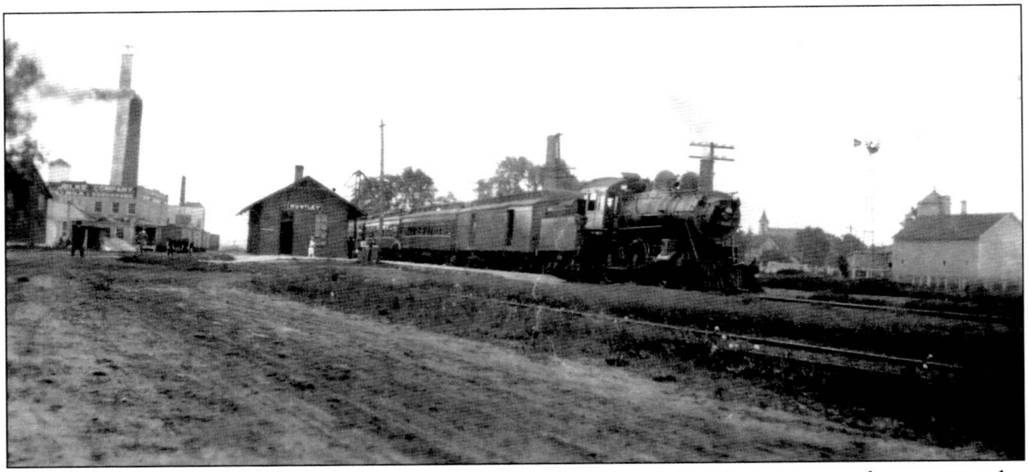

The bounteous output of local dairy herds, the proliferation of milk processing factories in the area, and the extension of the train line into town all made for prosperity for Huntley. Here the Chicago and North Western Railway train reaches the Huntley depot. To the left is the Jelke milk factory. The smokestack showing above the train is from the Wood and Weltzien (later Cornell) milk plant. The barn and windmill on the right belong to Edward Keating, a cattle dealer. (Courtesy of Huntley Area Public Library.)

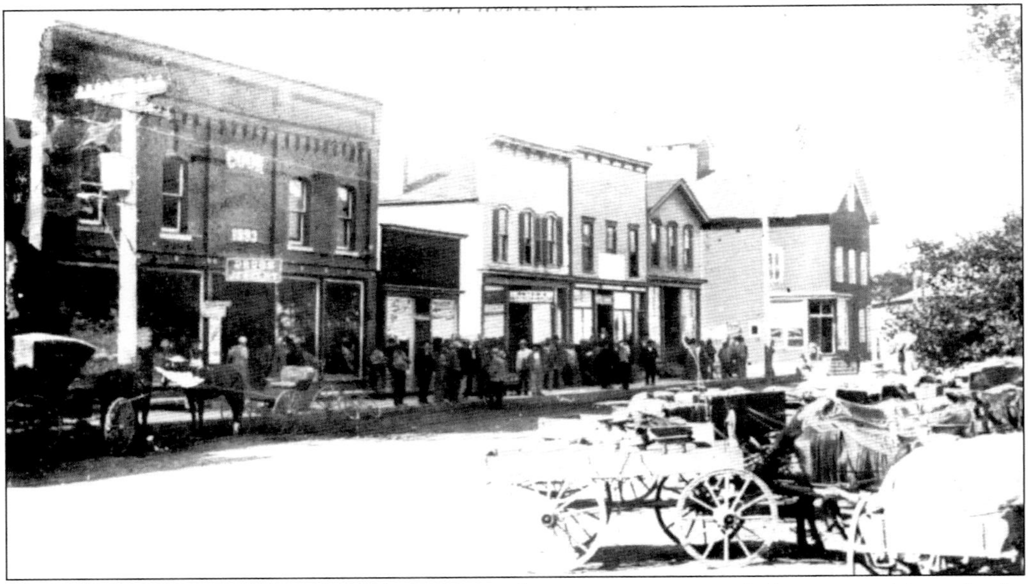

Chicago milk dealers visited Huntley early each spring to meet with farmers and bargain for a year's supply of milk. Farmers and dealers met on contract day to sign agreements for future milk delivery. The practice began soon after the railroad came through Huntley in the 1850s, allowing for easy transport of fresh milk into the city. Each morning, farmers loaded cans of milk onto their wagons, hitched the wagon to a team of horses, and drove into Huntley to meet the 8:00 a.m. milk train bound for Chicago. (Courtesy of Huntley Area Public Library.)

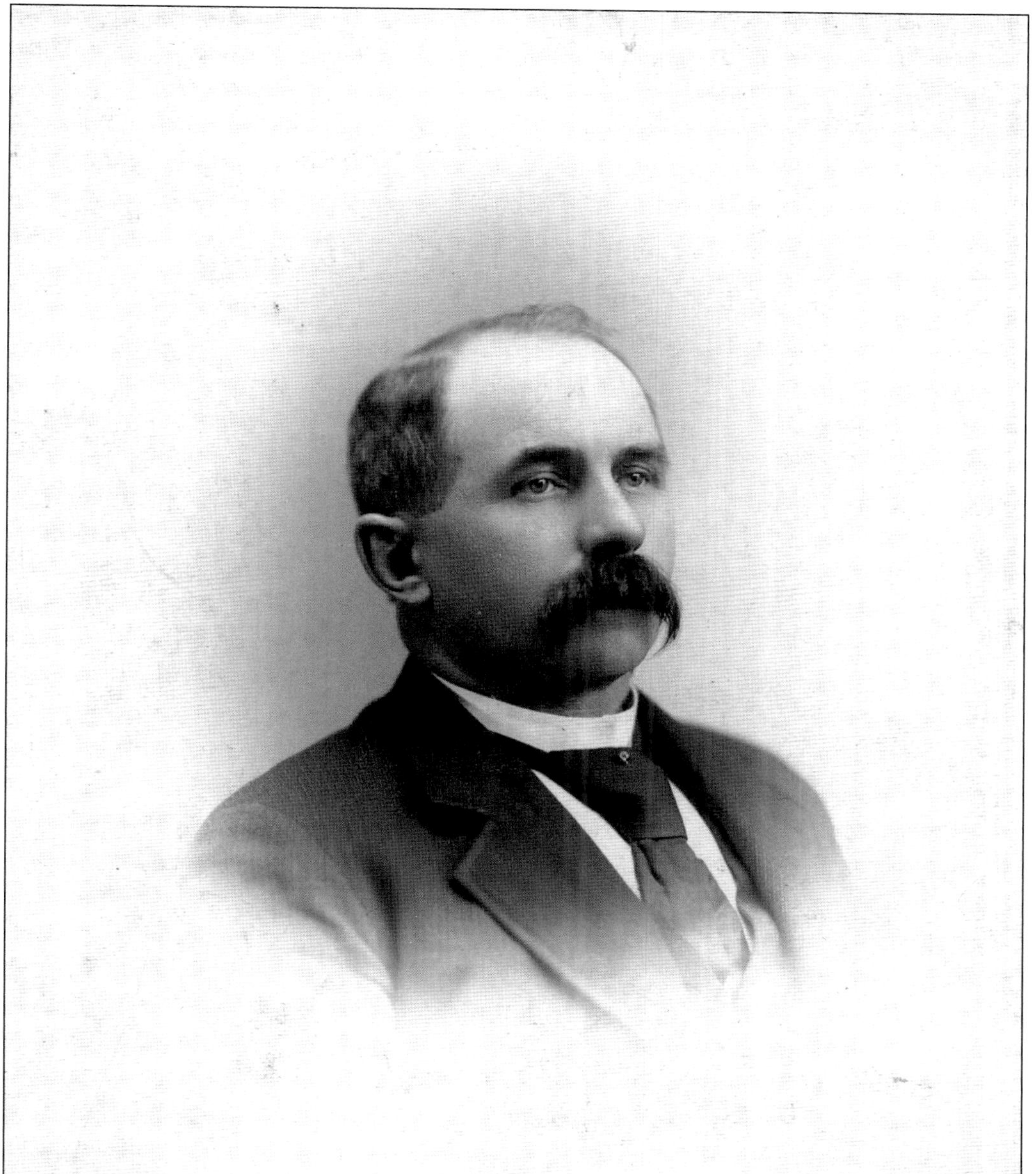

John G. Weltzien (1847–1916) came to Huntley in 1860. He farmed for many years and later moved to town where he was in business with D. E. Wood in the manufacture of cheese and butter. Their factory had the latest technology, including a refrigeration plant, the first without using ice. When Wood retired, Weltzien went into business with the Cornell brothers. An article in the July 21, 1894, *Huntley News* reported, "The Huntley cheese factory owned by Messrs. Weltzien and Cornell is the largest in capacity and output of any in existence." The article stated, "The average receipts of the creamery are not less than ten tons of milk for every day of the year." Weltzien was a prominent political figure, serving as president of the Huntley Village Board for many years. (Courtesy of Tom and Barb Conley.)

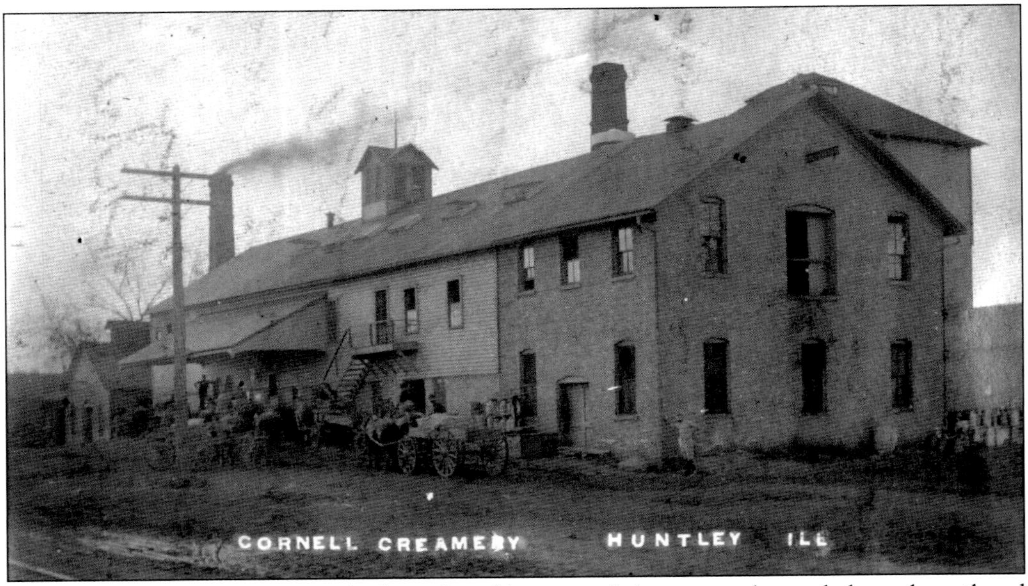

The Cornell Brothers factory, which produced butter and cheese, was located along the railroad tracks between Main and Mill Streets. Milk was purchased from farmers on a contract basis, ranging from 55¢ for 100 pounds in the spring to $1.20 in October. This factory burned to the ground on May 7, 1907. Cornell Brothers subsequently moved its operation to what recently was the Catty Corporation on Church Street. (Photograph by Ed Cook; courtesy of Tom and Barb Conley.)

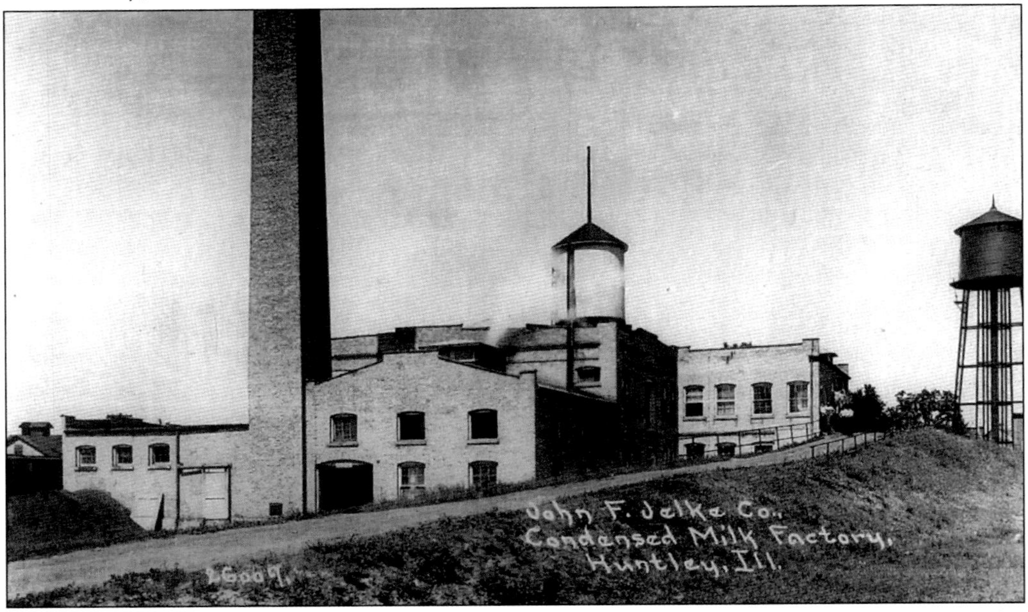

This building at Church and Mill Streets, near the Chicago and North Western Railway tracks, served as home to the Cornell milk factory then the Jelke Condensed Milk factory. After prohibition ended, it was a brewery (see chapter 9). During World War II, it was the William Fencil Gasket Company (see chapter 5). It most recently served as the Catty Corporation, a manufacturer of foil papers for food packaging. (Courtesy of Tom and Barb Conley.)

The large towers on the Cornell Brothers milk factory were under construction in this undated photograph. The Cornells moved to this location after their prior plant burned in May 1907. The towers were the vantage point for many of the aerial photographs taken of the town. The milk plant was situated along the railroad tracks, fronting on south Church and Mill Streets. (Courtesy of Huntley Area Public Library.)

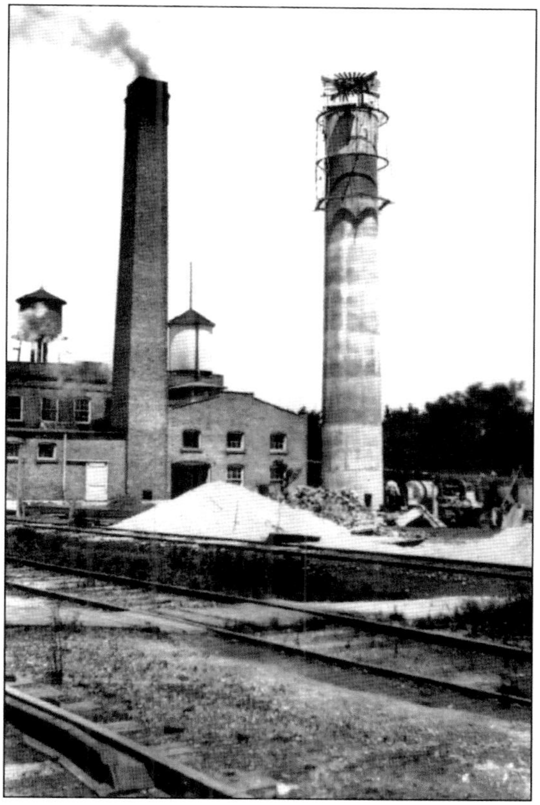

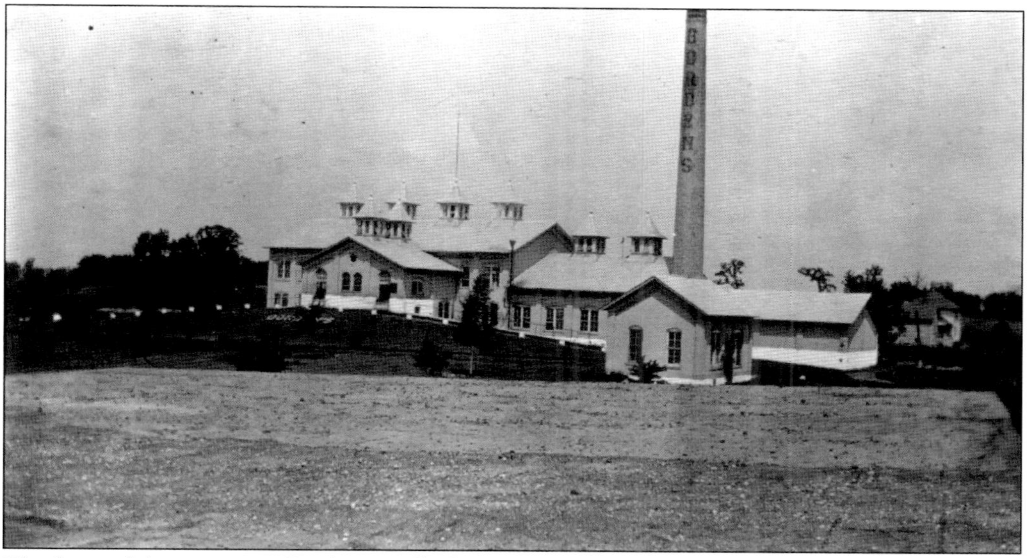

The beautiful, expansive Borden's milk factory was a Huntley landmark at the dawn of the 20th century. This photograph, dating to about 1906, shows the impressive scope of the building. It sat along Vine Street (now Route 47), and now, significantly changed, is occupied by Union Special, a manufacturer of industrial sewing machines. (Courtesy of Huntley Area Public Library.)

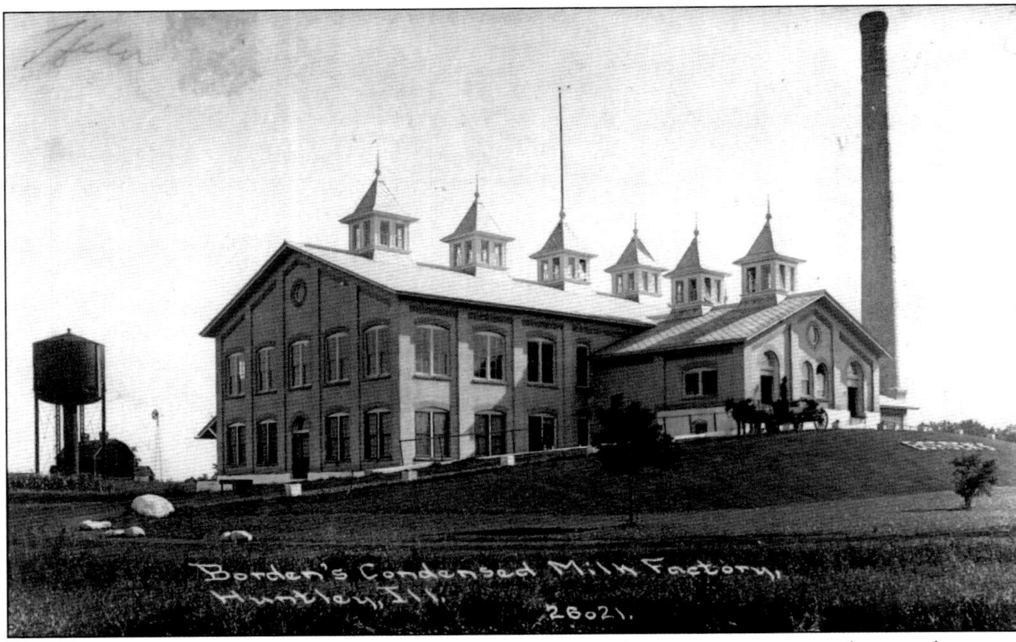

The Borden's condensed milk factory looked like a palace sitting just to the northwest of downtown Huntley in the early 1900s. The local factory was a success due to the surplus of milk available from area farmers. The convenience of the railroad system made it easy for Borden's to ship its products to Chicago. Local milk plants operated until new roads and trucking made transporting the raw milk into newer pasteurizing plants a more efficient process. When Borden's ceased production at the Huntley location, the Victor Mey milk plant moved into this building. (Above, courtesy of Noel and Lillian Hansmann; below, courtesy of Tom and Barb Conley.)

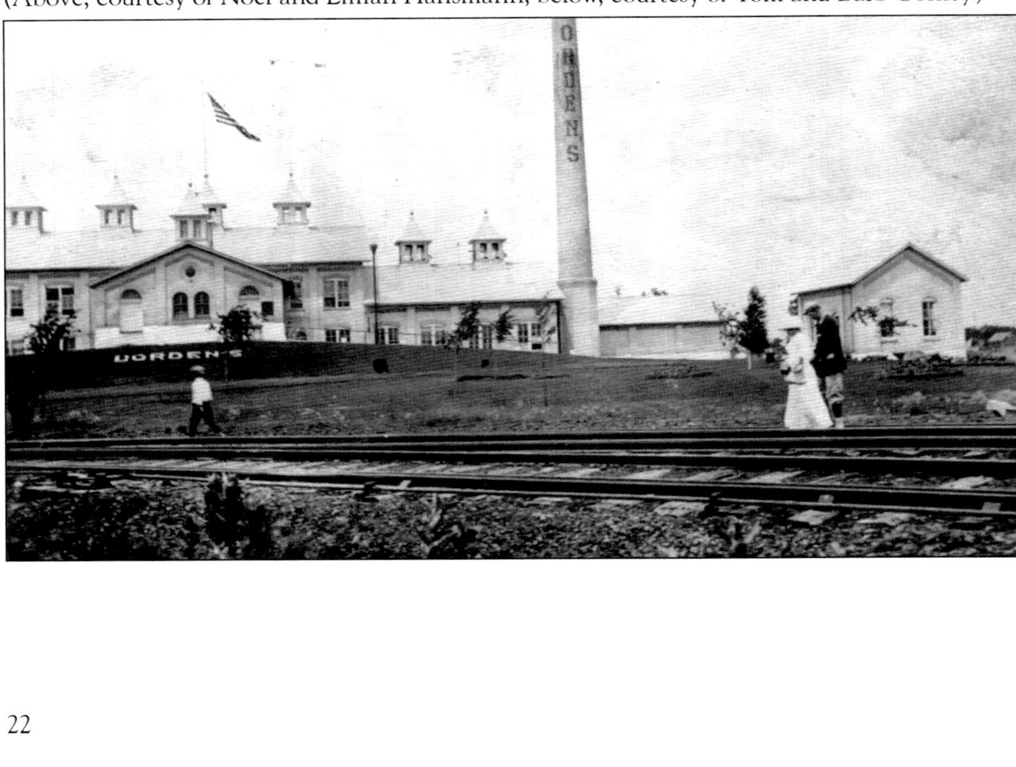

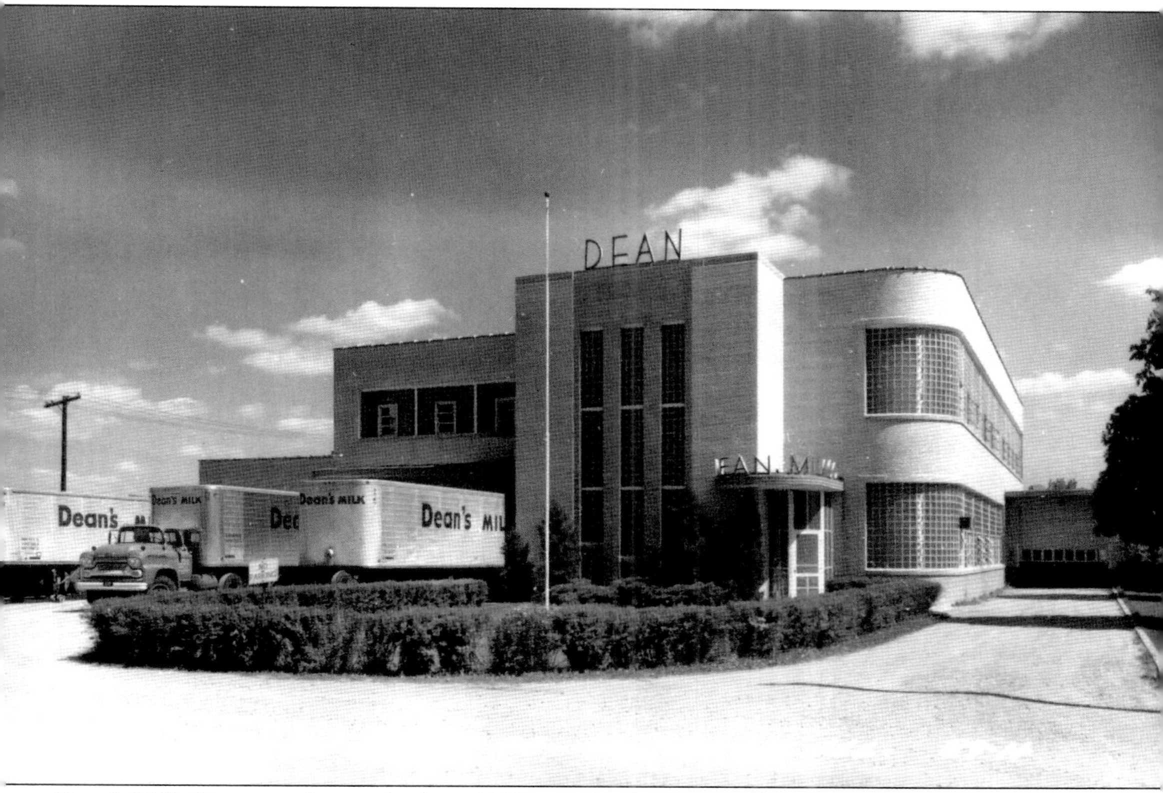

Dean's Milk Company factory, built in 1946, was the first new milk processing plant in Huntley since the 1920s. The plant, located on Mill Street, was built to bottle milk in cartons and jugs for consumer use. At the time it was built, to produce Country Charm Milk, all the milk processed at the plant was received from farmers within a 15-mile radius of Huntley. The plant still operates at the same location. In 1976, Mary Sue Seiler won $10 from the Huntley Lion's Club for coming up with Huntley's hometown motto, "the Friendly Village with Country Charm." (Courtesy of Tom and Donna Kalsow.)

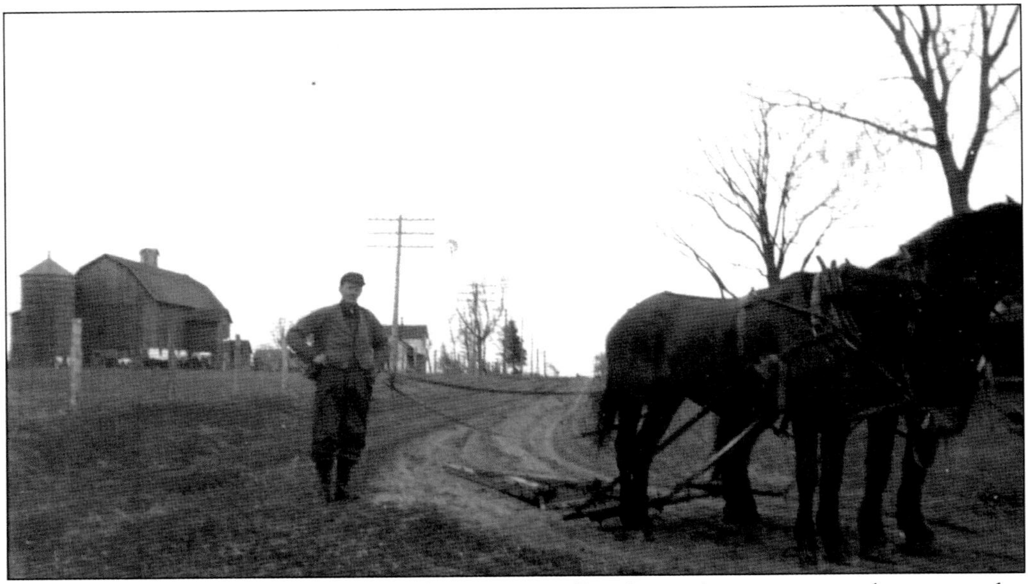

Charles Kreutzer Sr. stands on what today is Kreutzer Road near the entrance to the present-day St. Mary Church. In the background is the original Kreutzer homestead. His grandfather John Kreutzer purchased the farm on July 10, 1868, and brought his four sons, Paul, John II, Frank, and George, to the area. Eventually, all four sons owned farms within a three-mile radius. (Courtesy of the Kreutzer family.)

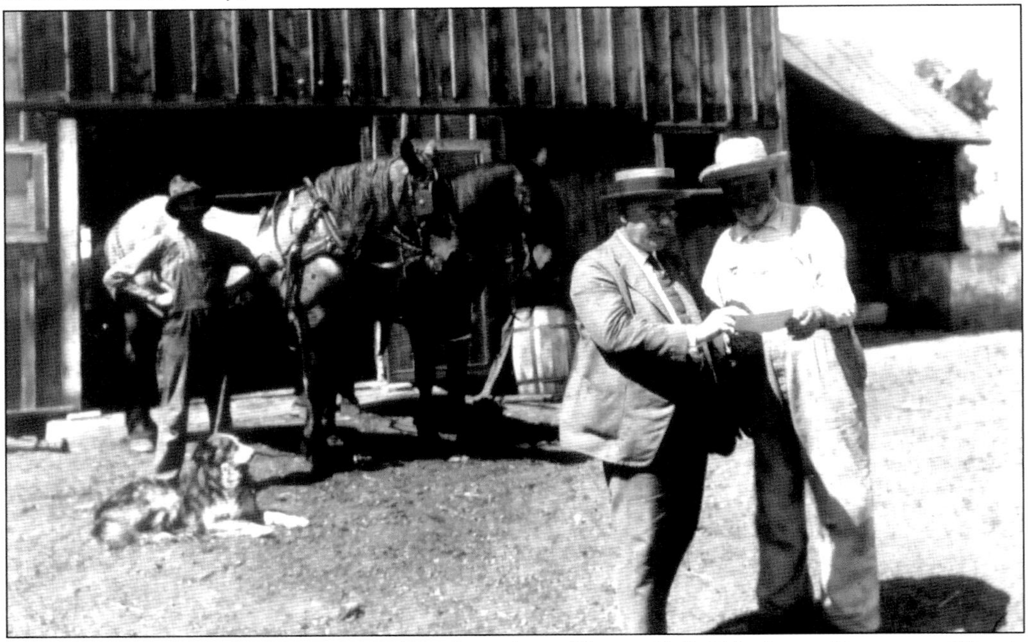

In August 1923, Paul Kreutzer purchased stock in Illinois Bell Telephone Company. Illinois Bell officials took this picture of the transaction and later sent a copy of the photograph to the Kreutzer family. Paul is at right, and the Illinois Bell official is to the left. Paul's son Joseph is in the background. The farm pictured is located across Kreutzer Road from the present-day entrance to St. Mary Church. (Courtesy of the Kreutzer family.)

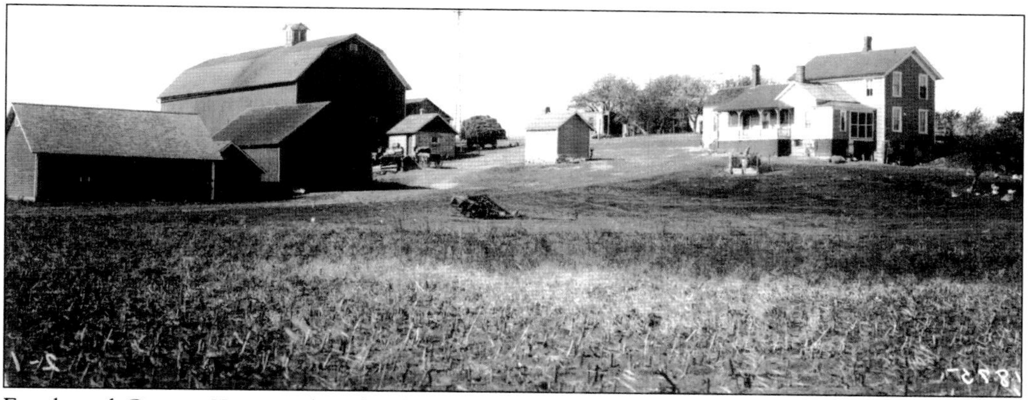

Frank and George Kreutzer bought this Miller Road farm in 1878. They paid $25 an acre for 160 acres. The farm remained in the Frank Kreutzer family until the 1990s. (Courtesy of the Kreutzer family.)

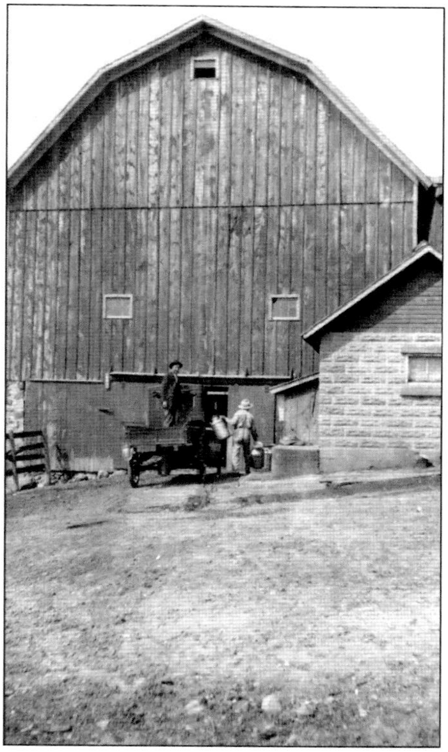

Daily life on the Frank Kreutzer dairy farm along Miller Road included loading milk cans onto the truck to transport the milk each morning to the train depot. The cement milk house is at right. Bill Kreutzer is in the pickup truck. (Courtesy of the Kreutzer family.)

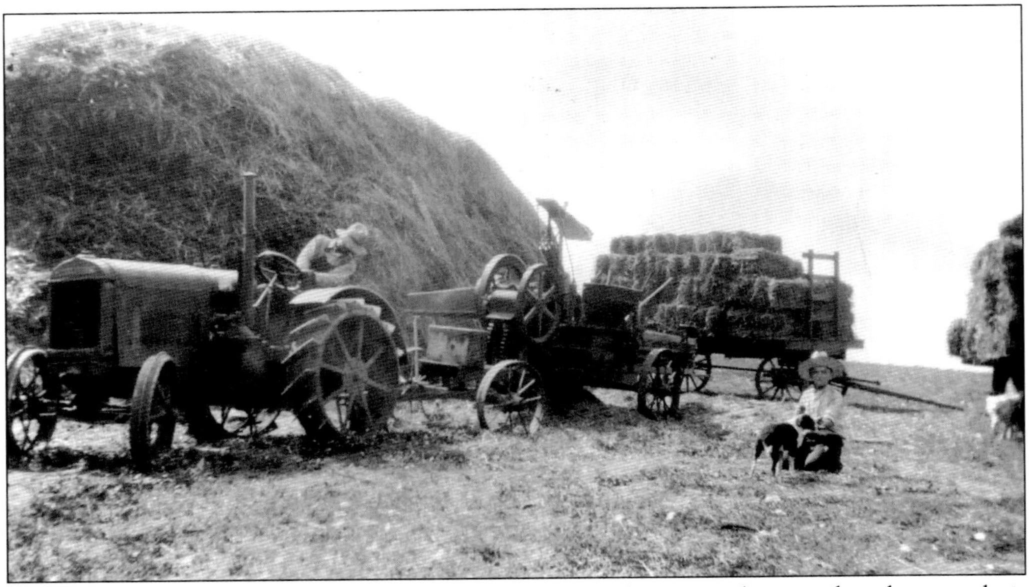

Joseph Kreutzer bales hay on his farm around 1910. The young boy in the photograph is unidentified. (Courtesy of the Kreutzer family.)

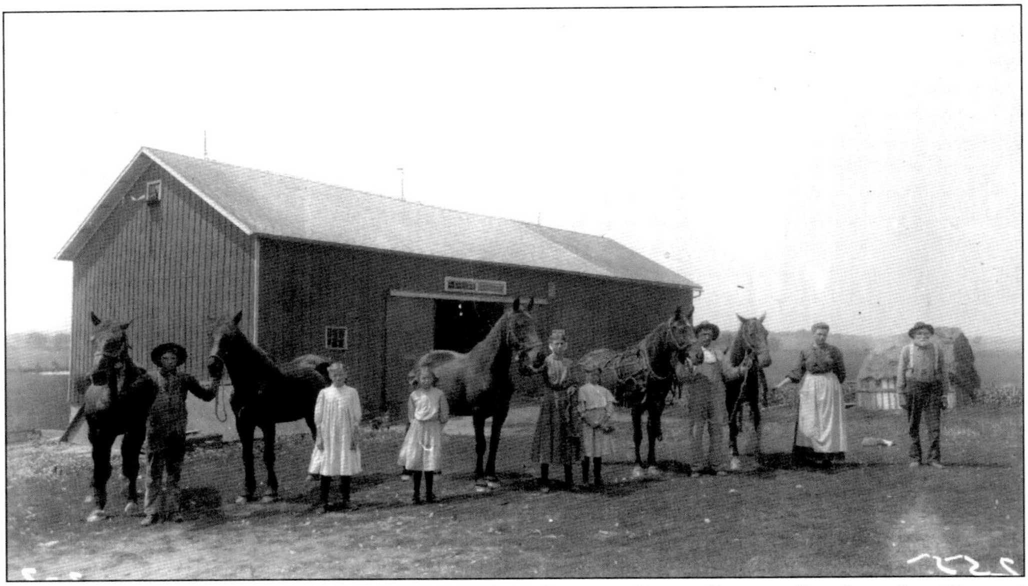

The Karsten family shows off their horses at their farm on Coyne Station Road south of Ernesti Road in this photograph most likely about 1915. Pictured from left to right are Frank Karsten, Gertrude Karsten, Elsie Heuer, Helen Karsten, Leta Karsten, Henry Karsten, Bertha Karsten, and Henry Heuer. Henry was Bertha's father and the grandfather of all the other children pictured. (Courtesy of Mary Ellen Moerke.)

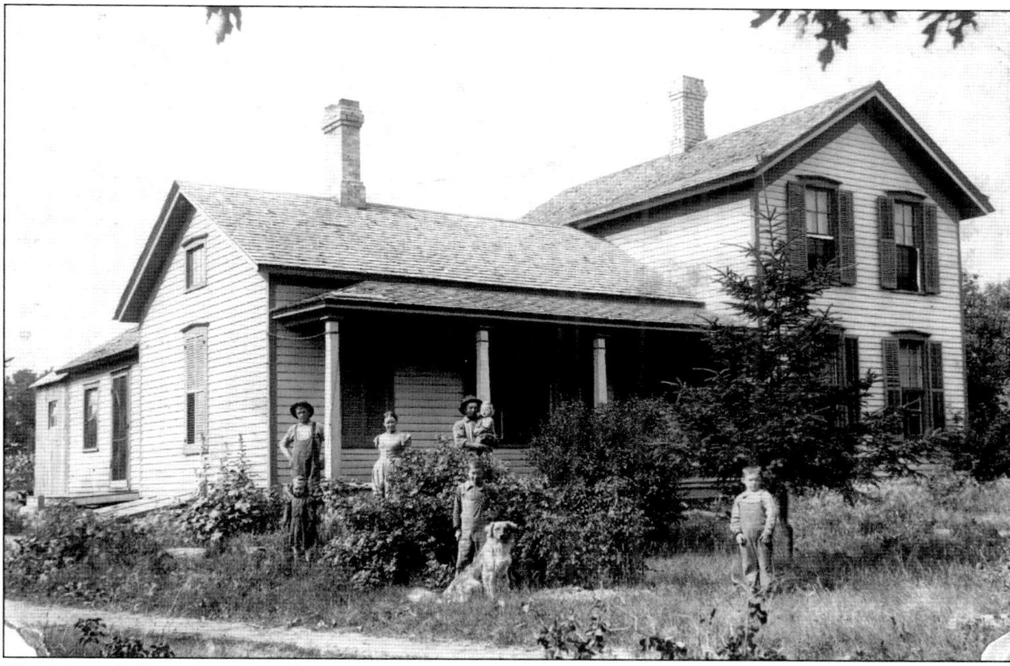

The Daniel Donahue family never would recognize their farm today. The Huntley Wal-Mart is located at the site of their homestead at Kreutzer Road and what is today Route 47. The farm first was owned by Daniel Donahue Sr., who arrived in the Huntley area in 1849. Above, Daniel Donahue Jr. is pictured holding baby Georgiana, who was born in 1895. At right is his oldest son, Daniel, who died about a year after this 1896 photograph was taken. The girl to the left is Margaret Donahue, whose adult success is related in chapter 5. Below, family and farmhands work the Donahue farm around 1896. The farmstead was purchased in 1850 and held by the family until it was sold on March 2, 1944. (Courtesy of Mary Beth Manning.)

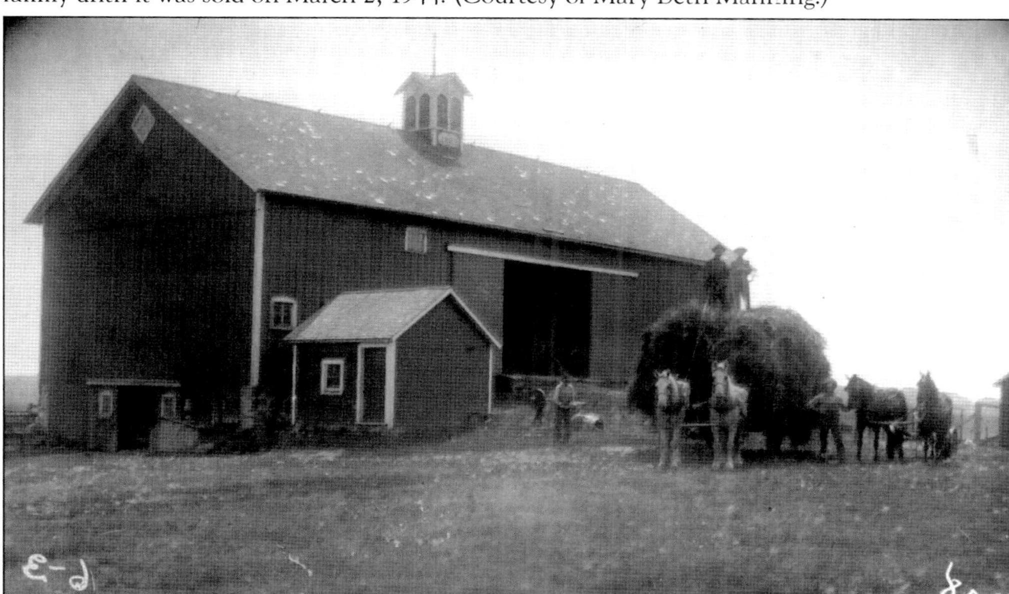

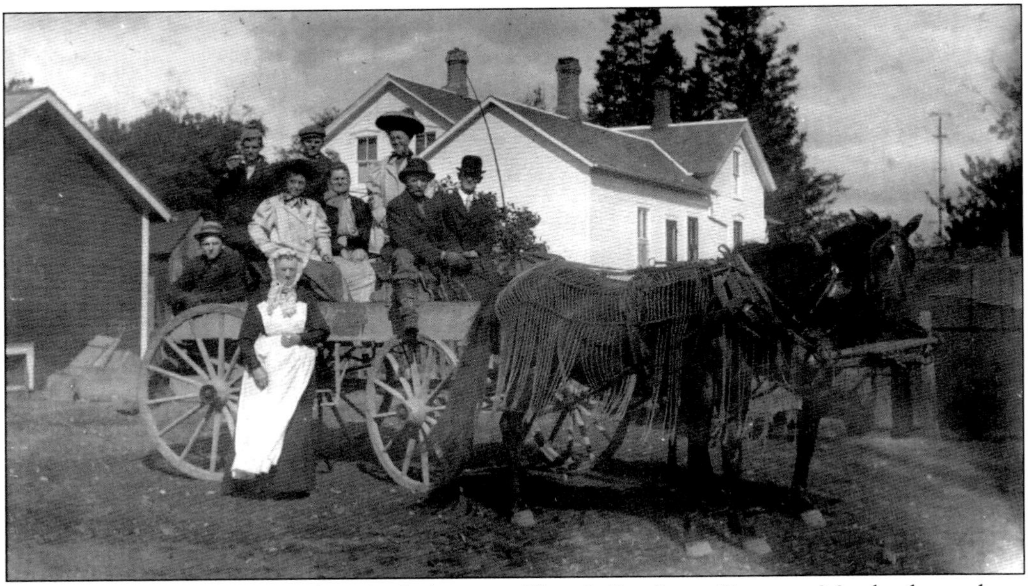

The first woman to live on the Marsh farm on Church Road was Susanna Marsh, shown here in front in the white apron. She and her husband, Nelson Marsh, were the first settlers, arriving in 1853. This photograph dates to after 1887, as the house pictured was built between 1886 and 1887. Every Marsh woman to live on the farm was left a widow but kept the farm going until the next generation took over. The farm is still in operation more than 155 years later. (Courtesy of Doris Marsh.)

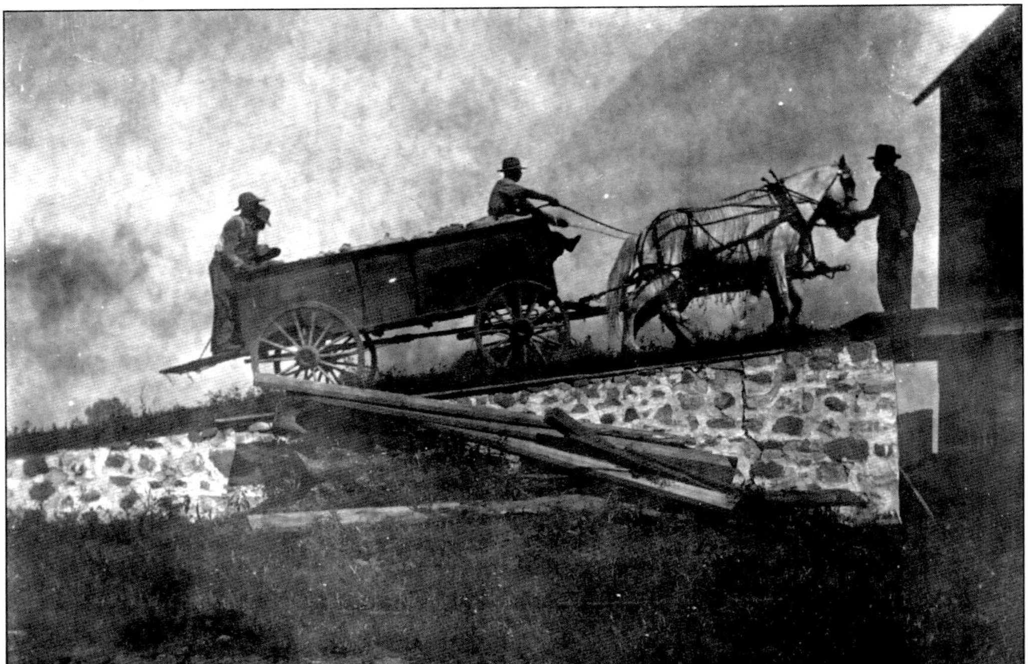

Threshing time on the Marsh farm along Church Road is shown in this undated photograph. James M. Marsh holds the horses as others load hay into the barn. (Courtesy of Doris Marsh.)

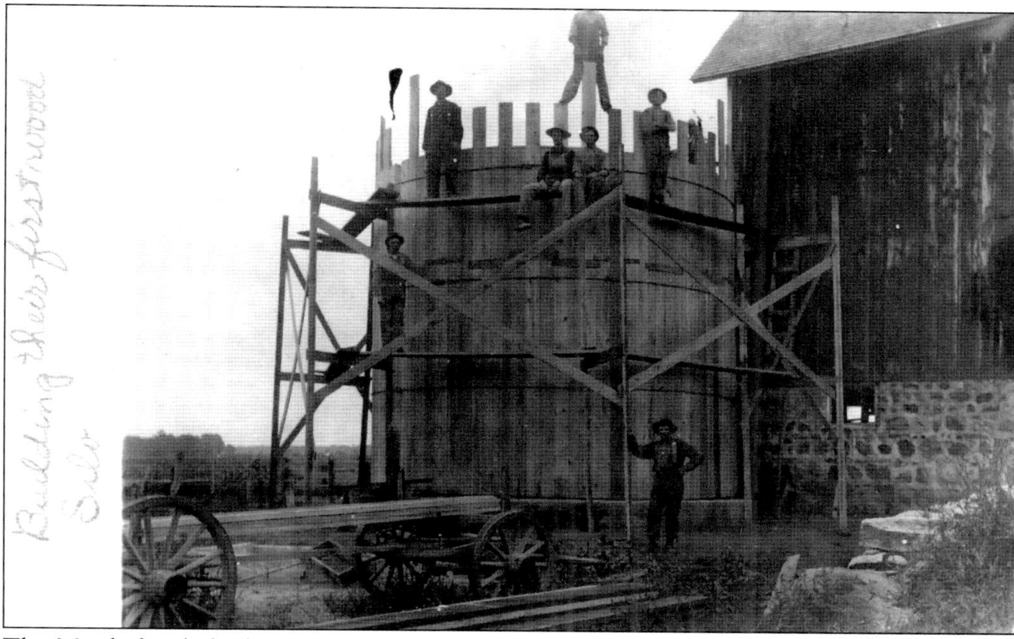

The Marsh family built its first wooden silo around 1900. Standing on the ground is George Marsh. On the middle platform at left is an unidentified hired man. At the top are James M. Marsh, Floyd Marsh, Clay Marsh, Lee Marsh, and Ralph Marsh (behind the boards). The man at the top is unidentified. (Courtesy of Doris Marsh.)

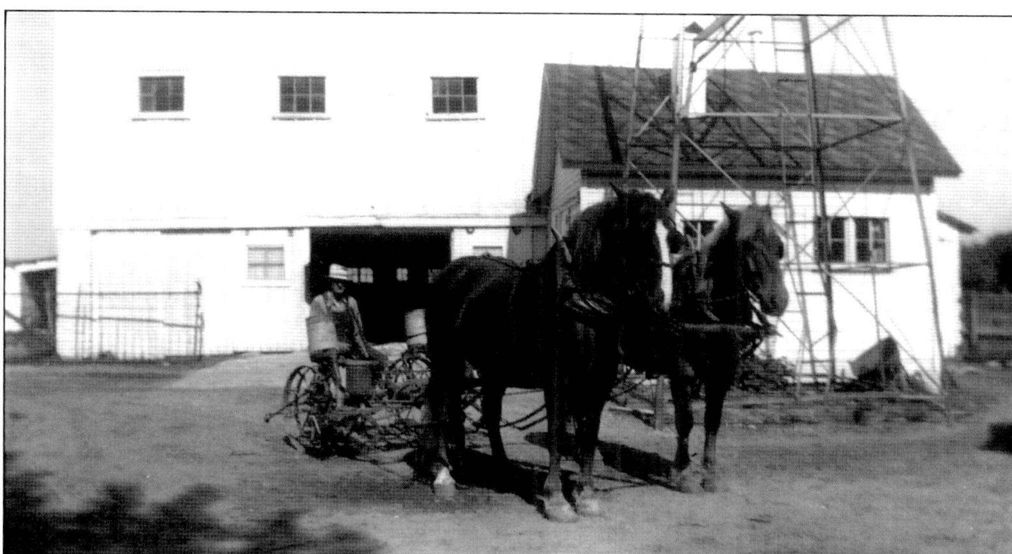

Lee Marsh, born in the Huntley area in 1893, is ready to plant corn with his two-row planter in the late 1930s. He was the third generation on the farm, which was settled in 1853. The farm, situated along Church Road west of town, grew corn and hay and had a dairy operation. The farm still is owned and operated by the Marsh family. (Courtesy of Doris Marsh.)

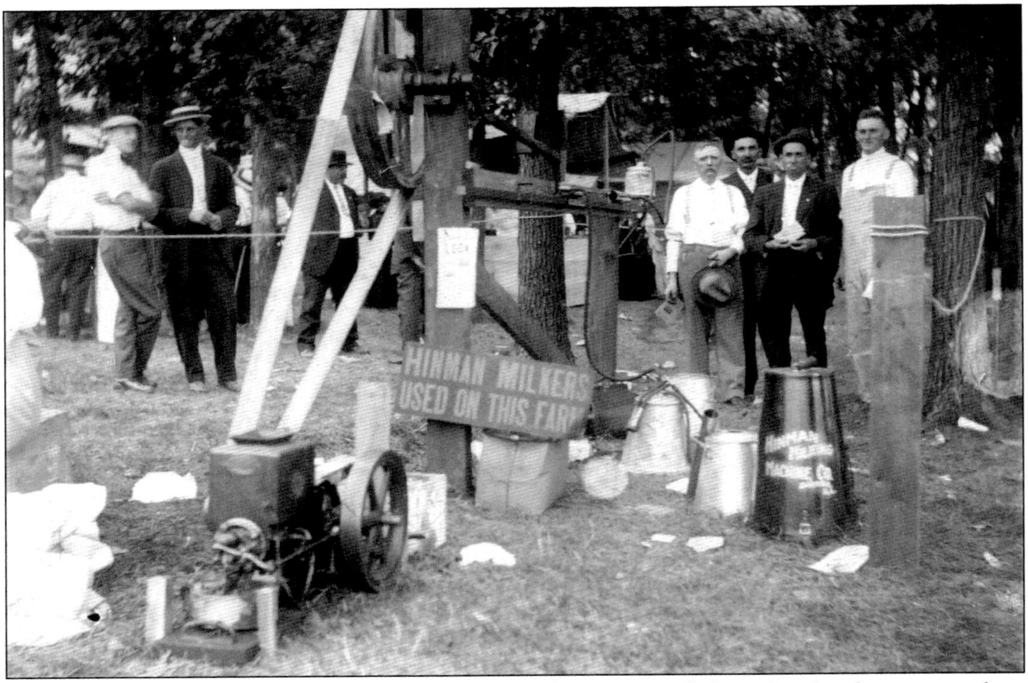

The first automated milking machine in the Huntley area was believed to be this one used on the Marsh family farm in the 1930s. At far right is Lee Marsh. James M. Marsh is in the white shirt to his left. (Courtesy of Doris Marsh.)

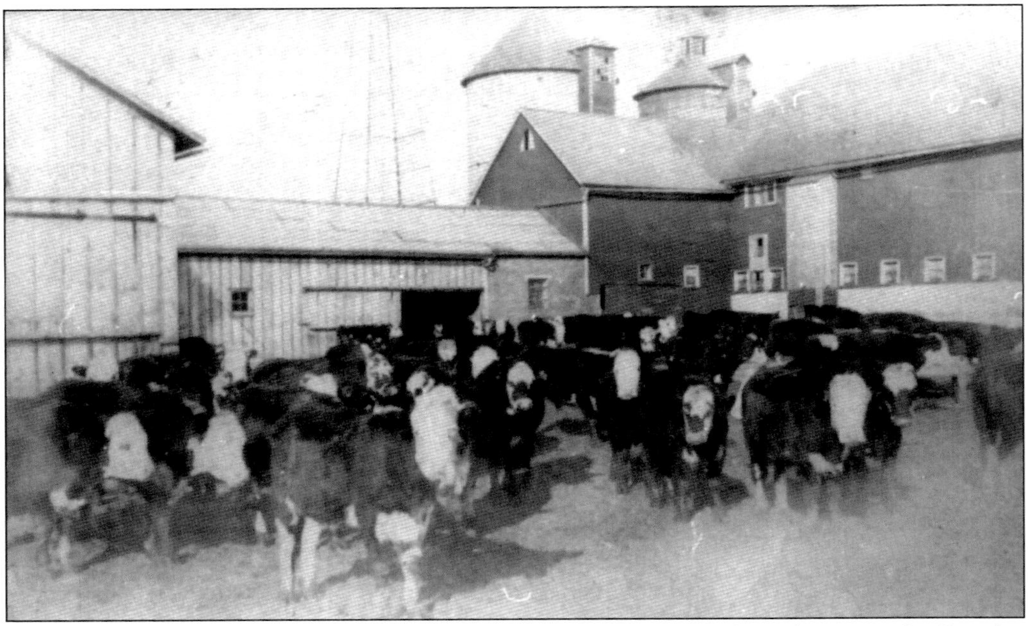

James Winne was one of the earliest settlers of the Huntley area. His farm along Huntley-Dundee Road east of town, which was later owned and operated by son and daughter-in-law Platt and Elizabeth Winne, was one of the showplaces of Huntley. Their barn and dairy herd are shown in this undated photograph. (Courtesy of the Kreutzer family.)

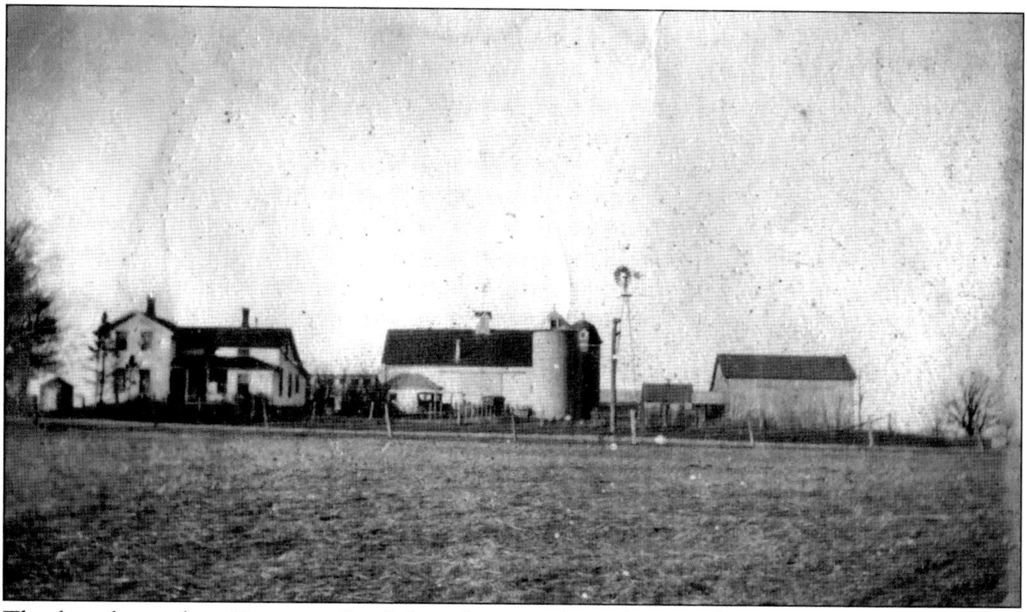

The farm located on Harmony Road directly across from the Huntley High School campus was at one time owned by the James Williams family. The farm was purchased in the 1840s for $75 and later sold to Williams, who arrived in 1850. Most of the farms along Harmony Road were built or owned by members of the Williams family. Louis Borhart purchased this farm from the Williams family in 1944 and sold it to School District 158 in 1990. (Courtesy of Vi Williams.)

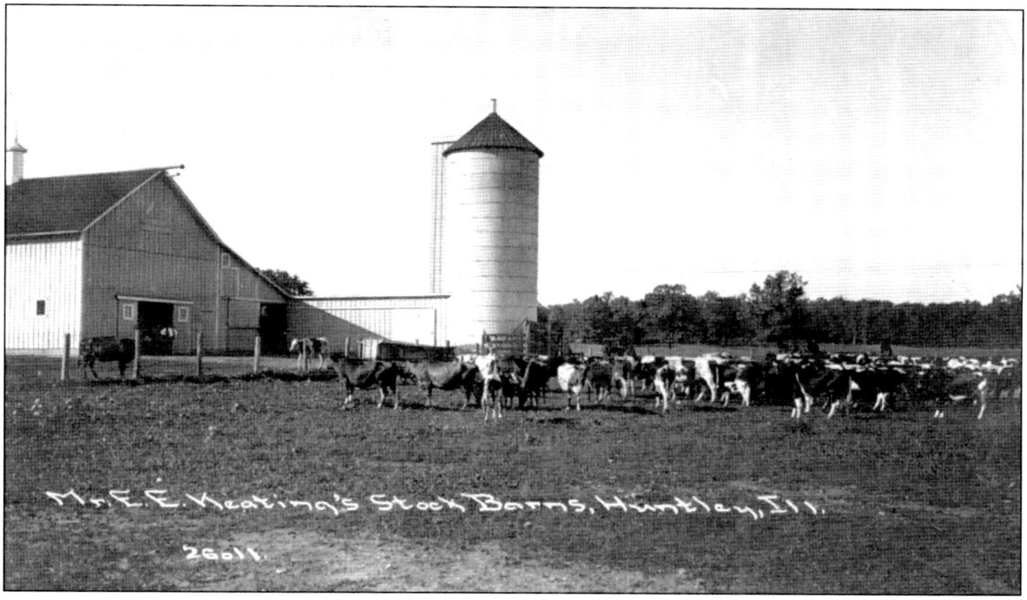

This undated photograph of the Edward E. Keating (1871–1937) stock barns shows a typical scene of Huntley's past. The Keatings were wealthy cattle dealers who owned numerous acres of land around Huntley. (Courtesy of McHenry County Historical Society.)

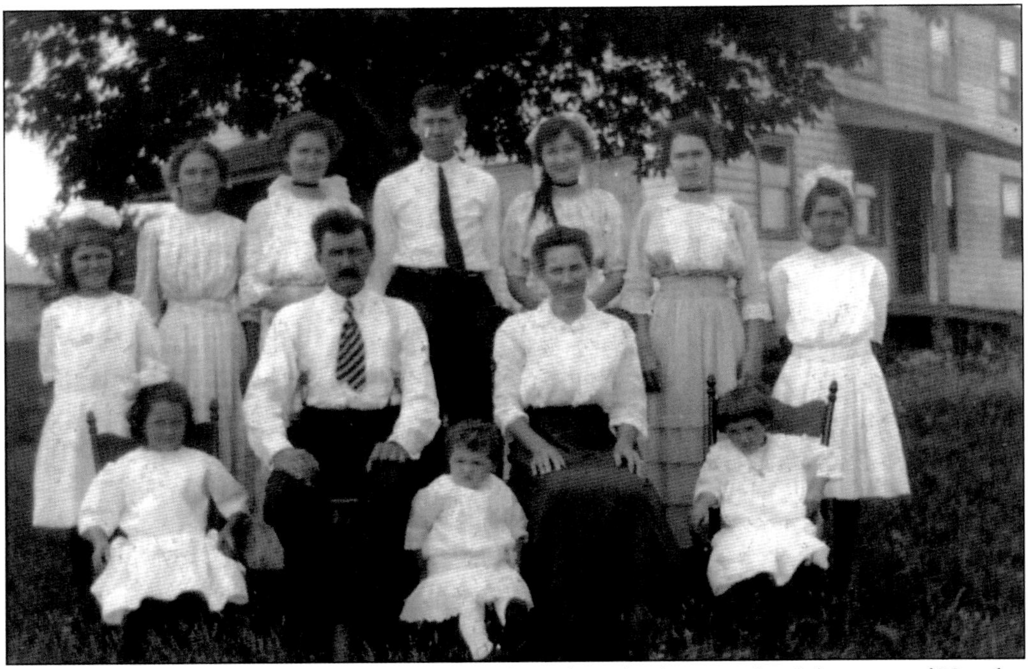

George and Mary Drendel married in 1894 and purchased a farm south of the town of Huntley about 1908. Their family consisted of 10 children, nine of them girls. Son Frank is standing at center. (Courtesy of the Vernon and Shirley Drendel family.)

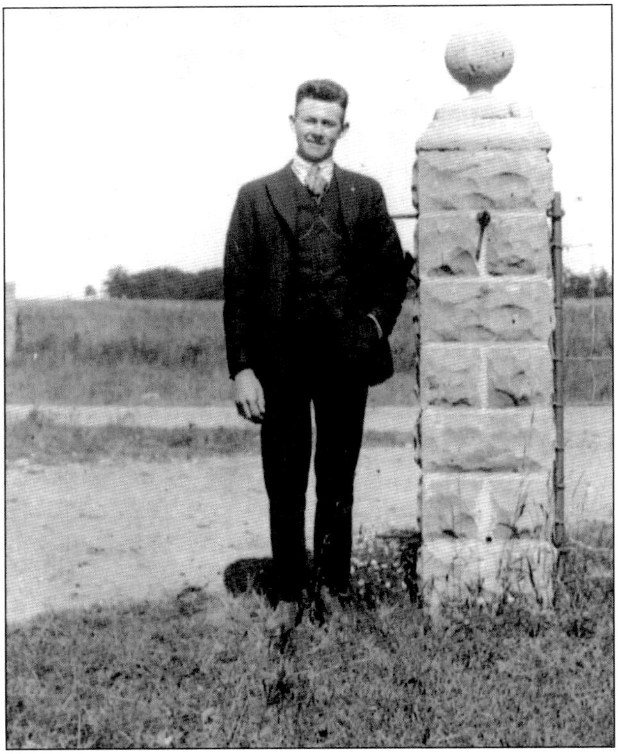

Frank Drendel stands next to a cement block column on the family homestead. During the 1920s, Frank's father, George, made these concrete blocks in wooden forms on his farm and on building sites and sold them locally. The Drendel home was constructed of these blocks, as were many area homes. Some can still be seen today, including those used on the Pabst building at the southwest corner of Main and Church Streets. (Courtesy of the Vernon and Shirley Drendel family.)

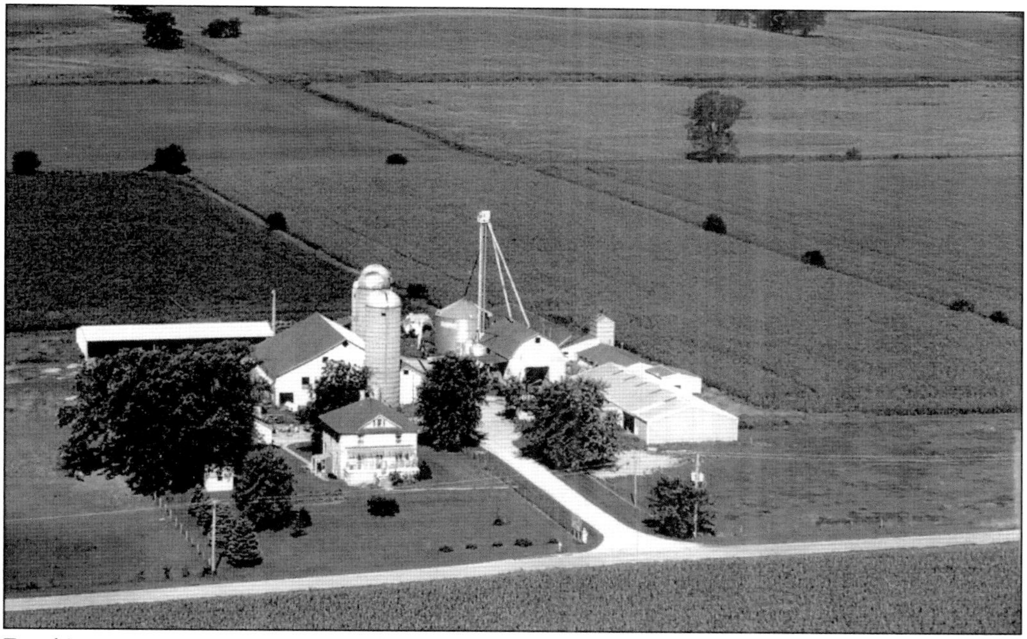

Frank's youngest son, Vernon, and wife, Shirley Drendel, moved to the farm after they were married and built it up to its modern facilities. They raised five children and lived there for 35 years. The farm was operated by Drendel family members for nearly 90 years before it made way for what today is Del Webb's Sun City. (Courtesy of the Vernon and Shirley Drendel family.)

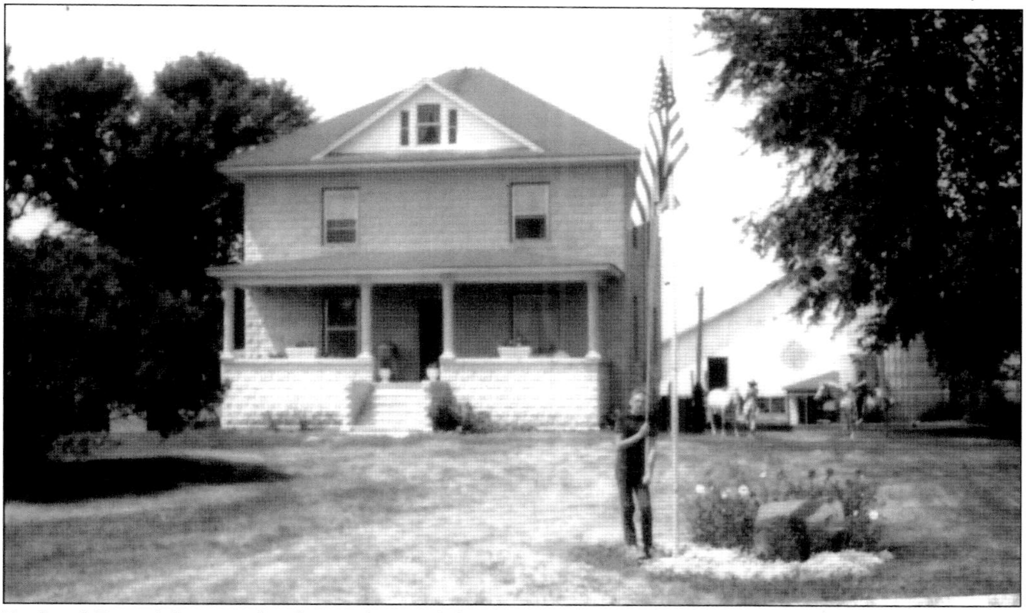

Richard Drendel raises the flag in front of the family home in this 1970 photograph. Richard, the great-grandson of first settler George Drendel, was the last of the Drendel family to reside in the home. Richard and his wife, Elke, moved off the farm in 1998 to make way for Del Webb's Sun City development. The concrete bricks made by George Drendel can be seen in the construction of the house. (Courtesy of the Vernon and Shirley Drendel family.)

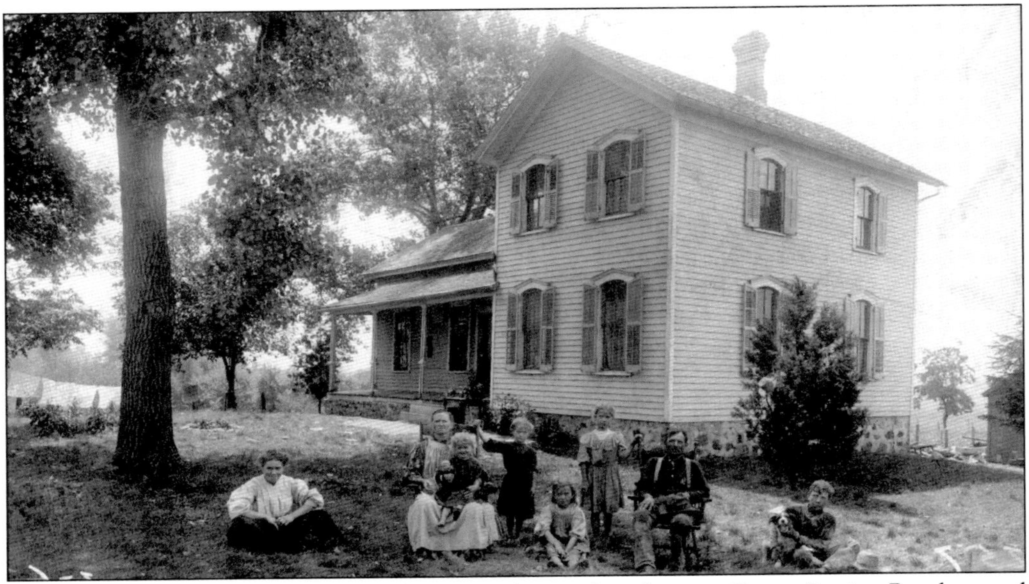

The August and Mathilda Jaster family enjoy a day on their farm on Coyne Station Road around 1900. The family owned the farm until 1964. (Courtesy of Ralph Drafall.)

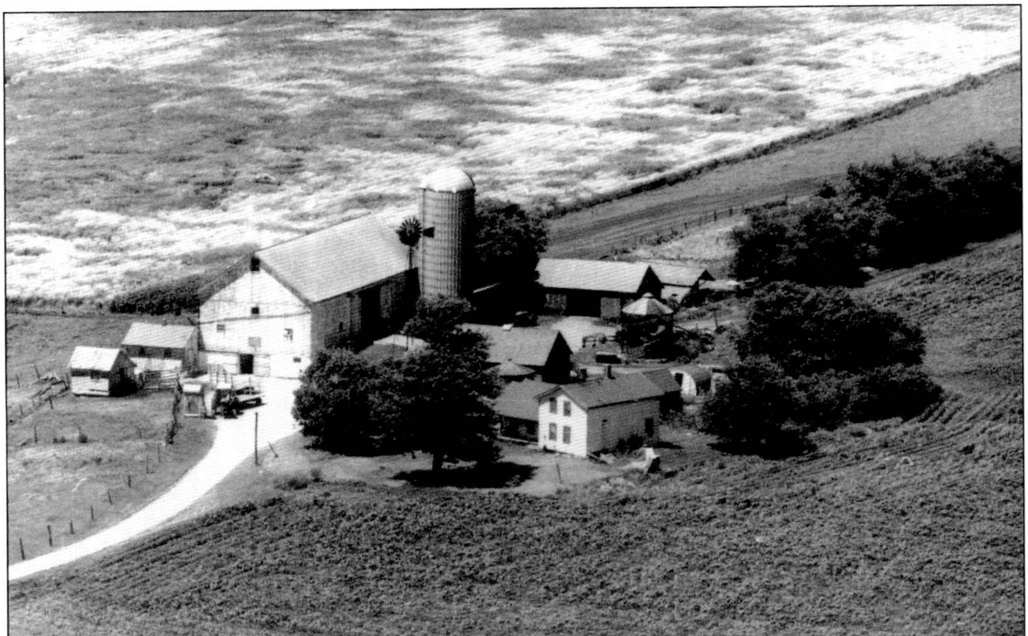

This photograph of the Enos Conley farm on East Main Street was taken around 1950. Conley owned several area farms. The small building at far left was once the ticket station for the Elgin-Belvidere trolley (see chapter 8). The building was moved to the farm after the trolley line ceased operation in 1930. (Courtesy of Ralph Drafall.)

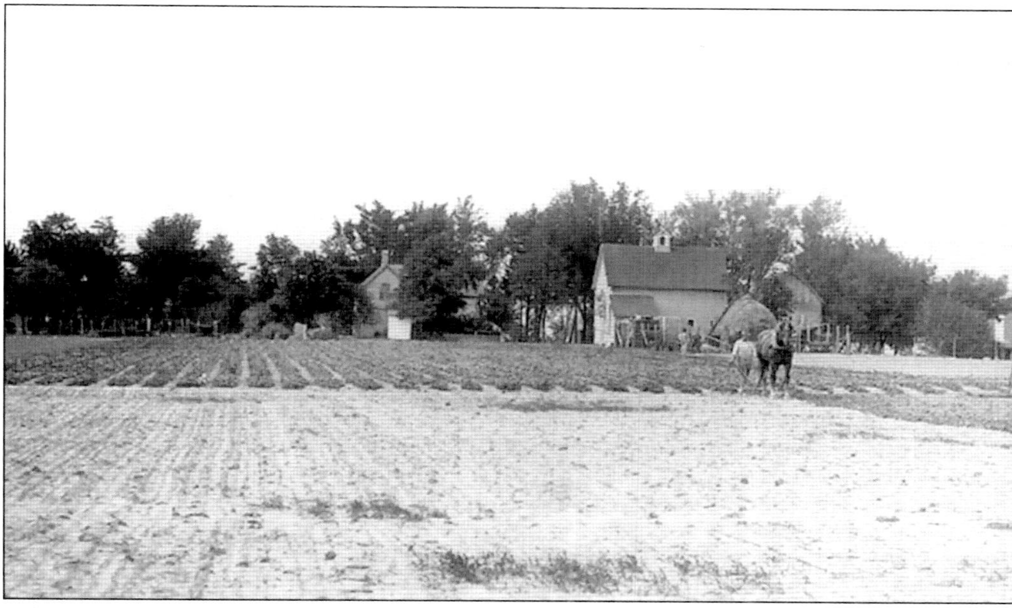

What could go better with all the milk and cream in Huntley than strawberries? The Mackeben family strawberry farm along west Main Street provided not only a convenient source of fresh fruit for local residents but also jobs for many Huntley children. The Huntley Berry Farm was started by Henry Mackeben in 1911. His children Ida and Harley Mackeben continued to raise strawberries and raspberries into the 1950s. (Courtesy of Huntley School District 158.)

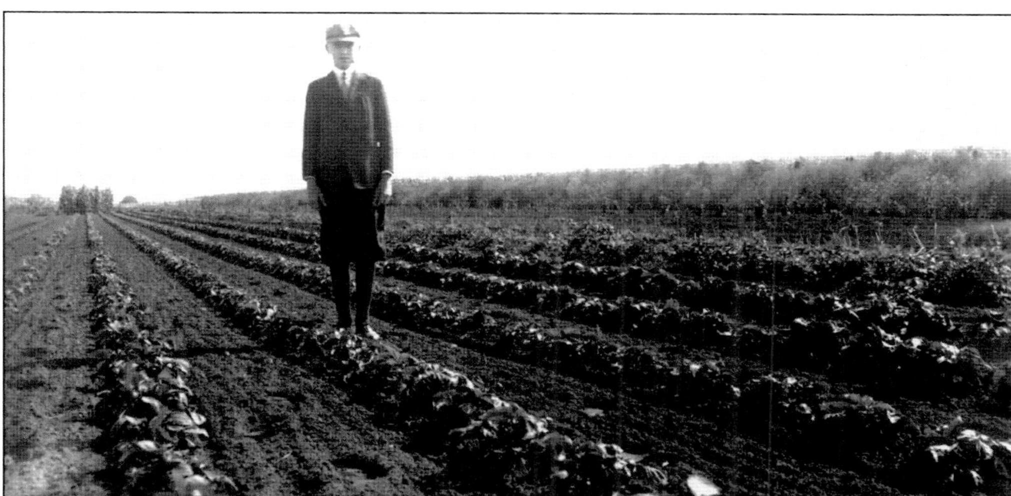

Harley Mackeben (1903–1984) stands in his family's strawberry patch around 1920. Many Huntley children earned their first paycheck picking strawberries for the Mackebens. Harley went on to serve on the school board for 18 years, was a member of the village planning commission, and served as McHenry County Board chairman. A school is named for him and his sister Ida. (Courtesy of Tom and Barb Conley.)

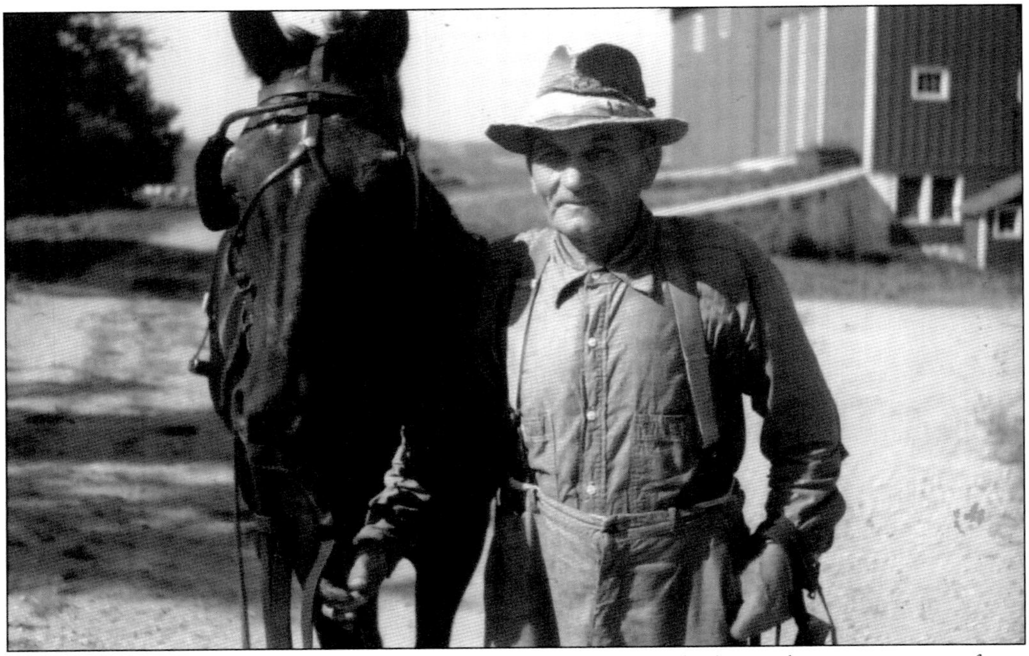

Alva (Alvie) Ritz was the last Huntley-area resident to give up the horse-drawn carriage in favor of an engine-driven vehicle. Here, Alvie is shown on his farm with one of his favorite horses. (Photograph by Harley and Mabel Swanson Mackeben; courtesy of Lonni Swanson Oldham.)

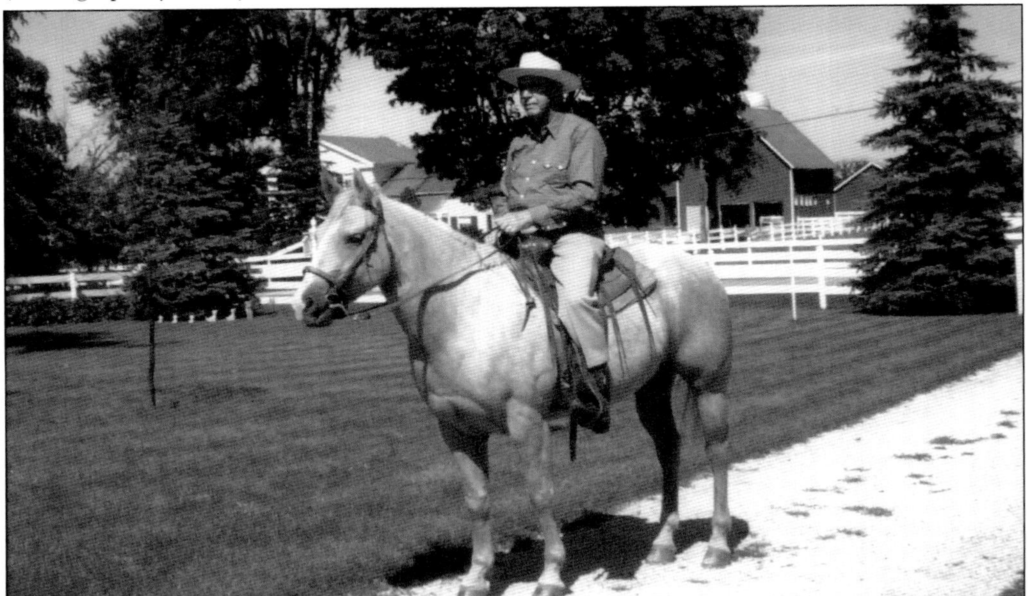

Edwin Deicke enjoyed his horse Dorsey at his Sun Valley Farm along west Main Street. The date was October 3, 1965. At one time, Deicke owned five farms totaling more than 1,000 acres in the Huntley area. Deicke often invited friends to Sun Valley Farm to enjoy hunting and riding. The Huntley Park District now owns the farm. (Photograph by Harley and Mabel Swanson Mackeben; courtesy of Lonni Swanson Oldham.)

Three

CHURCHES

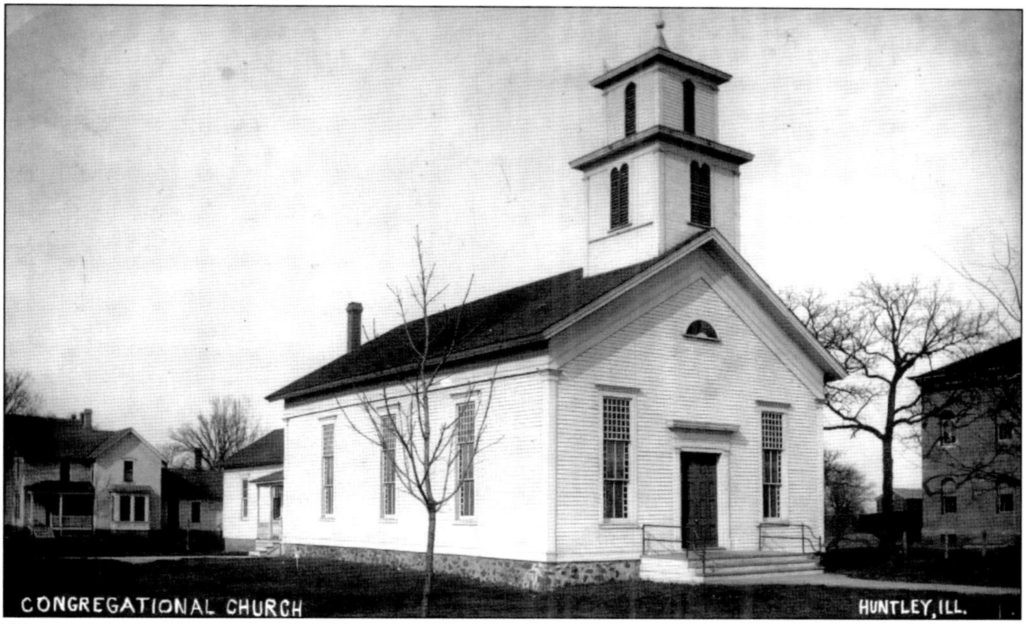

Thomas Stillwell Huntley was a founding member of the First Presbyterian Church of Ellicottville, New York, before immigrating to northern Illinois. A deeply religious man, Huntley donated land from his holdings for three churches, a Congregational, a Catholic, and a Lutheran, in the newly forming town named in his honor. The First Congregational Church, shown here in 1909, was built in 1864. Huntley was among the founders of the church and served as a trustee for many years. This is the oldest church in continuous use in McHenry County. (Courtesy of Tim and Ann Essig.)

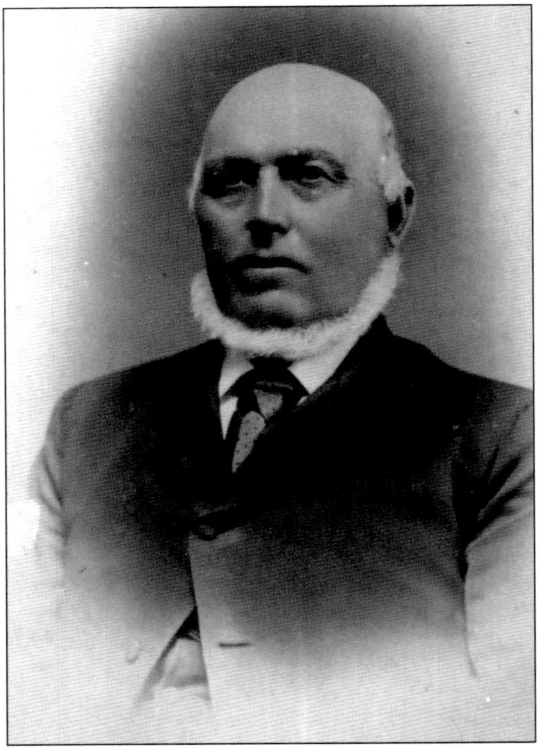

James "Deacon" Williams (1819–1898), his wife, and Thomas Stillwell Huntley, were among the eight charter members of Huntley's First Congregational Church. Williams arrived in the area in 1850. Plans to organize a Congregational church began in August 1852, and the church was built in 1864. (Courtesy of Vi Williams.)

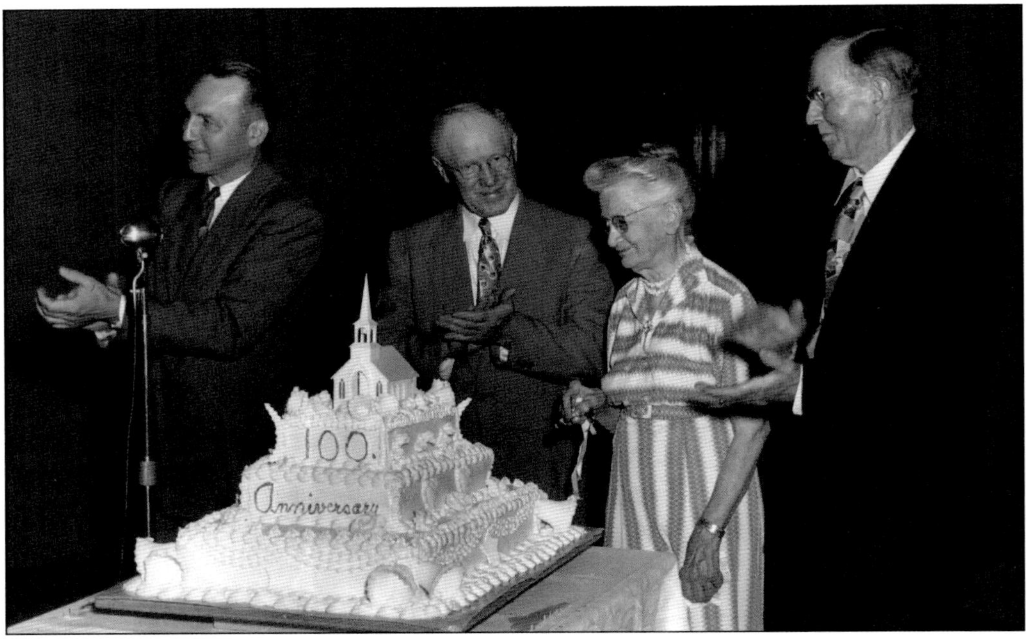

Henry Marlowe (left), Rev. Walter Heyl, Mary Bartholomew, and Vic Trumbull help celebrate the 100th anniversary of the founding of Huntley's First Congregational Church in 1952. Bartholomew (1865–1958), one of the longest-participating members of the church, had served as a nurse in the Spanish-American War. (Courtesy of Don Peasley.)

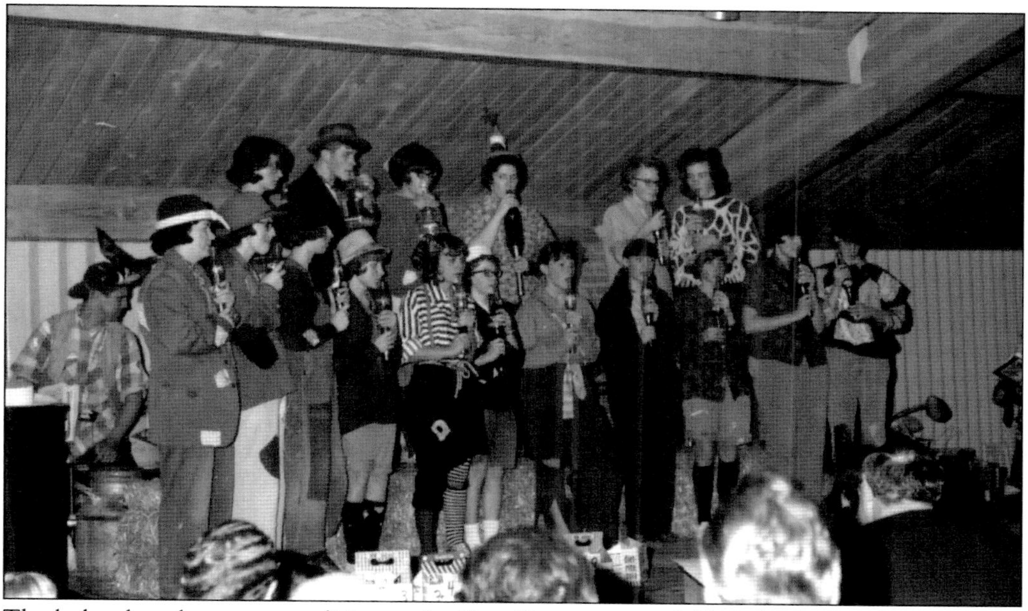

The hobo show became a tradition at the First Congregational Church after its debut in 1963. The show was begun to raise money to purchase hand bells for the church. A dinner of hobo stew is served on tin plates as audience members enjoy the show. Each year features a different theme centering on the hobo's antics. This late-1960s photograph shows the cast playing the bottles, a traditional part of the show. (Courtesy of Tim and Ann Essig.)

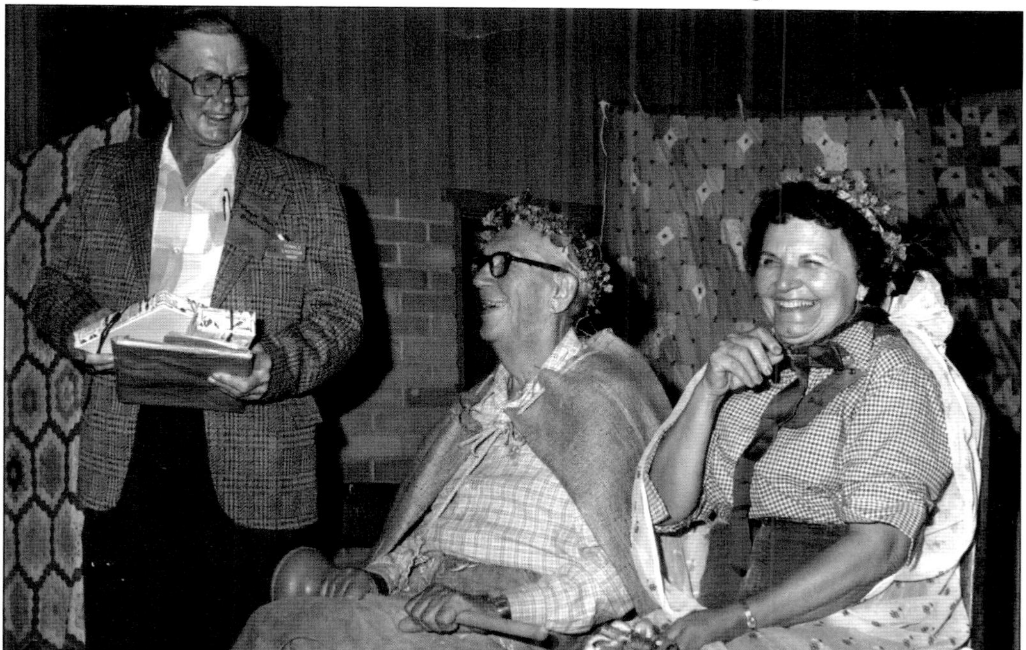

Edwin Deicke and his wife, Lois, are feted as king and queen of the First Congregational Church Hobo Show on his birthday. Acting as master of ceremonies is Don Enstrom (1925–2006), at left. (Courtesy of Don Peasley.)

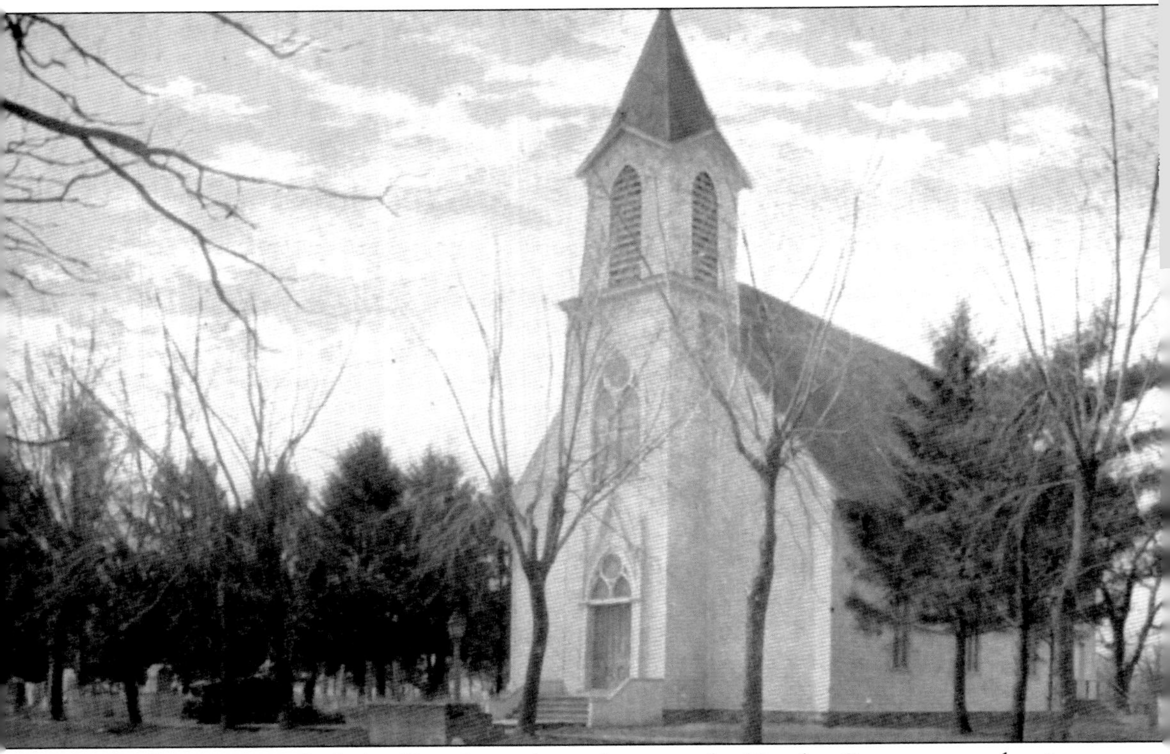

The first St. Mary Catholic Church was located next to the Huntley Cemetery on what is now known as Dean Street. In 1870, a group of Catholic men met in the John G. Kelley blacksmith shop on the north side of the town square to discuss building a church in Huntley. Among those present were John Kreutzer, Paul Kreutzer, John Coyle, Kelley, Philip Sheehan, Daniel Donahue, Michael Fitzgerald, John Zenk, George Hemmer, John Clinnin, and Henry Mountain. The church was built in 1873 on land donated by Thomas Stillwell Huntley. In front of the church is a stand for parishioners to dismount from their horses or carriages. This church was used until 1931. (Courtesy of McHenry County Historical Society.)

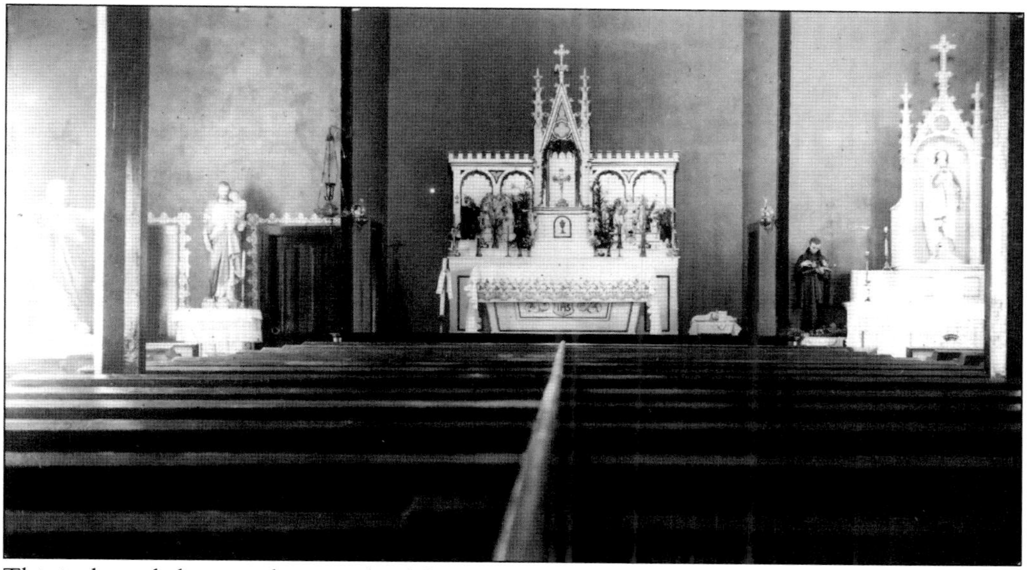

This is the only known photograph of the interior of the original St. Mary Church. The statues of St. Joseph holding the child Jesus, at left, and the blessed Virgin Mary, far right, as well as the communion rail were gifts to the church from the Paul Kreutzer family. (Courtesy of Mary Beth Manning.)

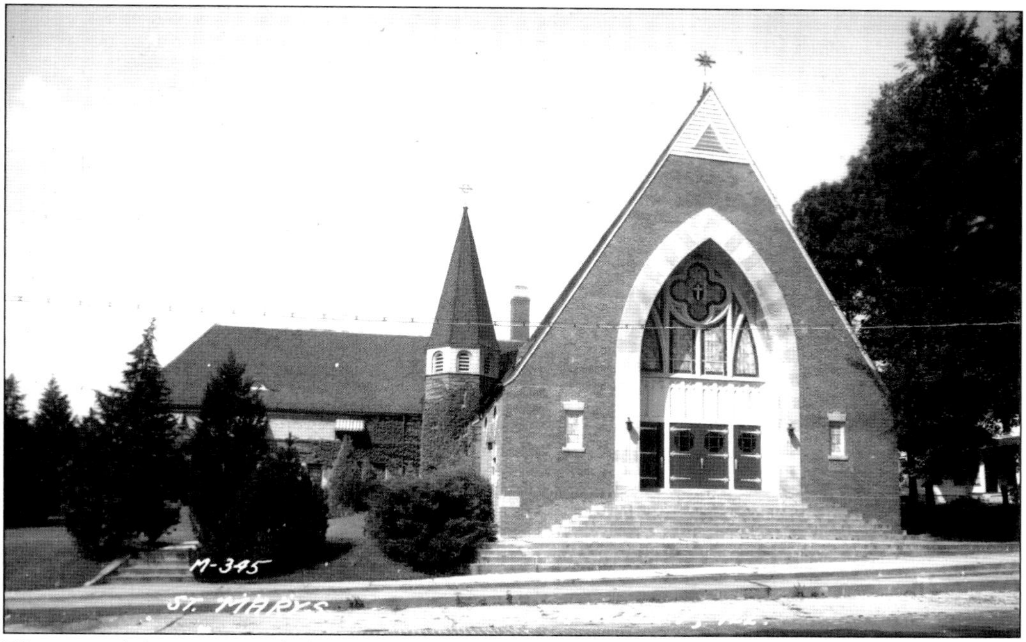

The second St. Mary Catholic Church on Woodstock Street was completed in 1931 when the Rev. Fr. Ivan Esser was pastor. When Rev. Fr. L. Dudley Day became pastor in July 1938, the church's indebtedness was more than $70,000. Although times were economically difficult, strong leadership by Father Day and an aggressive program of chicken dinner sales by parishioners helped to eliminate the debt in seven years. Father Day served at St. Mary for 40 years. (Courtesy of Tom and Barb Conley.)

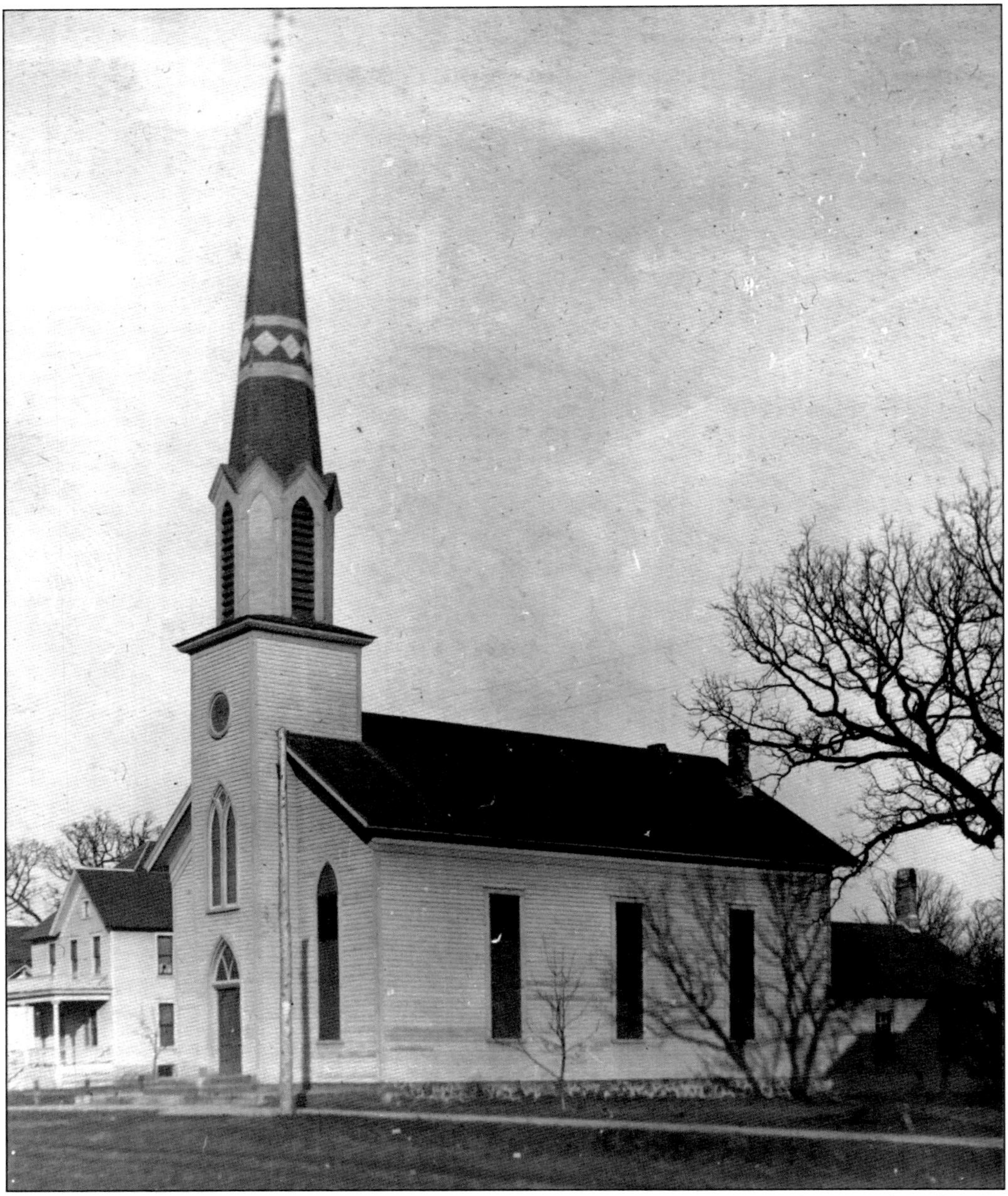

The German Evangelical Lutheran Church, today known as Trinity Lutheran Church, was located on land along Church Street donated by Thomas Stillwell Huntley. The Lutheran congregation was organized on March 1, 1871, and the church was built in 1874. In 1878, Rev. John Baumgartner added a steeple and bell, weighing 1,545 pounds, to the church. The steeple later was struck by lightening and the bell and tower removed. This photograph, found in an album from the late 1800s, is from a glass negative made by town pharmacist Ed Cook. (Courtesy of Tom and Barb Conley.)

Trinity Lutheran Church, in an undated photograph, is shown with its shorter steeple. The original church had the short steeple, and the bell tower and larger steeple were added four years later. A lightening strike to the steeple caused it to be reconfigured back to its original shorter size. (Courtesy of McHenry County Historical Society.)

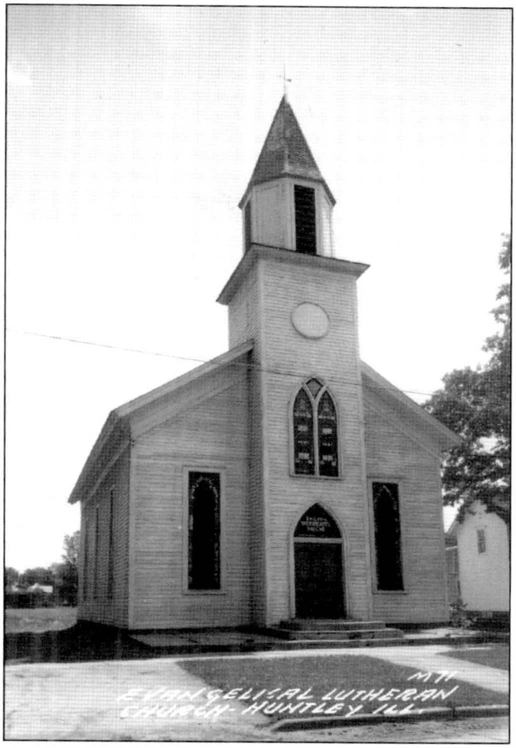

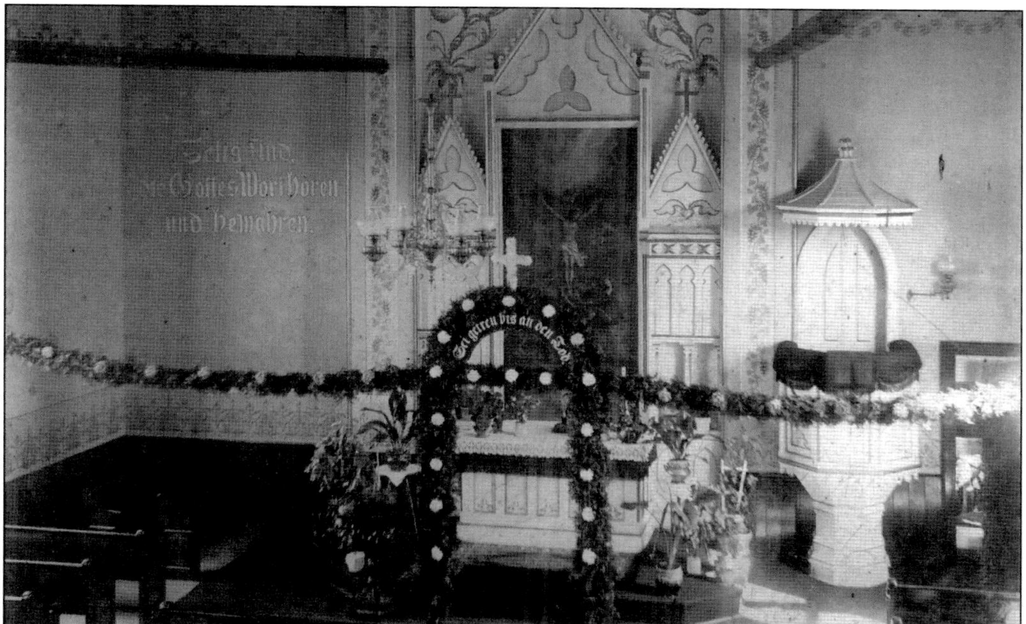

This photograph of the interior of the early German church, now Trinity Lutheran Church, shows it decorated for confirmation on Palm Sunday in 1910. German text on the wall and a banner can be seen. The congregation operated a German school nearby until 1923. (Courtesy of Ralph Drafall.)

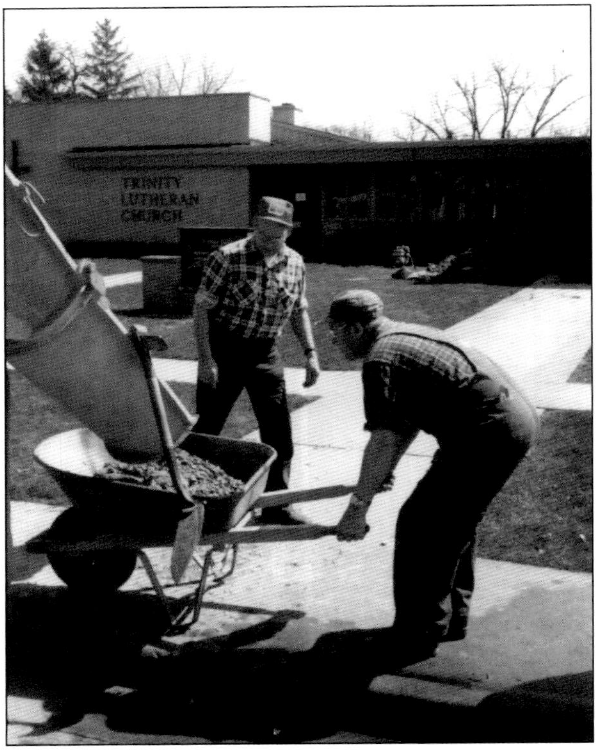

Congregation members agreed in 1983 to build a tower to house the church's original bell on to the front of their modern Trinity Lutheran Church on Church Street. Groundbreaking for the tower was held in April and the job was finished on June 23, 1983. The bell was rung in the new tower for the first time on July 10, 1983. Parish members Art Kahl, standing, and Chris Kahl, with the wheelbarrow, pour cement for the tower construction. (Courtesy of Trinity Lutheran Church.)

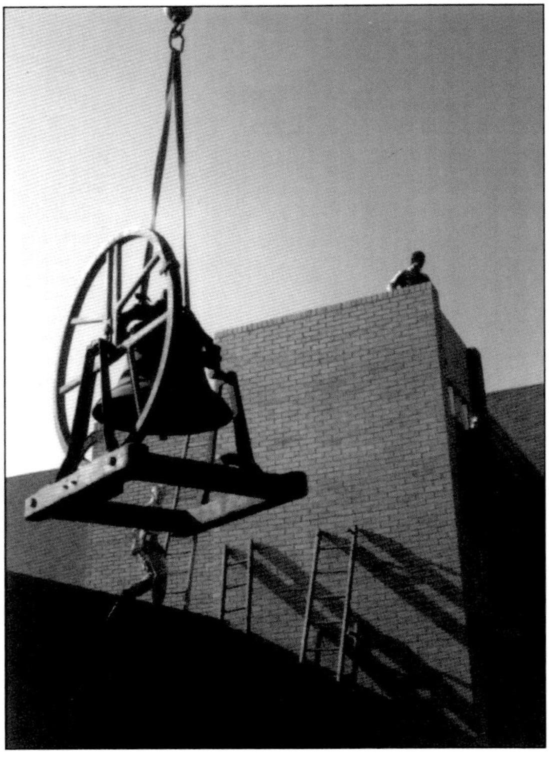

The bell is lifted into the new tower at Trinity Lutheran Church. The bell was housed in the tower of the original Lutheran church until the tower was struck by lightening. The bell later was stored in Delwin and Fran Borhart's barn for many years. In 1983, parishioners voted to build a tower on their modern church to house the bell. According to information on the bell, it was cast in Troy, New York, in 1878. (Courtesy of Trinity Lutheran Church.)

Four

School Days

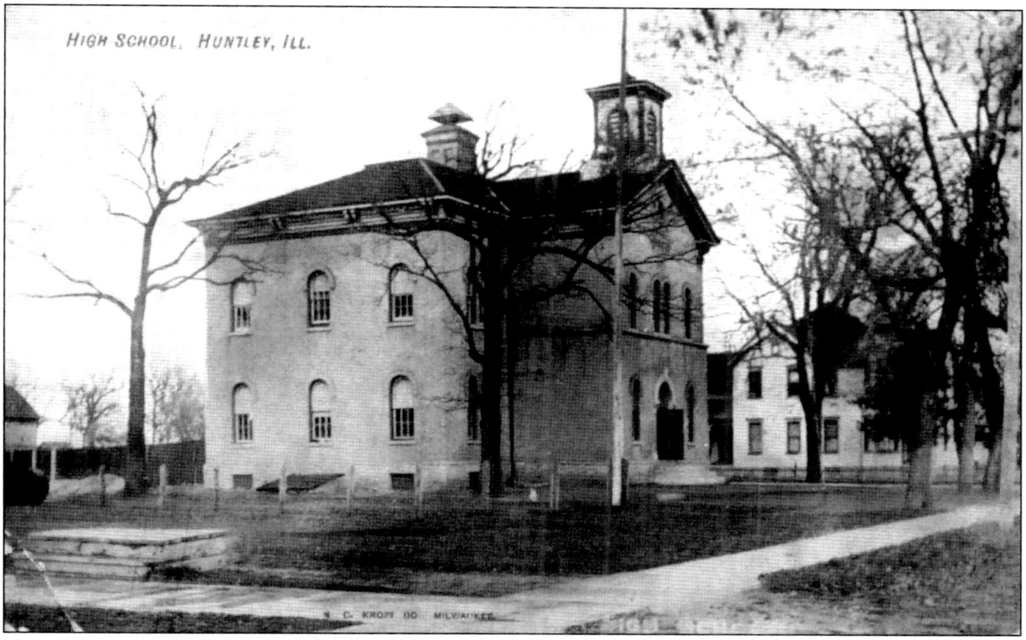

Huntley was proud of its brick town school, built in 1875 to house elementary and high school students. It replaced a frame building that was built in 1860. Located on Main Street east of the First Congregational Church, the 1875 school had four classrooms, four teachers, and 150 students when it opened. It cost $7,475 to build the school in 1875. This postcard is dated December 4, 1900, and shows the school before a 1909 addition was built. This school was in use until 1955. (Courtesy of Noel and Lillian Hansmann.)

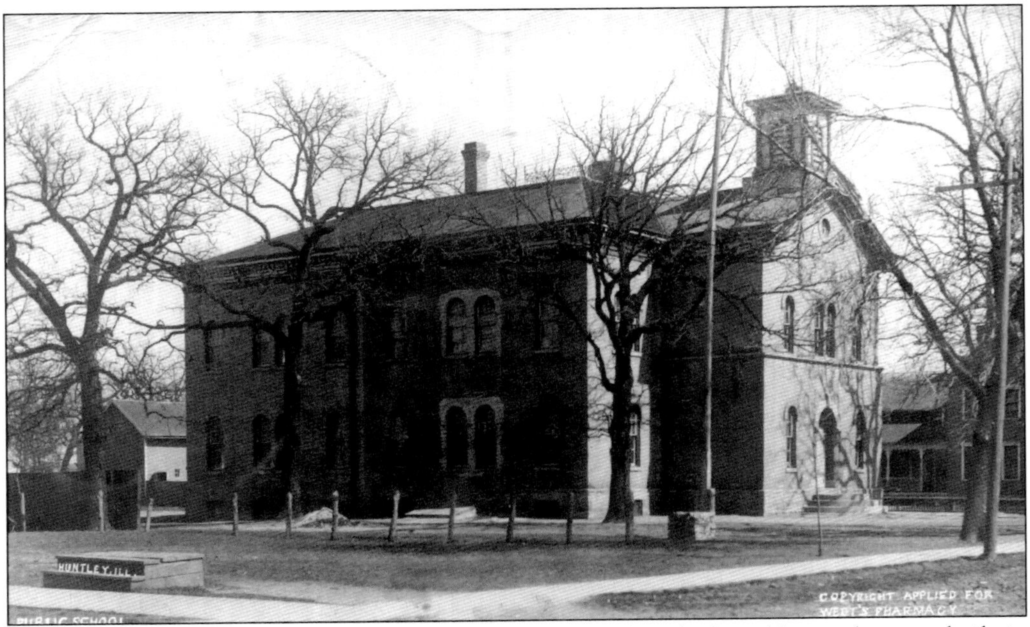

This postcard dated 1910 shows the 1875 Huntley School with the addition that was built in 1909. The bigger school, with six rooms, continued to be used for elementary and high school classes until the district consolidated with the rural schools and in 1924 opened a new high school east of the original building. (Courtesy of Jake Marino.)

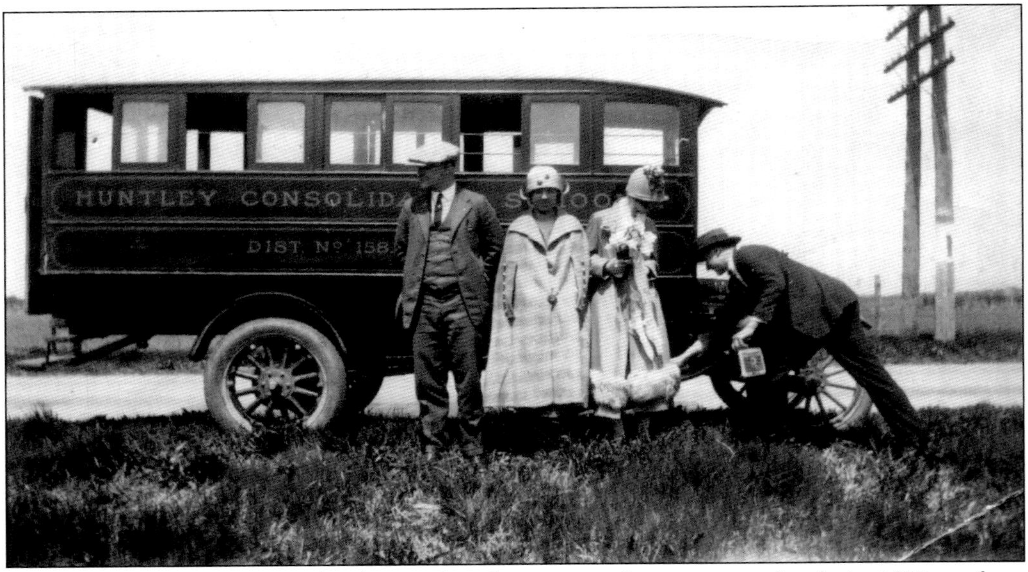

When the Huntley town school united with nine rural one-room schools in 1920 to form McHenry County's first consolidated school district, transportation was needed to bring the country students into town. This wood-sided bus, one of two, with long seats running the full length along the sides, did the job. Pictured are Fred Maushak, left, and Joe Hemmer. The women are unidentified. (Courtesy of Huntley Area Public Library.)

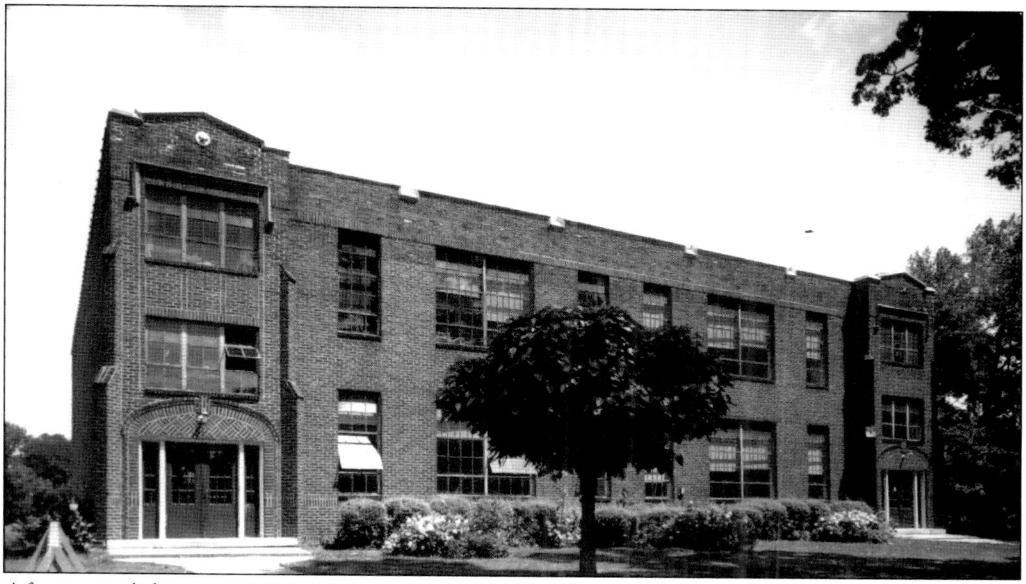

After consolidation in 1920, Huntley found its schoolhouse inadequate to house all elementary and high school students. Classes for upper grades were held on the second floor of the general store at Woodstock and Coral Streets until a new high school was completed in 1924 east of the earlier school. This school was in use as a high school until 1955. It was later used as Robinson Plastics factory and torn down in 1990. (Courtesy of Tom and Donna Kalsow.)

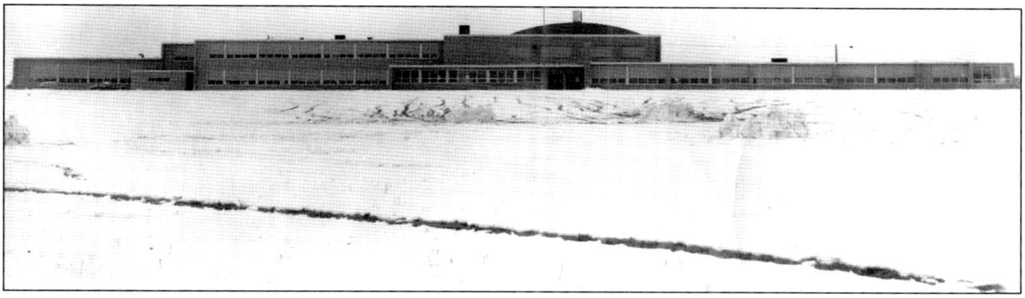

When it was opened in 1955, this school, located between Route 47 and Lincoln Street on the north side of Mill Street, housed all students for School District 158. The school later was known as Huntley Elementary, when in 1967, high school students were moved across Mill Street to a new building there. Still later, the elementary school became known as North Elementary, and the high school became South Elementary when a new high school was opened at the Harmony Road Campus. This building has been torn down to make way for development. (Courtesy of Mary Beth Manning.)

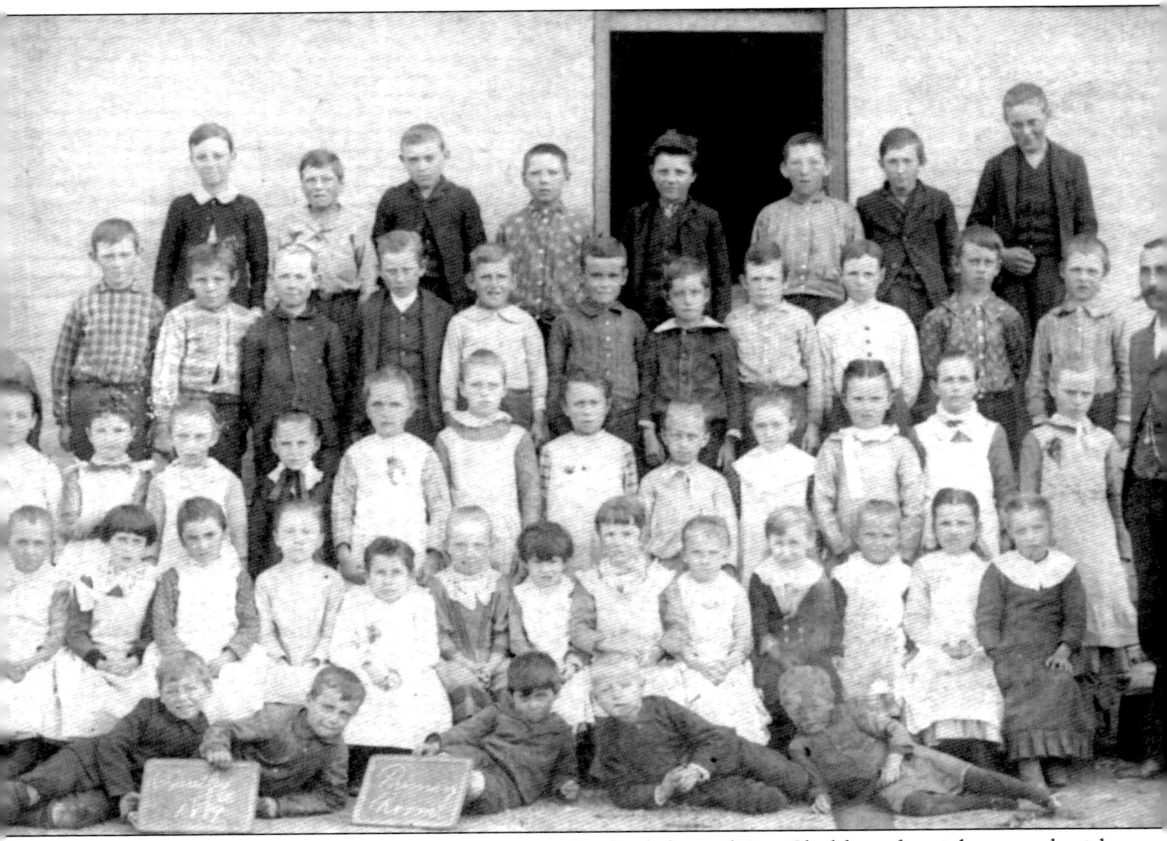

Teachers Nellie Pearsall, partially seen on the far left, and Jim Sheldon, far right, stand with Huntley elementary school students in 1889. Students from left to right are (first row) ? Werhorn, ? Ludwig, ? Ludwig, Roy Skeels, and Grant Skeels; (second row) Anna Graupner, Leslie Van Alstyne, Lizzie Schnelle, Etta Sheehan, Clara Schermerhorn, Bess Butler, ? Morck, ? Morck, Neva Hawley, Josie Clinnin, unidentified, unidentified, and Christina Weide; (third row) ? McNeeney, Florence Sawyer, Edith Hawley, Mary Alice Keating, ? Ross, Emma Heuer Ehlert, unidentified, Tillie Clara Hooker, Sophia Karsten, unidentified, Hannah Kausffert, and Minnie Zerbel; (fourth row) Dan Casey, Willie Weide, Willie McNeeney, Willie Wendt, Gus Graupner, ? Ludwig, Fred Ferris, Willie Casey, Walter Farley, Harry Van Alystyne, and Charles Mason; (fifth row) John Hadley, Louis Werhorn, Ernest Karsten, Ben Lawson, unidentified, unidentified, Eddie Carroll, and Charlie Zerbel. (Courtesy of Tom and Barb Conley.)

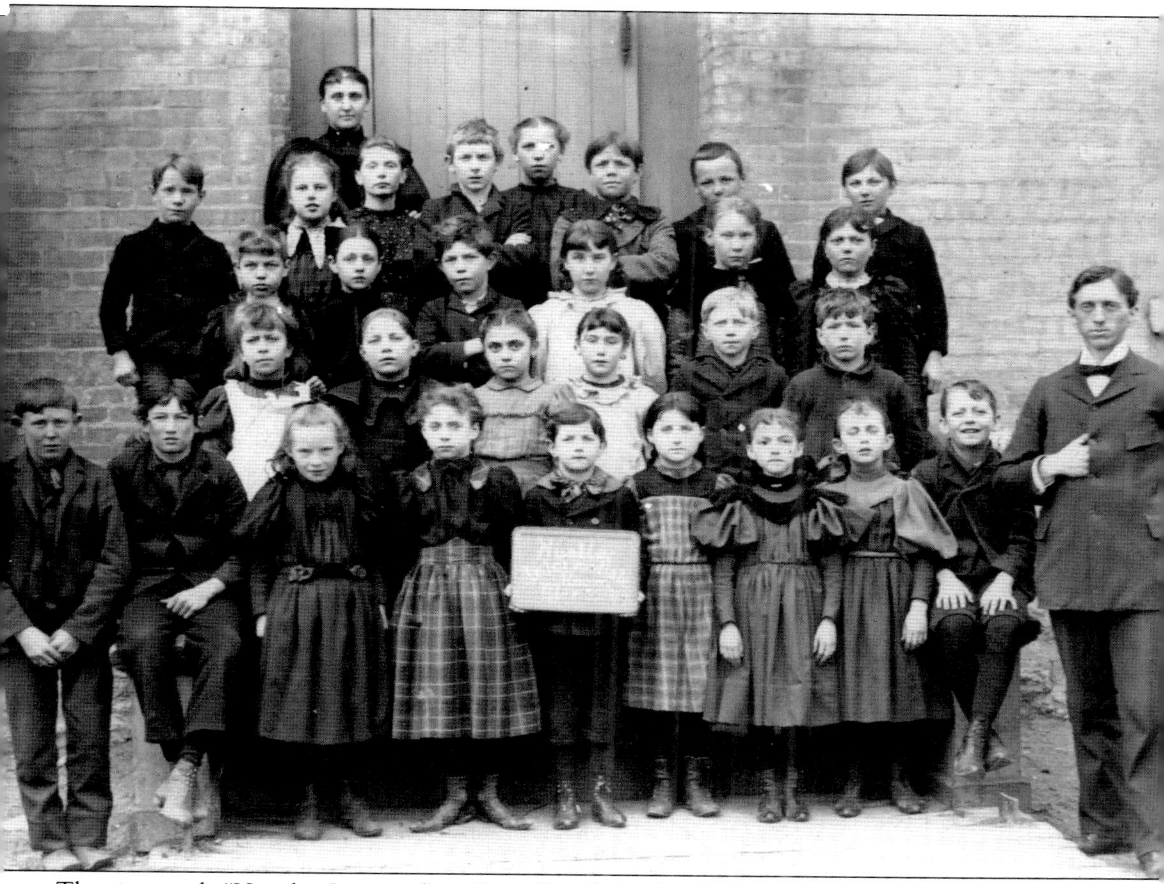

The sign reads "Huntley Intermediate Room" and the date is March 22, 1897. Future Huntley School teacher and School District 158 elementary school namesake Hannah Martin, at age nine and a half, is in the first row, third from the left. Also pictured are (first row) Will Meyers, Charles O'Malley, Hannah Martin, Hattie Weltzien, Fred Meyers, Anna Keating, Hazel Hadley, Lillian Hawley, and John Wendt; (second row) Mammie Wehrhorn, Alvina Frenck, Emma Schnelle, Jeannie Miller, Ed Pabst, and Frank Wales; (third row) Marguerite Elsholtz, Mabel Thomas, Joe Zenk, Mary Miller, Carrie Rammien, and Clara Henning; (fourth row) Frank Chase, Marjorie Kurant, Mae Casey, Alfred Casey, Bertha Graupner, Ned Chase, Lee Templeton, and Charlie Schnelle. Superintendent Mr. Ebershol is at far right in the first row, and teacher Nina Butler is behind the fourth row. (Courtesy of Tom and Barb Conley.)

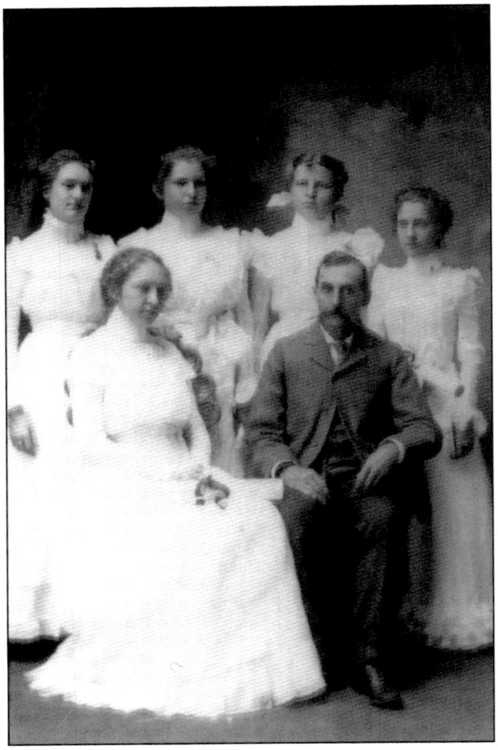

The Huntley High School graduating class of 1900 is shown with their teacher, Jim Sheldon. Standing from left to right, graduates include Iva Disbrow, Martha Kreimann, Tess Dwyer, and Neva Hawley. Bess Cook is seated in front. (Courtesy of Tom and Barb Conley.)

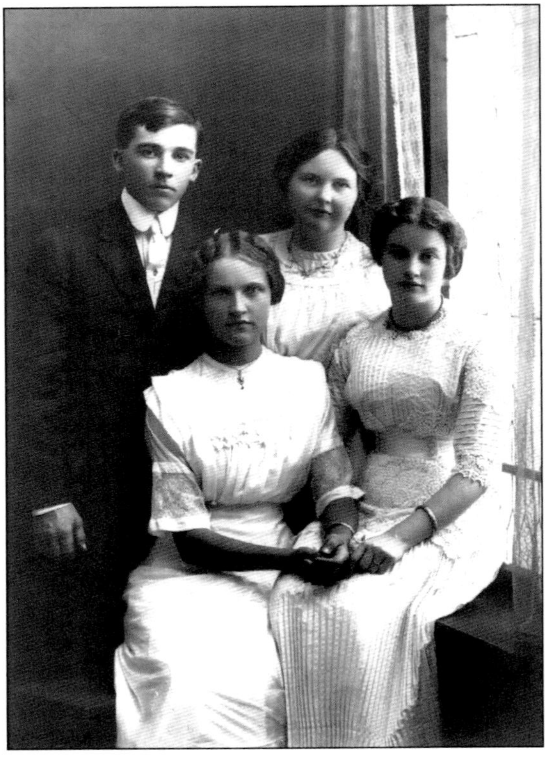

The Huntley High School graduating class of 1913 was a decidedly small group. Pictured from left to right are (first row) Lola Maushak and Marie Kelley Donahue; (second row) William "Pat" Williams and Georgiana Donahue. Huntley High School graduated its first class, consisting of five students, in 1887. (Courtesy of Mary Beth Manning.)

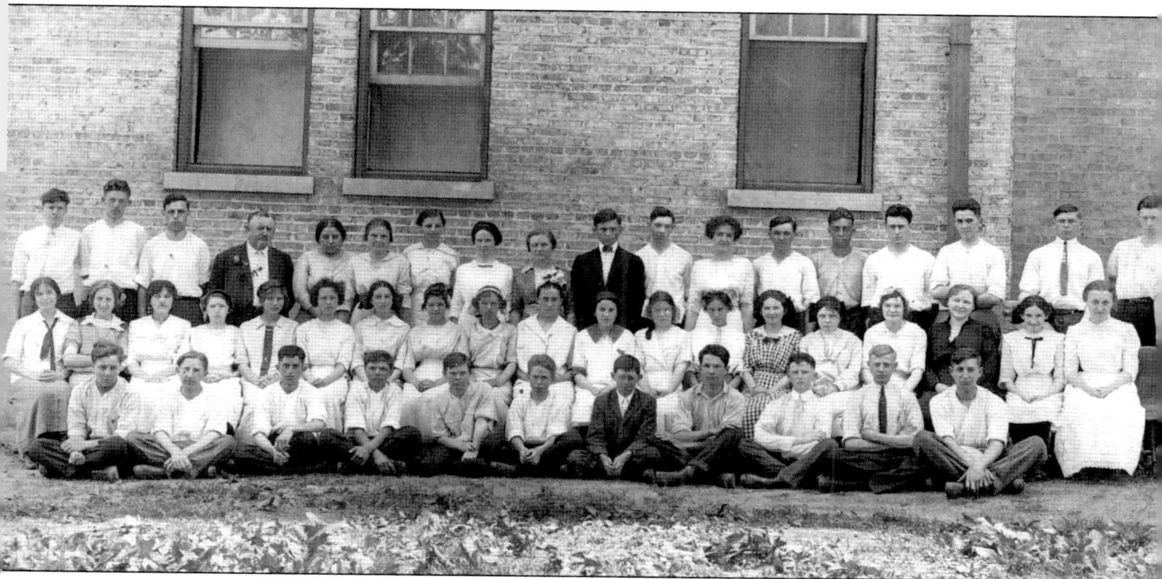

This 1914 photograph of Huntley High School students includes several members who went on to make names for themselves. Carl Schmalz became a professor at Harvard University and chairman and chief executive officer of R. H. Stearns Department Store in Boston. Frank Beu was president of Western Illinois University from 1942 to 1957. Mabel Donahue Hemmer, Bernice Heinemann, and Ida Mackeben became well-respected longtime teachers in the Huntley school district. One of the district schools is named for Ida Mackeben and her brother Harley, and another is named for Heinemann. Pictured are (first row) Edmond Hemmer, Herman Kunke, Glenn Keating, Walter Weltzien, William Donahue, Alfred Frenck, Arthur Heinemann, Harold Williams, Gordon Kelley, Frank Beu, and Clarence Frenck; (second row) Elsie Heuer Bandlow Hoy, Eva Frenck, Bernice Rehberg Michelsen, Emma Heideman, Marie Heuer Rugg, Lizzie Ehlert, Sue Manning Hein, Helen Karsten, ? Berner, Helen Sinnett, Mary Rehberg, Mary Donahue, Ruth Campbell, Jennie Williams, Jessie Ritz, Margaret Williams, Grace Hibbins, Loretta Powers Darby, and Ida Mackeben; (third row) Harold Heuer, Gordon Stringer, Carl Schmalz, George Sykes (superintendent), Pearl Hemmer, Mabel Donahue Hemmer, Bernice Heinemann, Ethel Williams, Marion Lawson Voss, Ed Heuer, Elmer Sewell, Grace Randall (teacher), Arnold Mortensen, Fred Campbell, Earl Williams, Percy Smith, Charles Hadley, and Hugh Williams. (Courtesy of the Edmond Hemmer Family.)

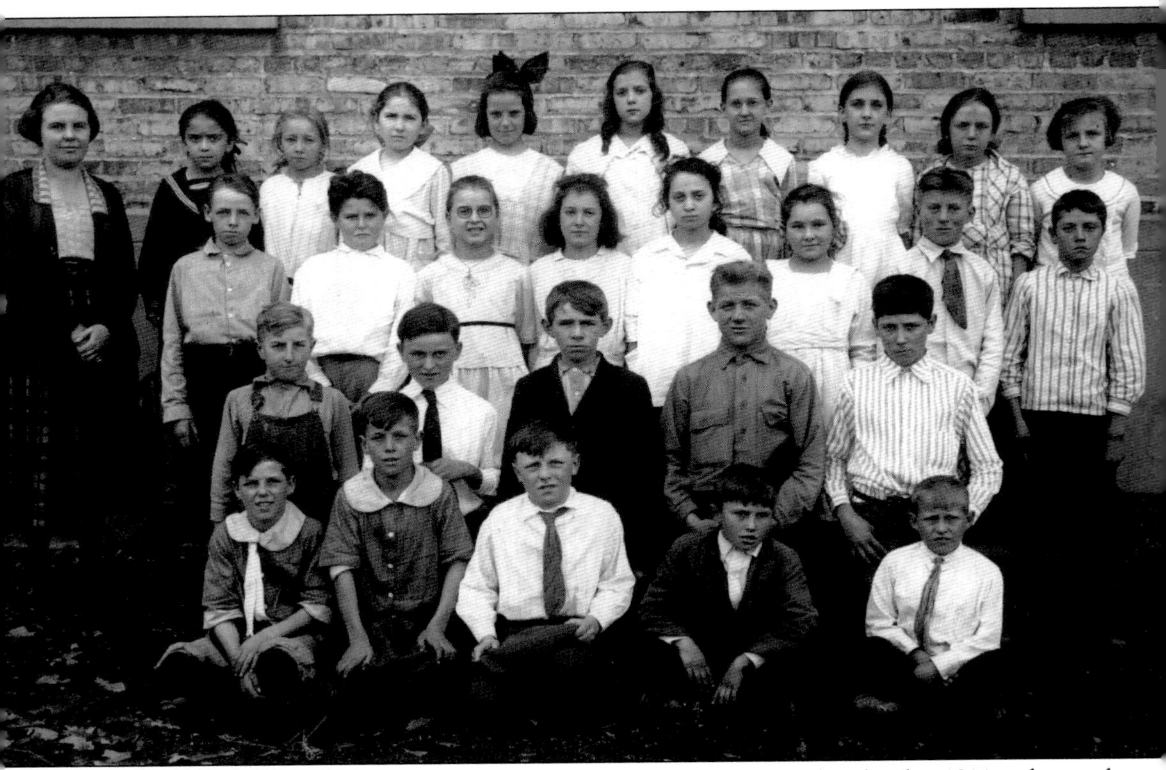

Mabel (Donahue) Hemmer (1896–1990) graduated from Huntley High School in 1914 and turned to teaching elementary school. She taught in the rural one-room schoolhouses and in the town school on Main Street. Here she is shown with her fifth-grade class in town in 1921. Pictured are (first row) William Schultz, Richard Schultz, George Schultz, Charles Lamz, and Earl Kalsow; (second row) Joseph Dryer, Lester Davis, unidentified, Fred Boxleitner, unidentified; (third row) Raymond Northrup, Harold Johnson, Elsie Guth, unidentified, Josephine Fabri, Marjorie Rugh Eggers, Lester Koppen, and Otto Olson; (fourth row) Loretta Van Vleet, Emily Miller, Garnet Olson Jones, Elizabeth Schultz, Marion Kreutzer Willer, Helen Drendel, Kathryn Burns, Merle Ritz, and Mary Louise Hoy. (Courtesy of Mary Beth Manning.)

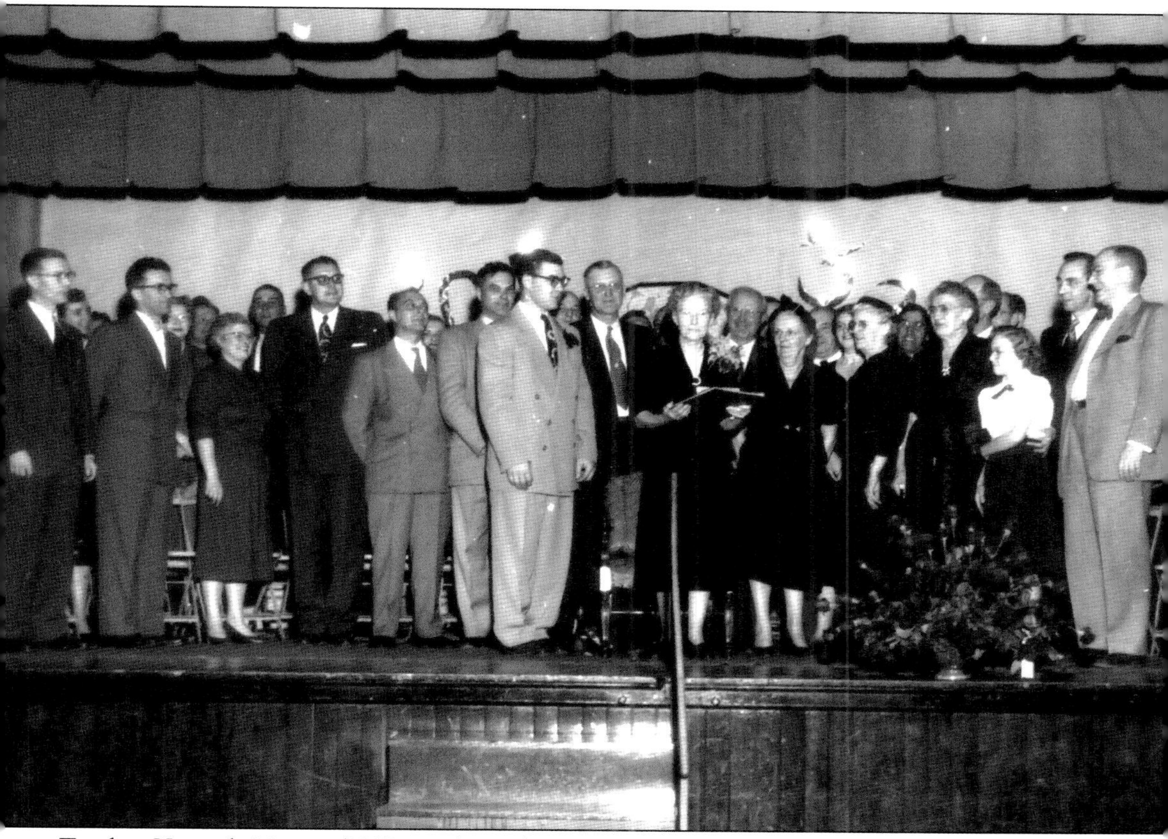

Teacher Hannah Martin (1887–1981) was honored in 1949 for her many years of teaching in the Huntley school district. Martin taught for 60 years in McHenry County, 55 of those years were in Huntley. She taught typing, bookkeeping, and shorthand at Huntley High School, and some of her students went on to win state typing competitions. The Huntley Parent-Teacher Association sponsored an open house called This is Your Life, to honor the beloved teacher. Pictured are (first row) Richard Tazewell (county superintendent), Huntley mayor Ed Williams, Marion Conley, James Davis, Clinton Swanson, Norm Kalsow, Alfred Jordi, Harley Mackeben, Hannah Martin, Margaret Connor, Hazel Lazansky, unidentified, Roxanne Stading, Ernest Stading Jr. (school board secretary), and Charles Scherer. (Courtesy of Mary Beth Manning.)

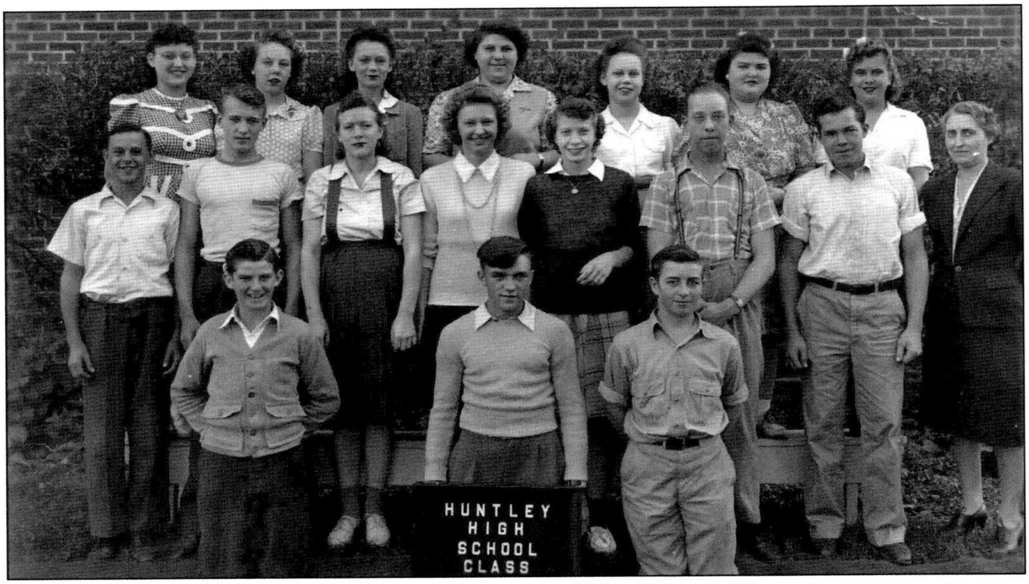

Teacher Margaret Morrissey taught this 1945 Huntley High School class in the building that was constructed along east Main Street in the early 1920s. Pictured are (first row) Wayne Donahue, George Finzel, and Donald Tessmer; (second row) Gene Wasserstrass, Richard Jacobs, Helen Ashbaugh, Arlene Hensel, Dorothy Hess, Alfred Krause, Larry Kramka, and Morrissey; (third row) Elmina Olson, Barbara Hemmer, Nina Hennegan, Geraldine Goodman, Iris Kunke, La Verne Bartelt, and Maida Dalby. (Courtesy of Wayne and Carol Donahue.)

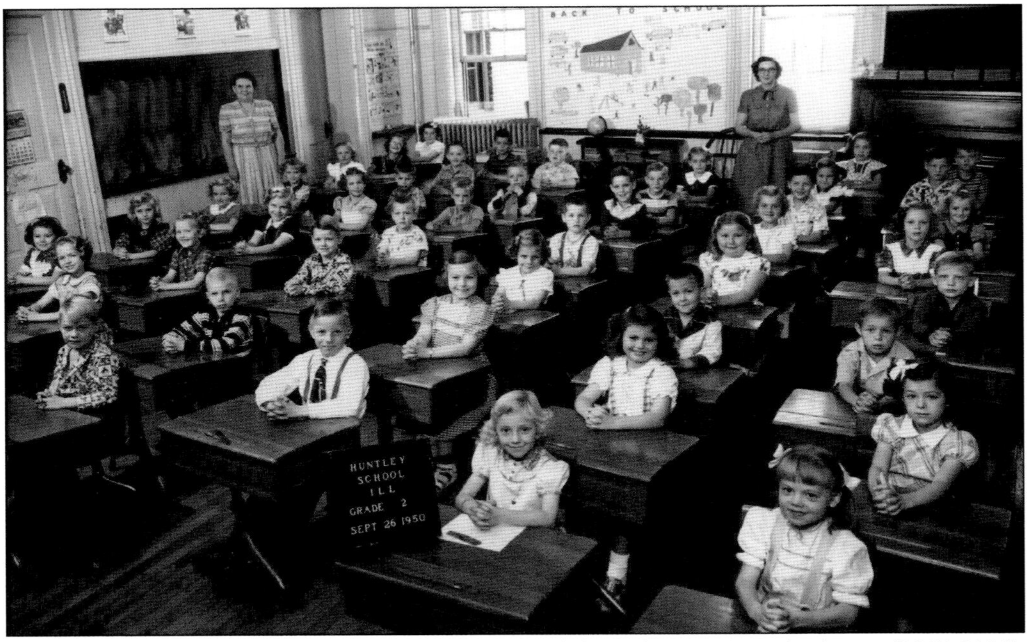

Teachers Mabel Donahue Hemmer (1896–1990), at left, and Betty Ann Anderson (1917–2005), back, pose with their second-grade class at the start of the school year in 1950. The photograph shows the interior of the 1875 building, which was used as a grade school until 1955. (Courtesy of Huntley Area Public Library.)

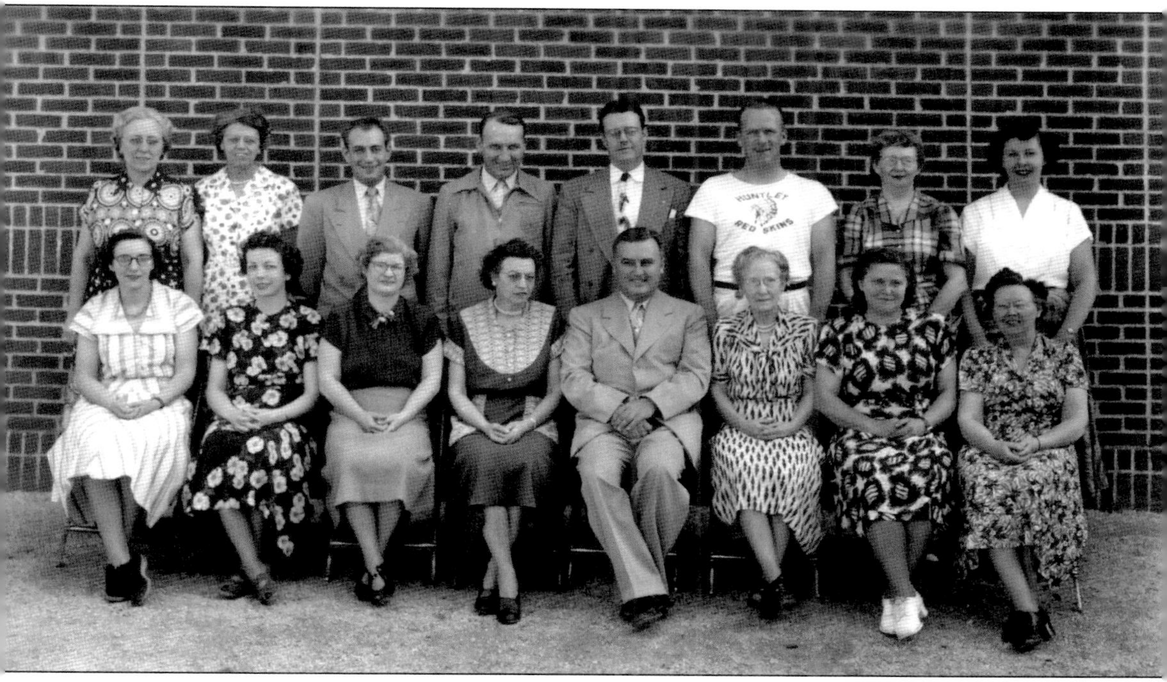

Sixteen teachers comprised the entire staff of School District 158 in 1951. Several of the pictured instructors today have schools in the district named in their honor. Pictured are (first row) Betty Ann Anderson (elementary grades), Marjorie Baker (fourth grade), Marion Conley (third grade), May Chesak (sixth and primary grades), Frank Hendricks (superintendent), Hannah Martin (commercial), Louise Wiese (substitute for Mabel Donahue Hemmer), and Georgiana Donahue (seventh and eighth grades); (second row) Ida Mackeben (fifth grade), Bernice Heinemann (English), Joe Ciontea (music), Henry Marlowe (agriculture), Harry Fairfield (social studies), Guy Leighton (coach), Frances Crowley (first grade), and Marie Kreutzer (home economics). (Courtesy of Huntley Area Public Library.)

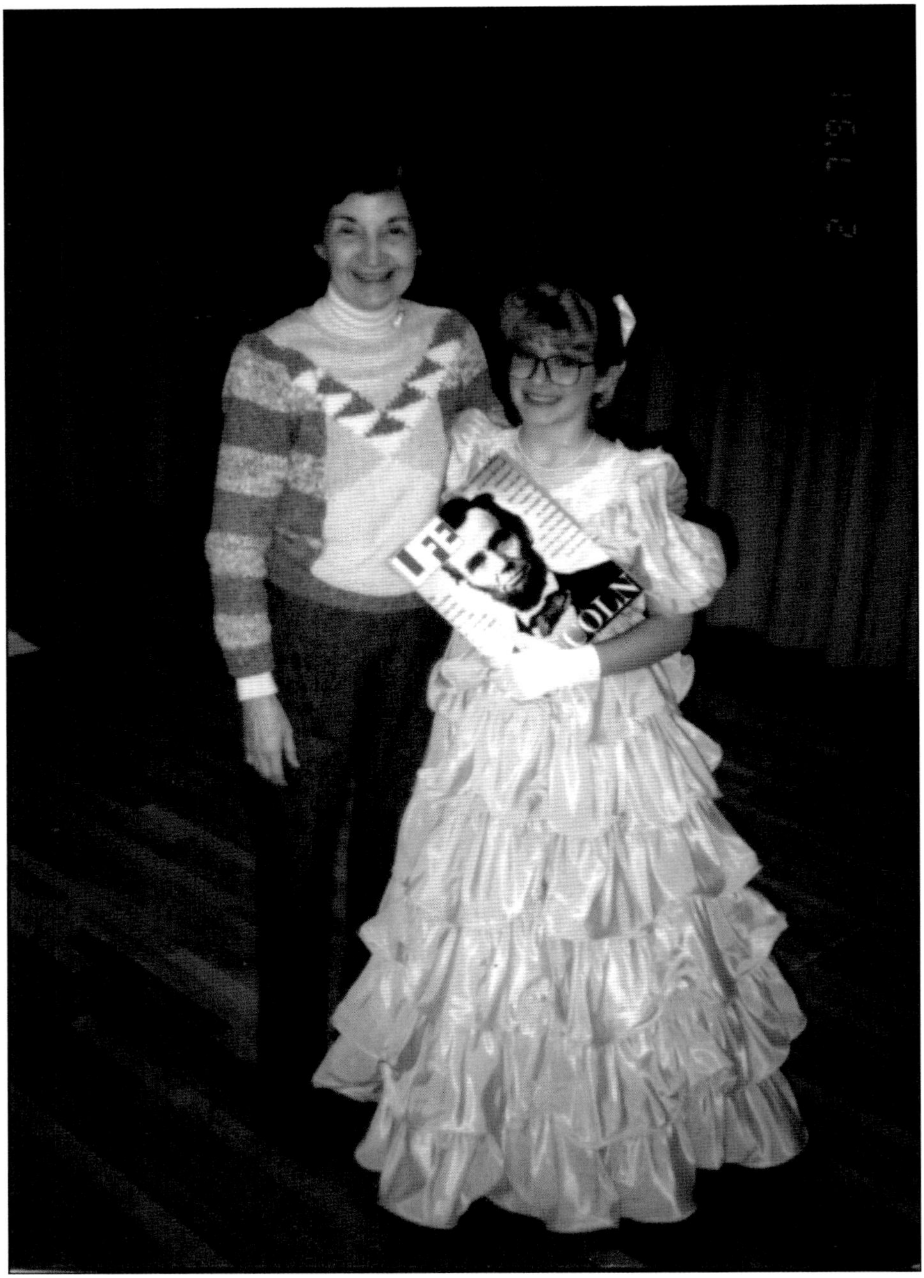

The first new School District 158 elementary school since 1955 was opened on the Harmony Road Campus in 2000 and was named for former teacher Katherine Leggee (1929–1994). Leggee was known for the Abraham Lincoln play that she developed for her third-grade class in 1971, the first year she taught in the Huntley schools. The play quickly became a highlight of the school year and evolved into three performances annually, one for the entire student body, one in the evening for parents, and another at a senior citizens' residence in Woodstock. Krista Jurs took part in the play in 1991. Jurs later went on to be chosen Miss Huntley in 2000. Leggee retired in 1993. (Courtesy of William Leggee)

Five

A Mark in the World

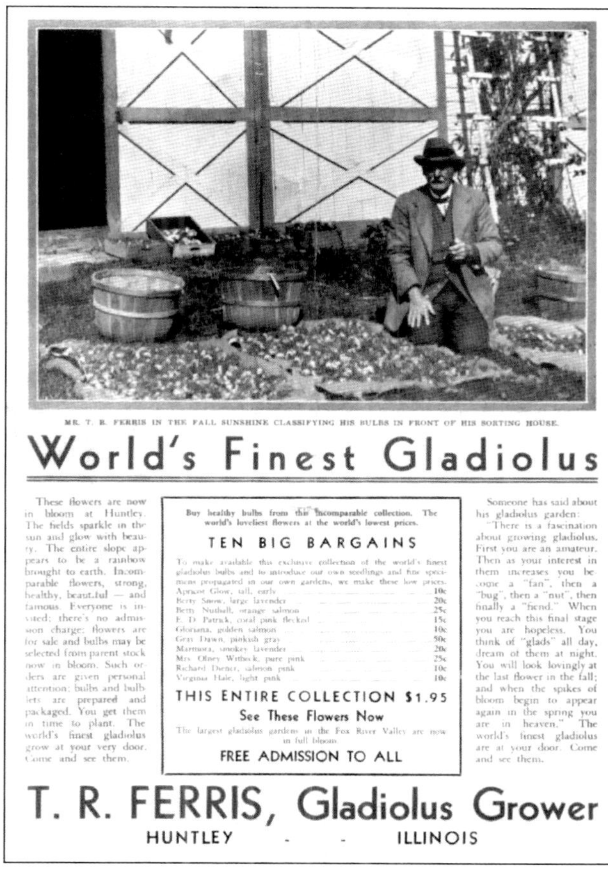

Although a small midwestern town, Huntley made itself known to the larger world in several ways. Theodore R. Ferris (1849–1939) put Huntley on the map with his prolific gladiolus gardens, which he started as a hobby at his home at the north end of Woodstock Street. The hobby eventually became a full-time business, with thousands of visitors, some from other countries, viewing the garden each year. This advertisement for Ferris's gladiolus was printed in a 1932 edition of the *Fox Valley Mirror*. At the time, Ferris, 83, was still actively pursuing business. (Courtesy of Mary Beth Manning.)

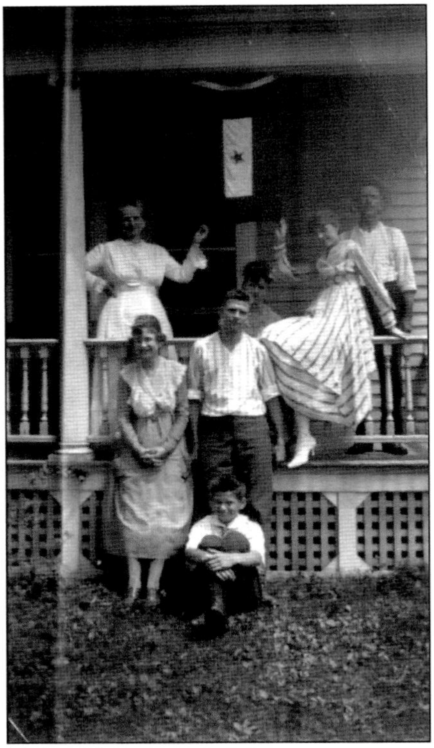

The Heuer family shows their patriotism and support during World War I by displaying a flag with a single star, indicating someone in their family was in active service. Edwin Heuer was in the U.S. Army, stationed in France. Pictured are his family members at their Vine Street (now Route 47) home. Lester Heuer is sitting on the ground. Standing behind him is Elsie Heuer and Harold Heuer. Marie Heuer is sitting on the railing. At left in back is Edwin's mother, Mary Heuer. Standing at back right is Paul Heuer. The woman in the background is unidentified. (Courtesy of Mary Ellen Moerke.)

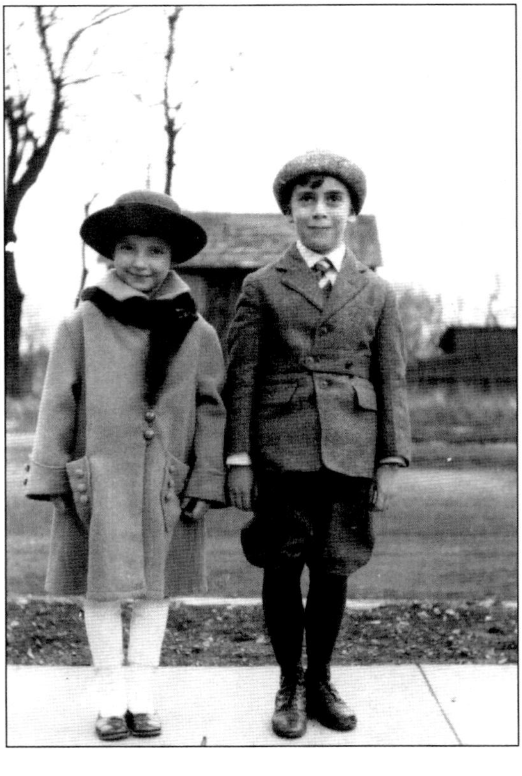

Cousins Betty Ann (Lazansky) Anderson and Oliver Hadley Statler were the descendants of early Huntley settlers Richard Scott Hadley and his wife, Olive Crego, and Henry and Jane (Van Wormer) Sinnett. The Hadley and Sinnett families arrived in the area in the early 1850s. Anderson became a much loved, longtime Huntley elementary school teacher, and Statler became an international best-selling author and noted authority on Japan. (Courtesy of Huntley Area Public Library.)

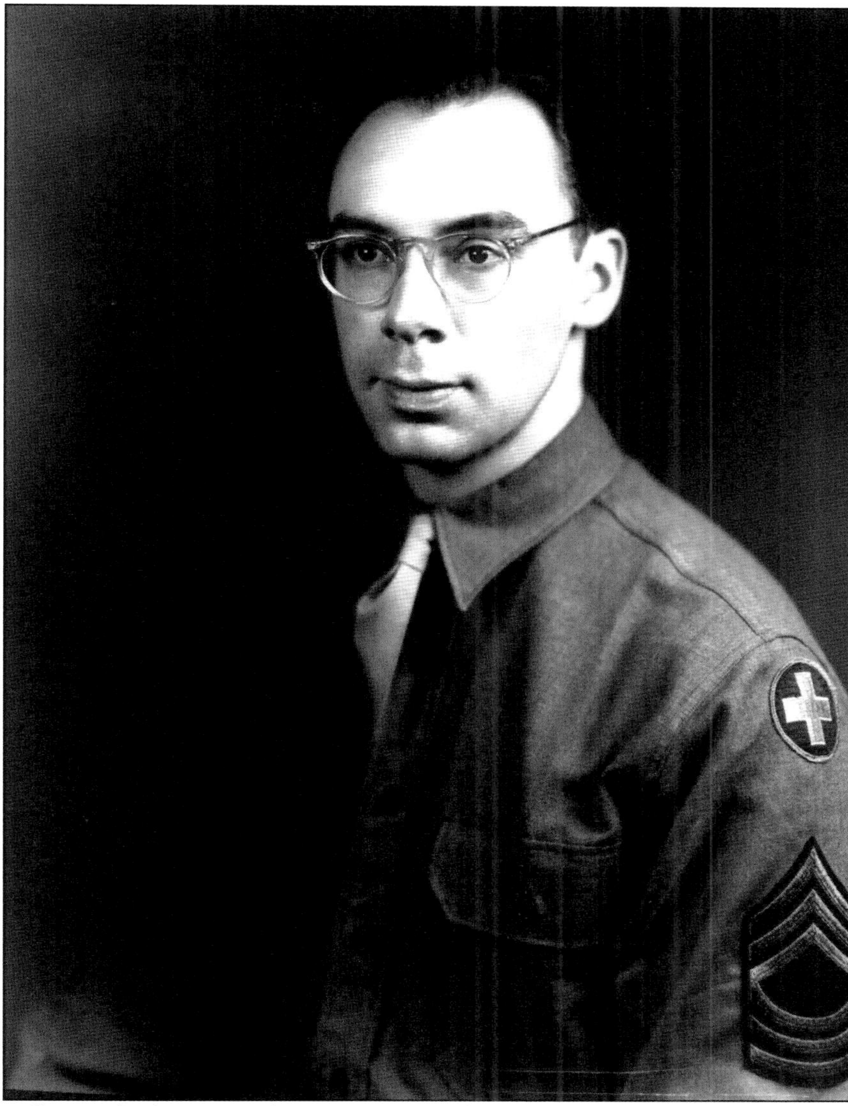

Oliver Hadley Statler (1915–2002) grew up on Woodstock Street and attended elementary school in Huntley. He served in the U.S. Army Quartermaster Corps from 1941 to 1945 in Hawaii, New Guinea, and the Philippines. Following service in World War II, he accepted a position in Yokohama, Japan, where he became interested in collecting Japanese woodblock prints. His collection of more than 1,000 prints is now housed at the Art Institute of Chicago. A mutual love of Japanese prints led Statler to a lasting friendship with Pulitzer prize–winning author James A. Michener. Michener encouraged Statler to prepare a book, and the result was *Modern Japanese Prints: An Art Reborn* (1956). His second book, a novel, *Japanese Inn*, was dedicated to Michener. The book was on the best-seller list for 25 weeks in 1961. Statler also wrote *The Black Ship Scroll* (1963), *Shimoda Story* (1969), and *Japanese Pilgrimage* (1983). He served as an adjunct professor and a fellow in Asian studies at the University of Hawaii where he taught courses in Japanese history. He was a respected authority on Japan, its art and culture, and wrote numerous articles, film scripts, plays, and lectured on Japanese topics. (Courtesy of Huntley Area Public Library.)

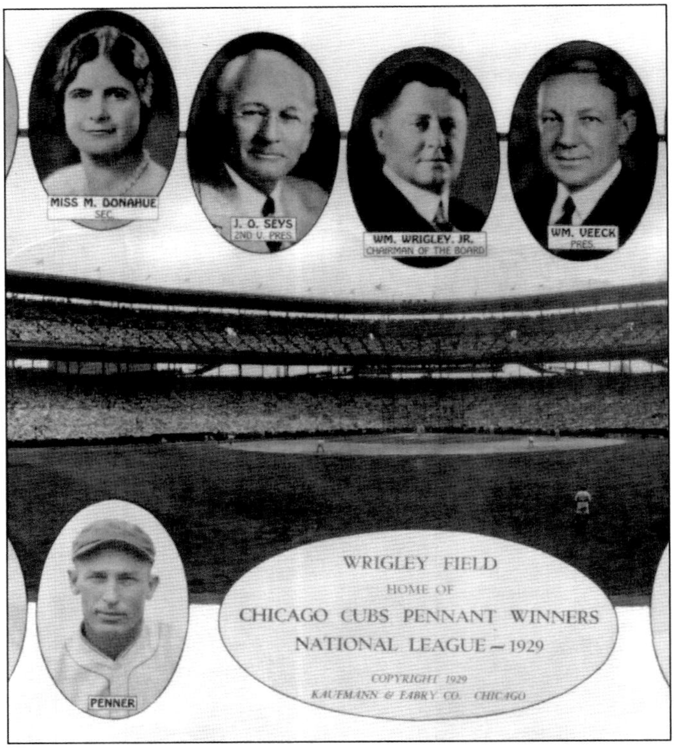

Huntley native Margaret Donahue (1893–1978) was secretary of the Chicago Cubs when this poster was made in 1929. The full panel shows a panoramic view of Wrigley Field, with photographs of team members and club officials. Donahue began as the Chicago National League Ball Club bookkeeper and stenographer in 1918. In 1927, she became club secretary and was elected vice president in 1950. She has the distinction of being the first woman official of a major-league baseball team. Donahue is credited with instituting season ticket holders and special ladies days at Wrigley Field. (Courtesy of the Edmond Hemmer family.)

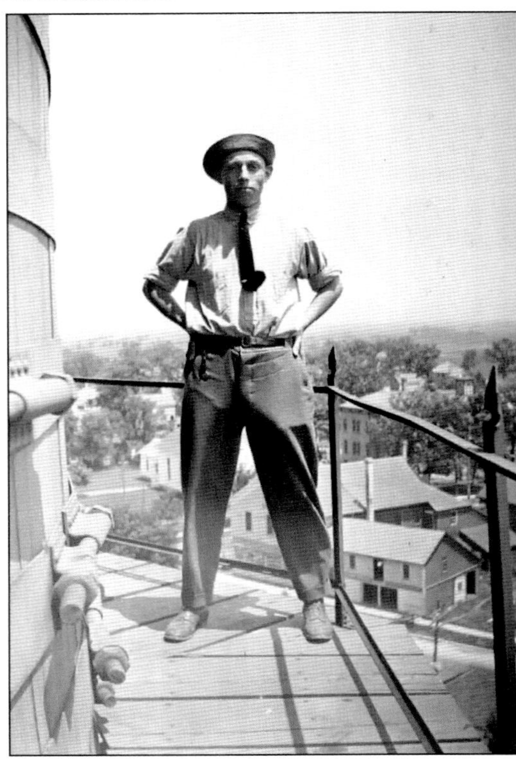

Carl N. Schmalz (1898–1979), son of the local general store owner, graduated from Huntley High School in 1915 and Harvard University in 1919. He became a business professor at Harvard and then chairman and chief executive officer of R. H. Stearns Department Store in Boston. He served as president of the National Retail Merchants Association. Here he is shown in 1915 atop the Huntley water tower, the vantage point for many of the photographs he snapped. The Congregational church and town school are behind him. (Courtesy of Robert Schmalz.)

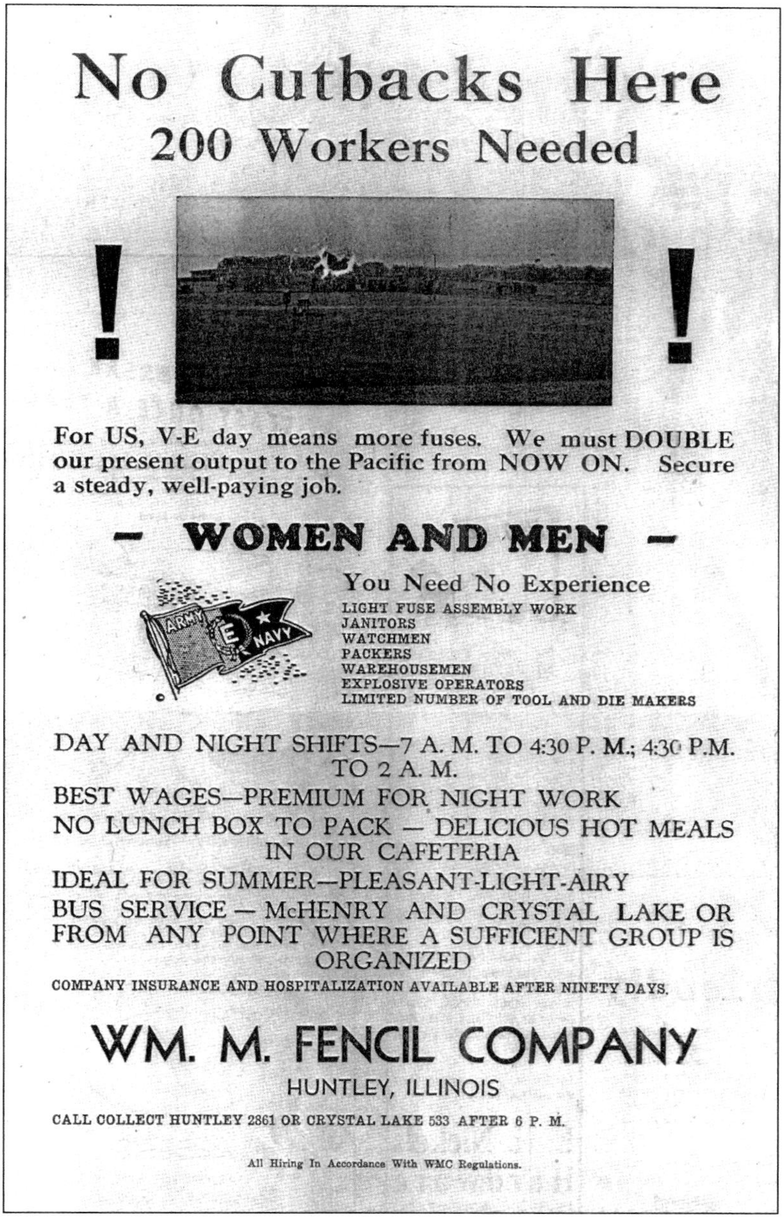

Local residents did their part on the home front during World War II. Detonator fuzes made in a Huntley factory were shipped to U.S. military sites around the world Advertisements for available jobs at the William Fencil Company fuze plant in Huntley ran in local newspapers. The plant, located on a 48-acre parcel of the Roy and Selma Hughes farm along the railroad right-of-way, operated from 1942 to October 1945. The site was marked off with cyclone fencing, barring the curious from views of the various buildings that served in the process of producing detonator caps for weapons. Security was high at the government-supervised location, known to locals as Powder Park because of the explosive powder used to fill the caps. Although advertised as pleasant work with high wages, many of the jobs were dangerous and several explosions occurred at the plant. (Courtesy of Huntley Area Public Library.)

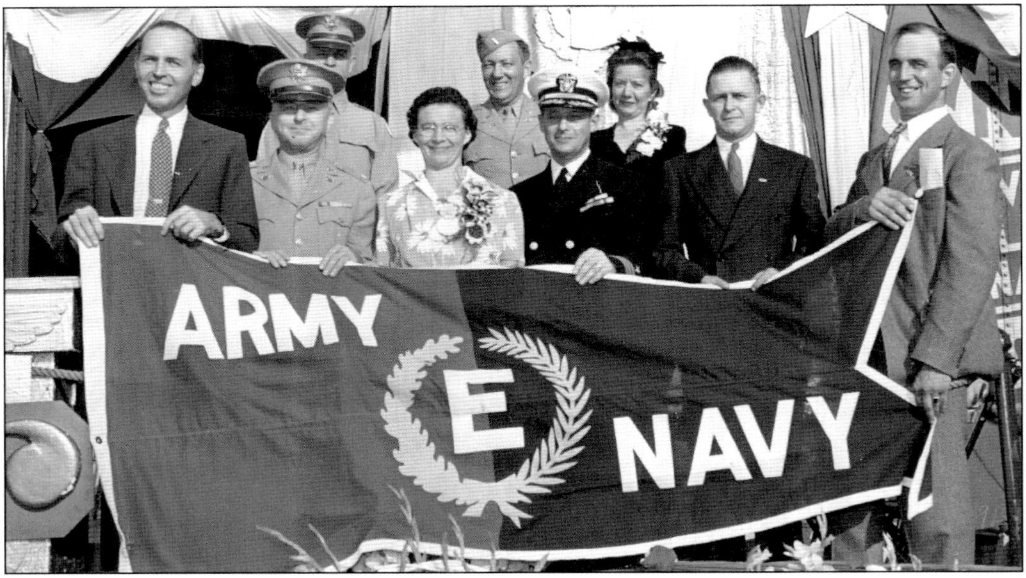

The William Fencil Company plant was very successful at producing mortar fuzes and timed artillery fuzes for the military. The plant received several awards for production, including the Army-Navy E award, the highest civilian honor for the war effort. The presentation, held on September 2, 1944, at the Huntley site, brought the military brass to town. Earl Fyfe, the plant manager (far right), and Meta Tessmer (center) the employee representative, accepted the honor for the local plant. (Courtesy of McHenry County Historical Society.)

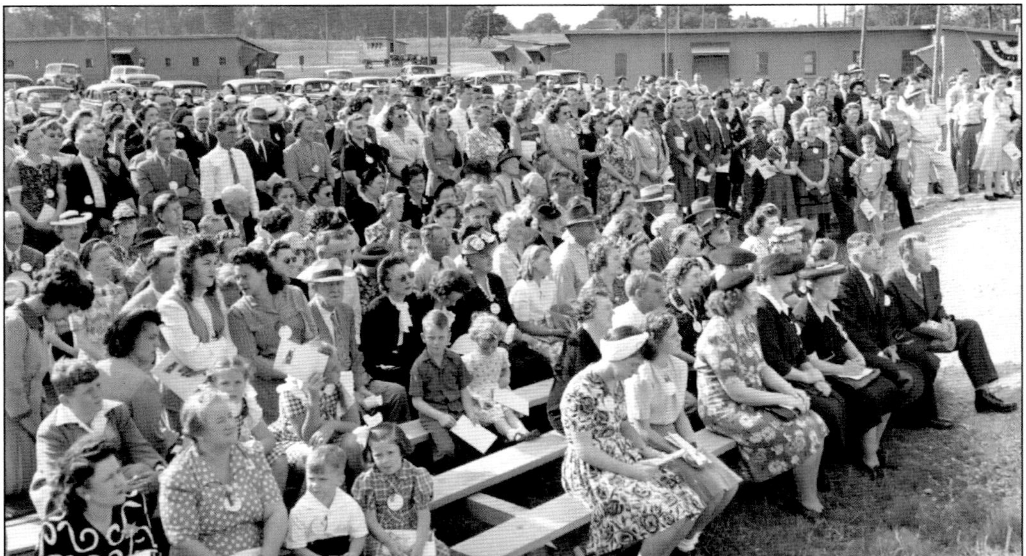

Normally off-limits to the public, the William Fencil Company invited Huntley residents to the ceremonies honoring the plant in September 1944. The town turned out in great numbers. Many viewed the ceremony from temporary seating, while others stood near the back. The award was given to plants that achieved outstanding performance on war production. Some of the facility's various buildings, now long gone, can be seen in the background. (Courtesy of McHenry County Historical Society.)

Six

Historic Square and Aerials

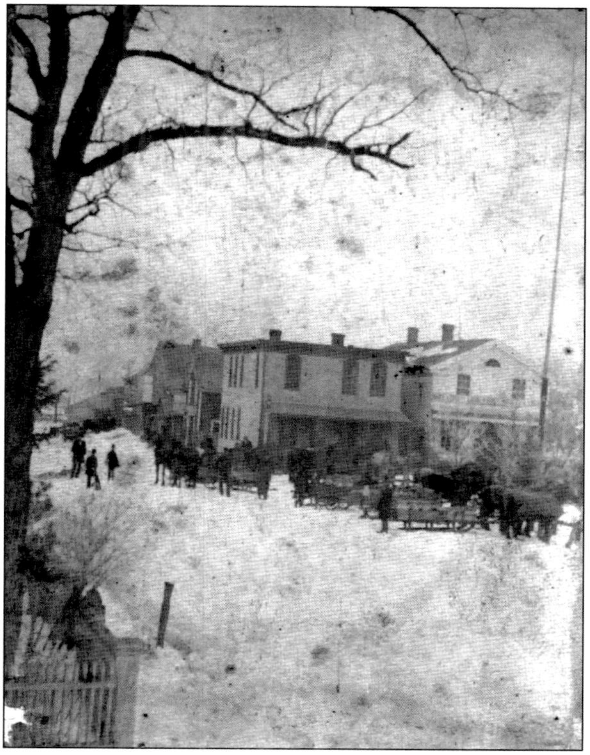

The oldest-known photograph of the village center of Huntley dates to about 1876. It was taken along Main Street looking toward Woodstock Street. The building on the left is one of the town's earliest. It first was used as a hotel, and then from 1881 to 1917, it was Devine and Skeels General Store. Over the years, it has been Otto Hart's General Store, Sigrist Restaurant, a laundromat, a dentist office, a pharmacy, a religious goods store, and a photography business. The building at right with the peaked roof, known as the Wales building, was owned by Willard and Clara Cummings, who sold it to John Hawley and his brother-in-law John G. Weltzien in 1878. Hawley built a new building on the site. The building still stands today. (Courtesy of Tom and Barb Conley.)

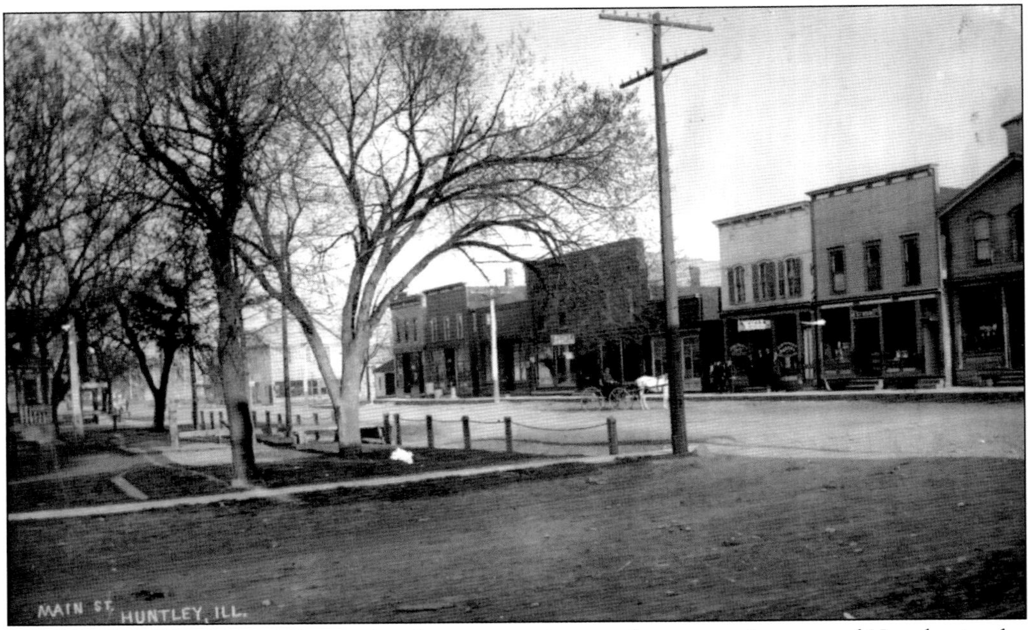

The horse and buggy was the mode of transportation on the unpaved streets of Huntley in the early 1900s. The southwest corner of the square is shown. Woodstock Street is in the foreground. Note the well and trough in the park for watering horses and the prominent telephone poles. In April 1897, a village ordinance granted the Chicago Telephone Company the right to erect and maintain its poles and cables in Huntley. (Courtesy of Huntley Area Public Library.)

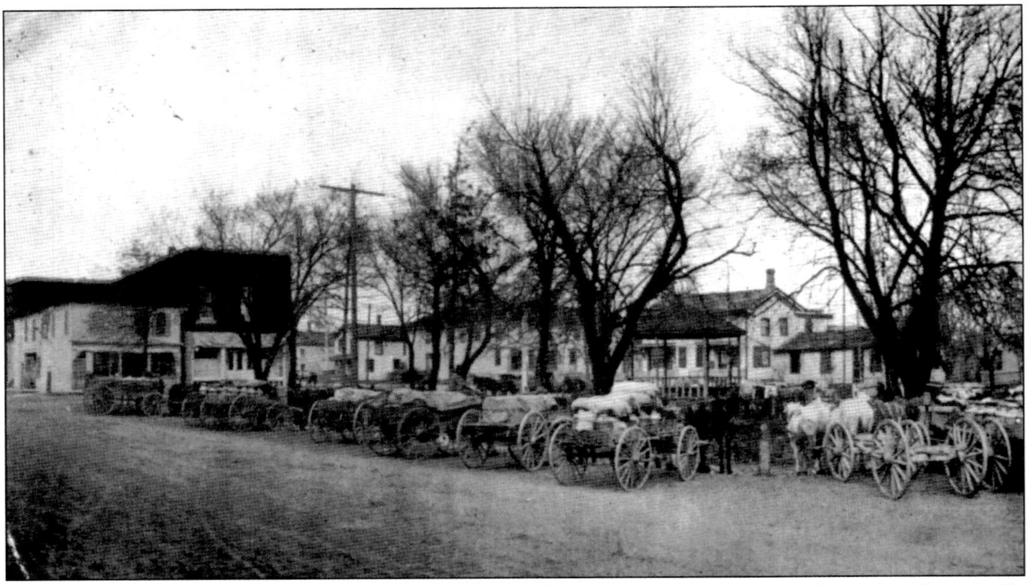
Huntley's town square was a bustling place in the early 1900s. Farmers brought their milk into town early each morning and stayed to shop for necessities. Several general stores were in business at the time, including Devine and Skeels, at the far left. Next to it, another general store was in operation. This photograph, dating to about 1910, looks to the northwest. (Courtesy of Huntley Area Public Library.)

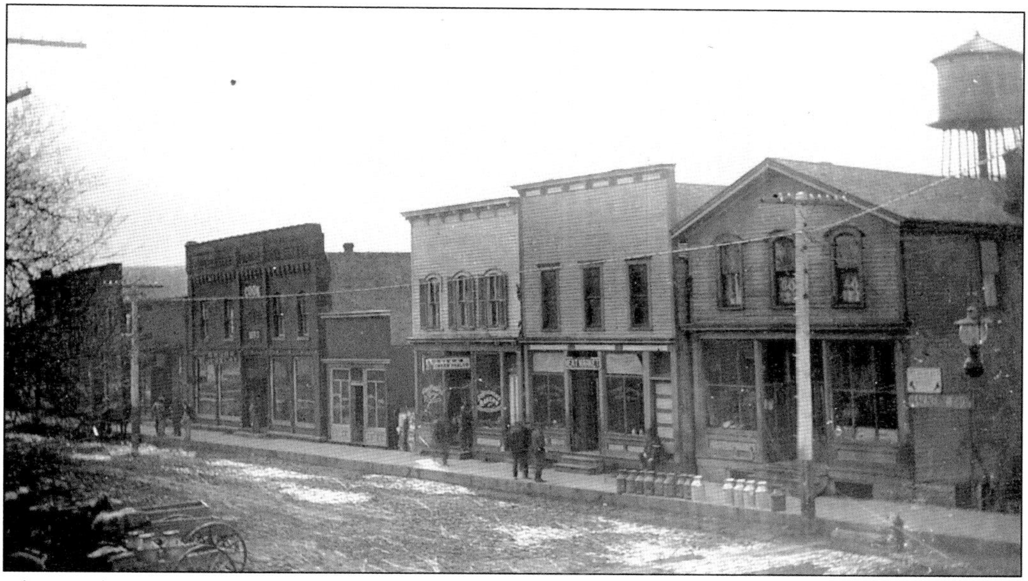

The south side of Main Street was the center of Huntley's business district in the early 1900s. Dry goods, meat markets, a bakery, ice-cream parlors, jewelry stores, and drugstores were among the many businesses in operation. The prospering milk trade was their reason for existence. Milk cans are seen lining the concrete sidewalks. A 1911 ordinance ordered, "All sidewalks in the village shall be cement sidewalks." Note the gaslight hanging over the street at the far right. (Courtesy of Tom and Barb Conley.)

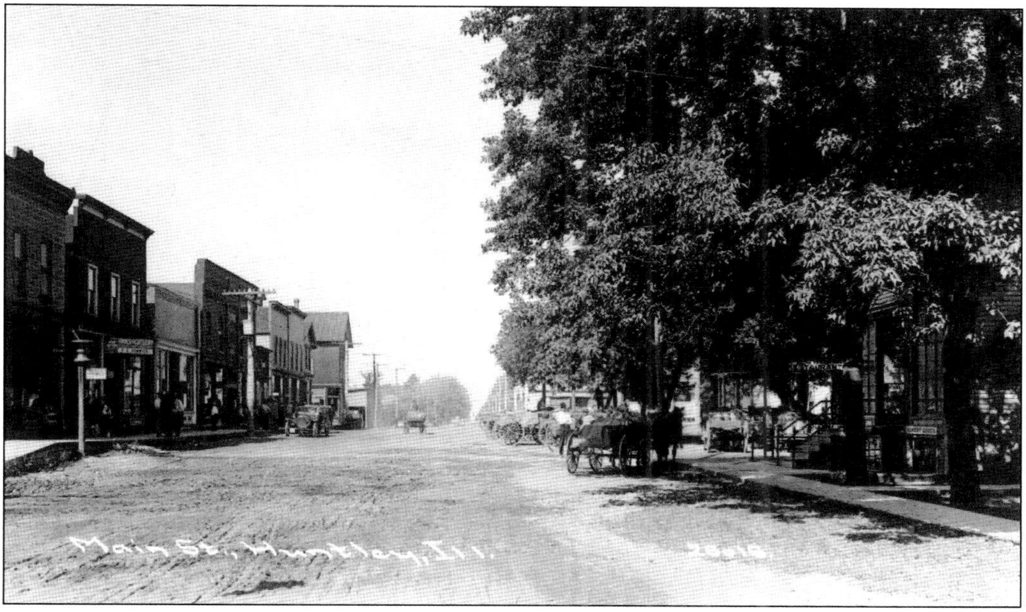

Businesses operated at the east end of the town square and can be seen at the right-hand side in this early 1900s photograph. The view is facing west. The upper level of the building at the far right housed a restaurant, and the lower level advertised bakery goods. Glazier's harness shop, and, in succession, Oakley's, Fisher's, and Ehorn's furniture stores also operated at this location. The buildings were torn down some time after 1918. (Courtesy of Tom and Barb Conley.)

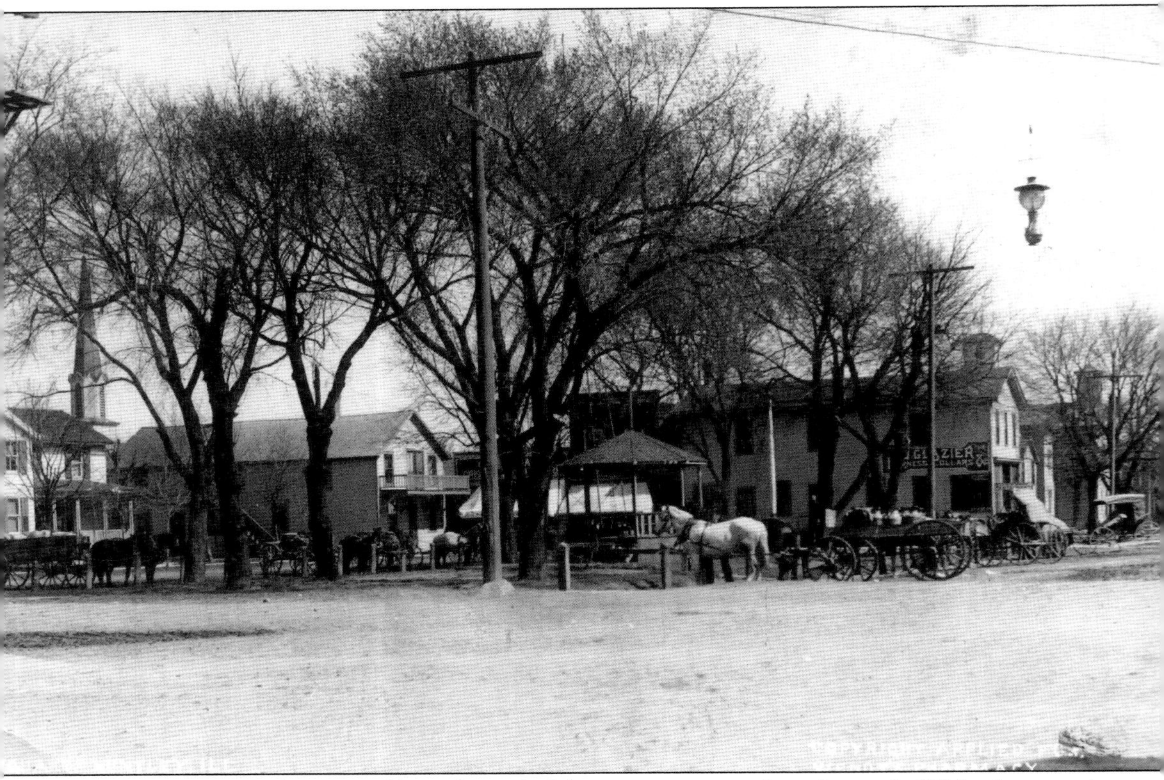

Glazier's harness shop is visible at the end of the town square park in this early 1900s photograph. Looking northeast into the square, the many buildings that once occupied that area of the downtown can be seen. Schmalz's General Store operated at the very eastern edge of what is today Coral Street on the northeast end of the square. Its marquee can be seen, barely visible, just to the right of the center building's second-story balcony. Note the Lutheran church's steeple to the left and the gas lantern hanging above the street on the right. One of the local milk plants began providing electricity for the town in 1913. Electric streetlights were not installed until the 1920s. (Courtesy of Noel and Lillian Hansmann.)

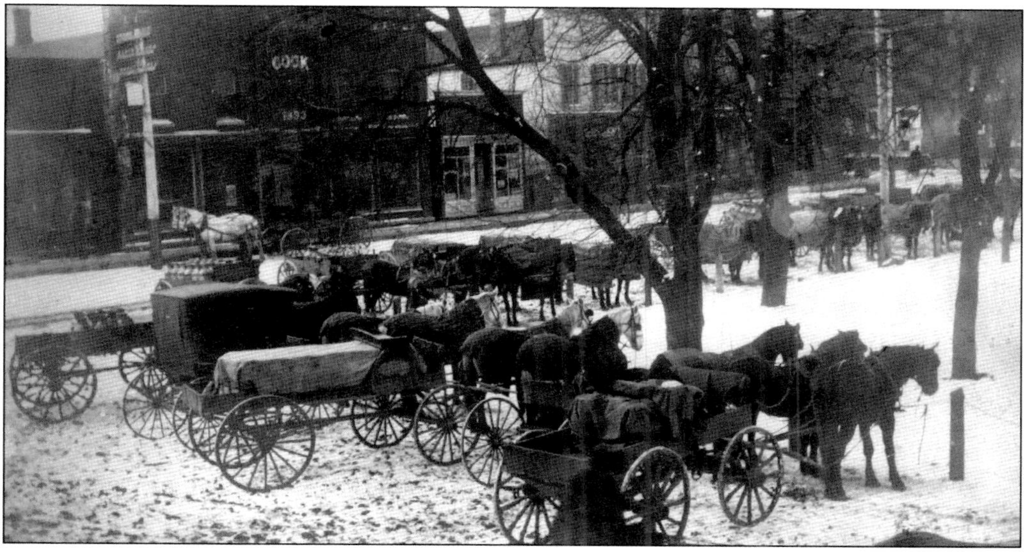

The Cook building is seen in this photograph looking south along Main Street. Dr. Charles E. Cook constructed the building in 1893 to house his medical practice and the first bank in town, the Farmers' Exchange Bank. After Cook died in 1904, his brother Ed Cook owned the building, housing his pharmacy and the bank, until his death in 1951. Ed Cook also was one of the town's undertakers and had a casket showroom in the upper level of the building. Today the building is one story. The street in the foreground now is part of the town square park. (Courtesy of Tom and Barb Conley.)

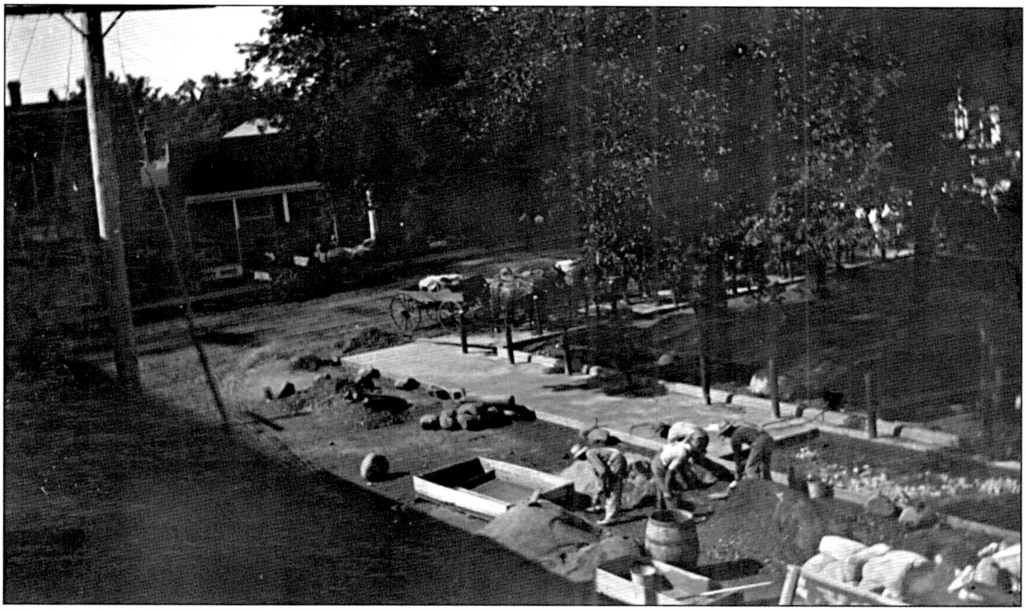

Workers cement an area for horse tethering at the east end of the square around 1915. The photograph most likely was taken from Schmalz's General Store, which would have been along this side of the square. Glazier's harness shop, Ehorn's furniture, a dentist, a bakery, and a lunchroom were some of the other business that operated at this end of the town square. Church Street was along the back of the stores. (Courtesy of Robert Schmalz.)

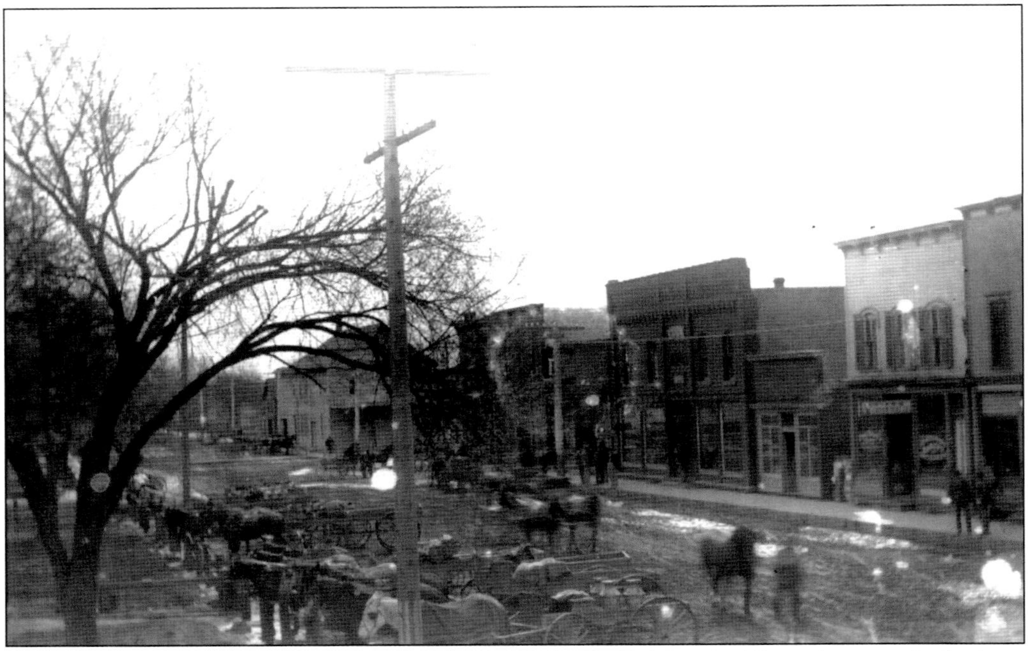

The busy town square is shown at the dawn of the 20th century. This photograph, looking southeast from Woodstock Street, is undated. However, the building seen in the center background with Disbrow's wagon shop open along the Main Street side has its second-story balcony, which dates it to before 1909. (Courtesy of Tom and Barb Conley.)

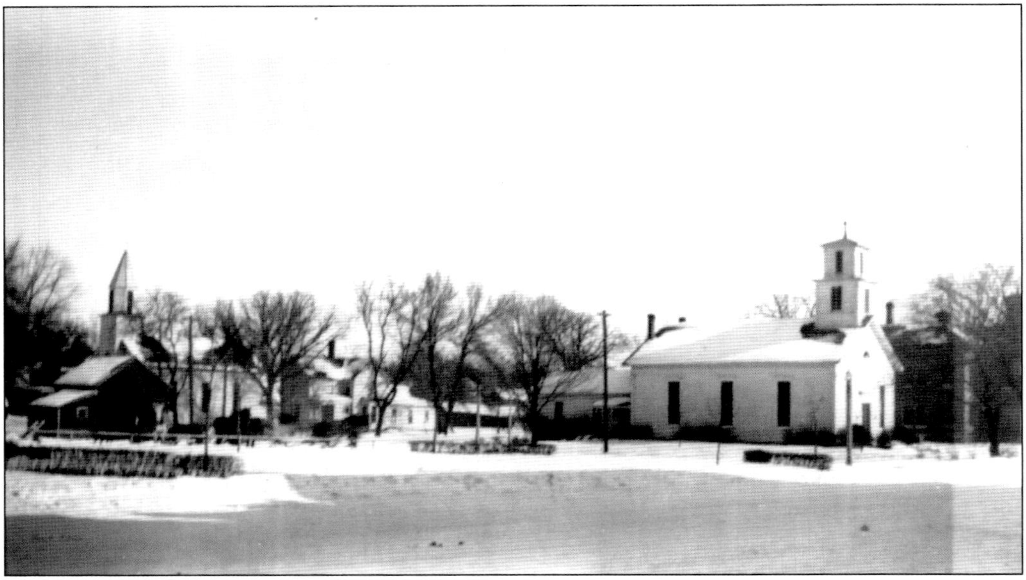

The Lutheran church has a shortened steeple (at left), and the east end of the square is free of buildings in this 1936 photograph. The First Congregational Church is at right. The exact dates as to when the Lutheran church steeple was struck by lightening and subsequently shortened and when the buildings in the square were torn down are two unknowns. This photograph gives a clue to the fact that both events occurred prior to 1936. (Courtesy of Earl Kalsow.)

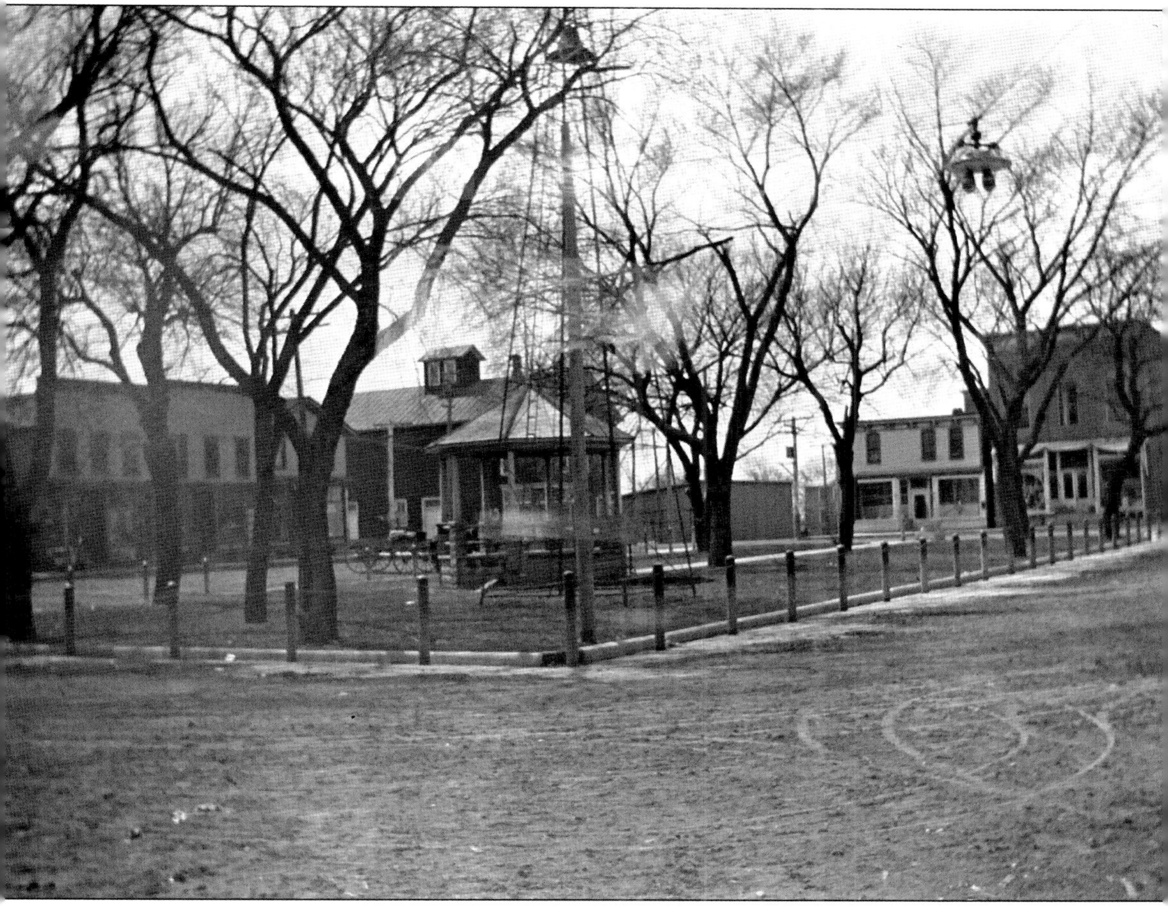

Huntley's town square has included a bandstand or gazebo since the earliest days. While the first structure's date is not documented, it is known that there was a bandstand in the park in the late 1800s. A second bandstand was built in 1910, with Andrew Schmitt of Huntley laying the foundation and brickwork. The McHenry County Historical Society honored the landmark as a historical site in 1992, but the village deemed the bandstand structurally unsafe and tore it down in December 1993. A new, third gazebo was built in 1994. This photograph, looking southeast, shows the second gazebo and the fire bell tower beside it. In the foreground is Coral Street, curving southward around the square. The buildings on the east end of the square would have been behind the photographer. The lower building at the far end of the square is Devine and Skeels General Store. (Photograph by Carl Schmalz; courtesy of Robert Schmalz.)

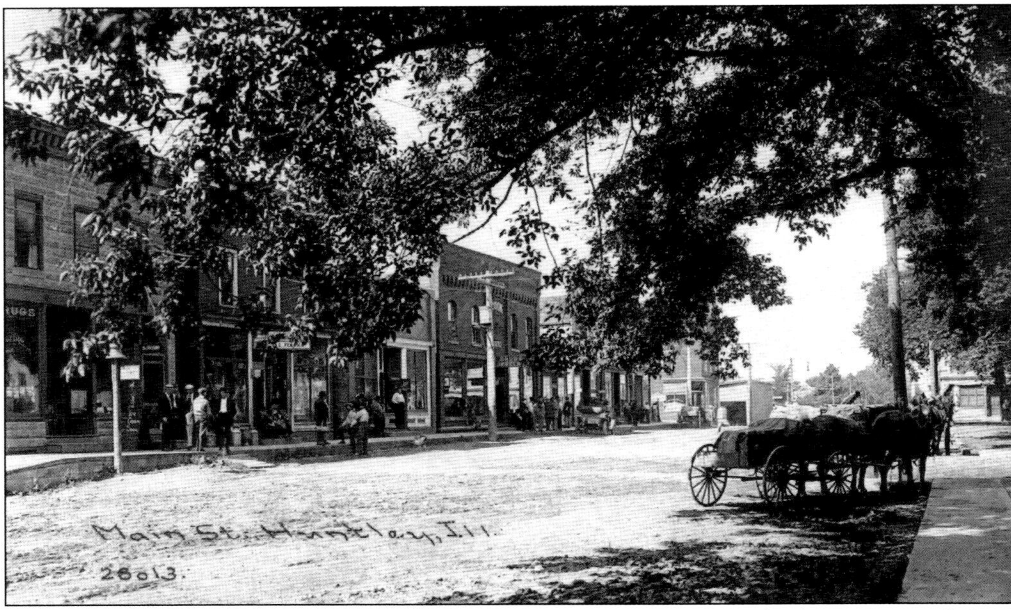

Huntley's Main Street still is unpaved in this postcard. The view is looking west and shows the many businesses along the south side of the beautiful central town area. The postcard is postmarked 1917, but the photograph probably dates to between 1911 and 1913. The building at far left is Wendt's Pharmacy. That building predates the 1916 Pabst building, which was constructed on the east wall of the pharmacy. The sign for Fenwick's Hardware shop is visible. (Courtesy of Jake Marino.)

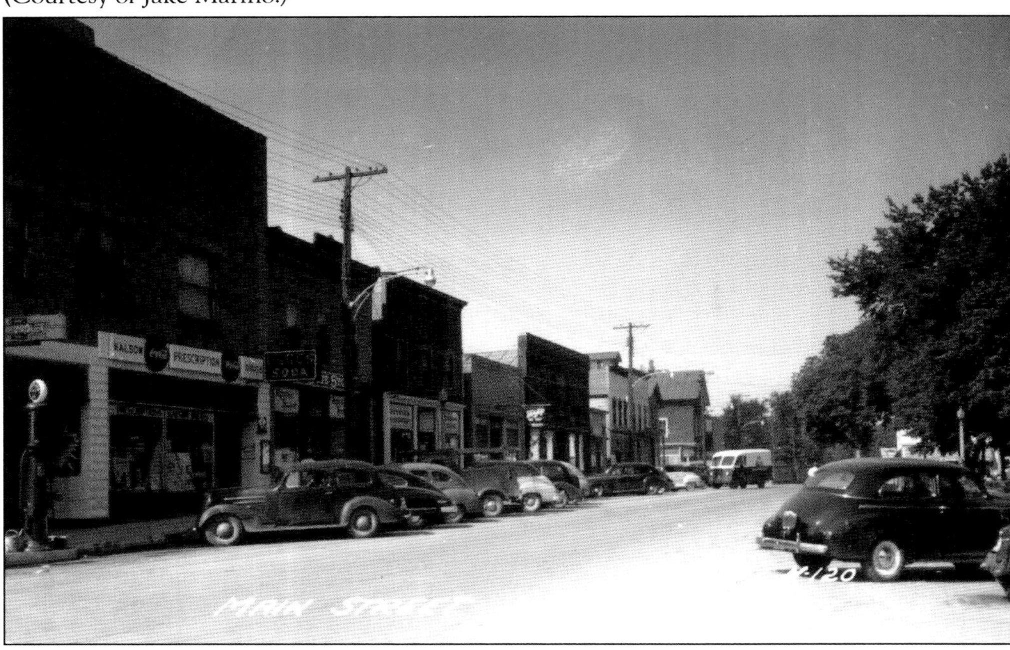

This photograph is similar to the one above but taken more than 20 years later. Kalsow's Drug Store is at far left, and Fenwick's Hardware Store is still in business in this picture from about 1940. (Courtesy of Tom and Donna Kalsow.)

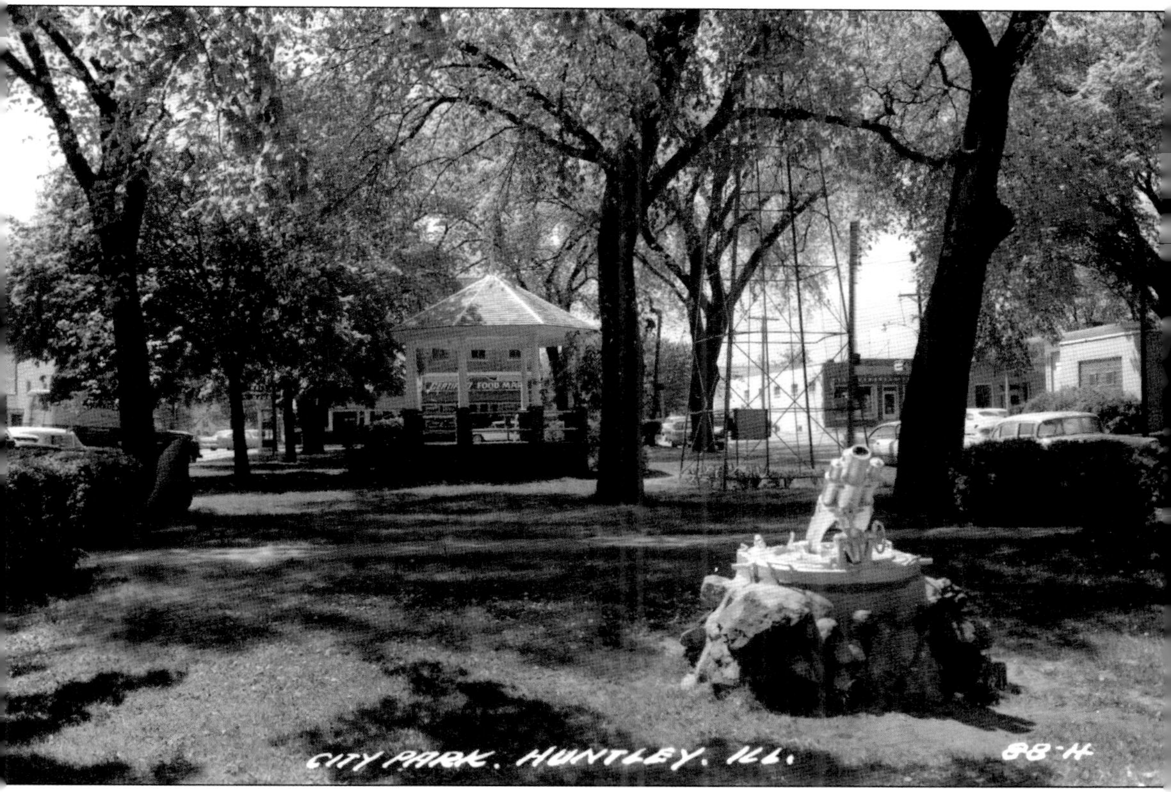

Huntley's town square park is shown in an undated postcard. The tower at right housed the village's fire bell, which called volunteer firemen to action. While the tower is now gone, the bell remains in the town square. The small World War I mortar also remains in the park today. The mortar's foundation was set by Andrew Schmitt, who also laid the foundation for the bandstand around 1910. A plaque placed by the Huntley Women's Club in 1923 on a large boulder near the cannon honored those who served in World War I. The park went unnamed for most of its existence until the 21st century when it was designated James C. Dhamer Park in tribute to the former village president, who died in office in 1999. (Courtesy of Tom and Barb Conley.)

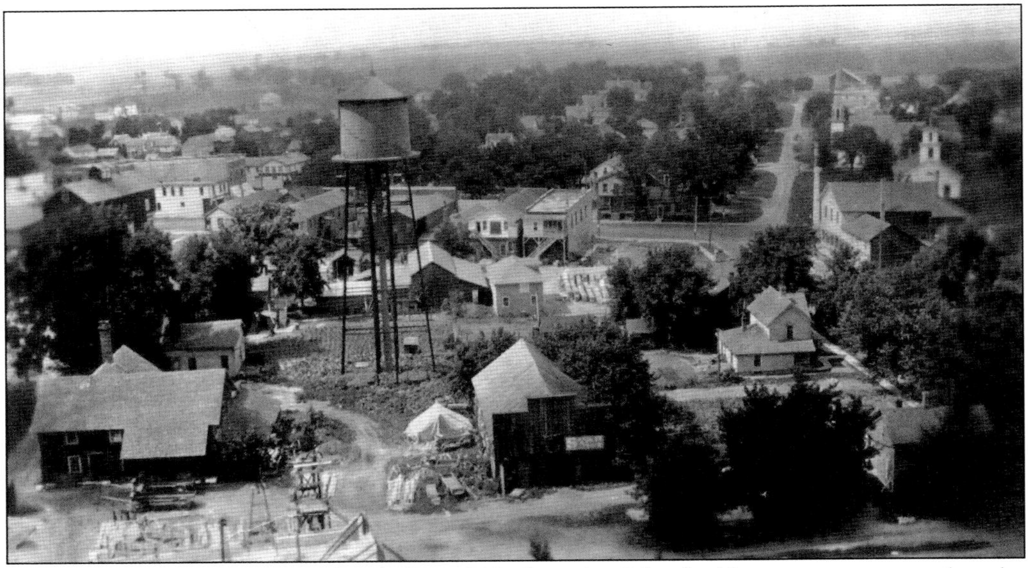

This aerial photograph was taken before 1916 when the Pabst building was constructed at the southeast corner of Main and Church Streets. Here the site is a vacant lot. Note the buildings at the east end of the town square park, partially hidden in the trees. The buildings were removed sometime after 1918. Afterward, the square was completely opened as parkland from Woodstock Street to Church Street, and Coral Street was extended east to Church Street. (Courtesy of Huntley Area Public Library.)

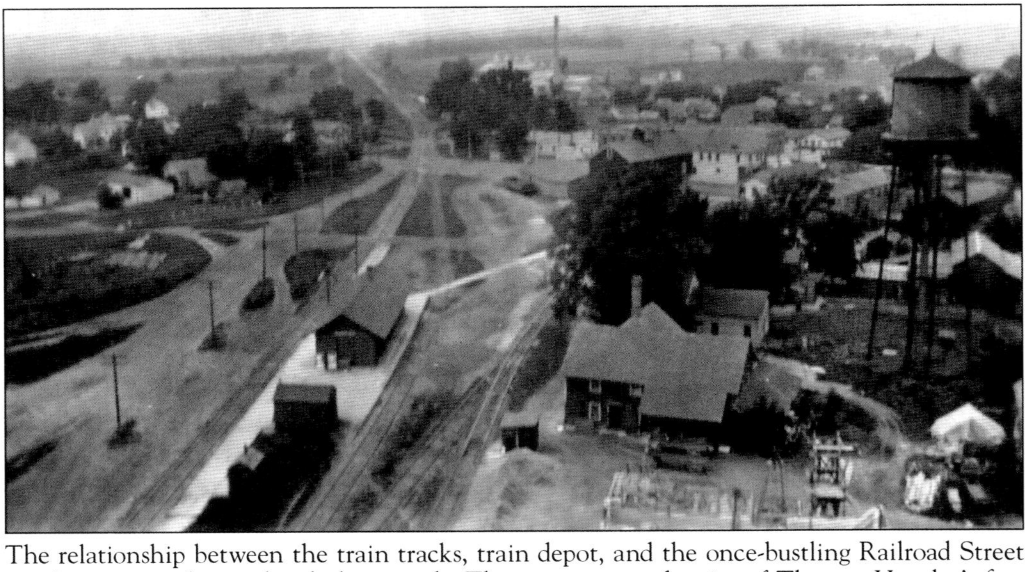

The relationship between the train tracks, train depot, and the once-bustling Railroad Street can be seen in this undated photograph. The street, once the site of Thomas Huntley's first general store, the first village hall, a hotel, a livery stable, a tailor, a warehouse, a creamery, and other businesses, has disappeared from Huntley maps of today. What is left of the road is now a parking lot. The prominent water tower at right was the vantage point for many photographs of Huntley. (Courtesy of Huntley Area Public Library.)

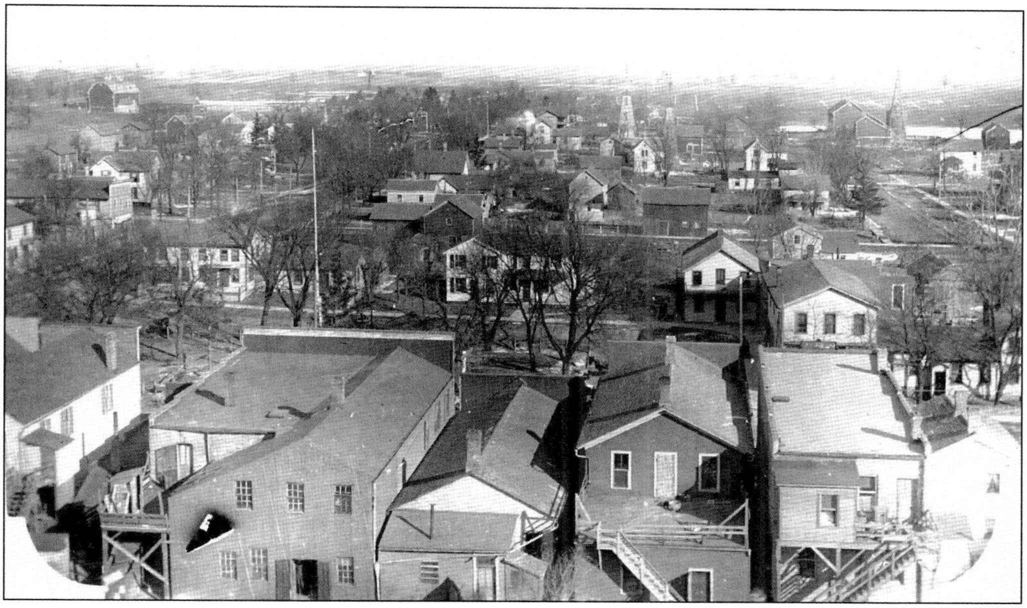

This undated photograph was made by Huntley businessman Ed Cook (1863–1951) from a glass negative. At the time, the town square still had buildings at the east end. The John Kelley house, which dates to the 1860s, can be seen behind the trees in the center of the photograph. Windmills are visible on the farms in the distance. This picture was one of many in Cook's photo album, now owned by Tom Conley.

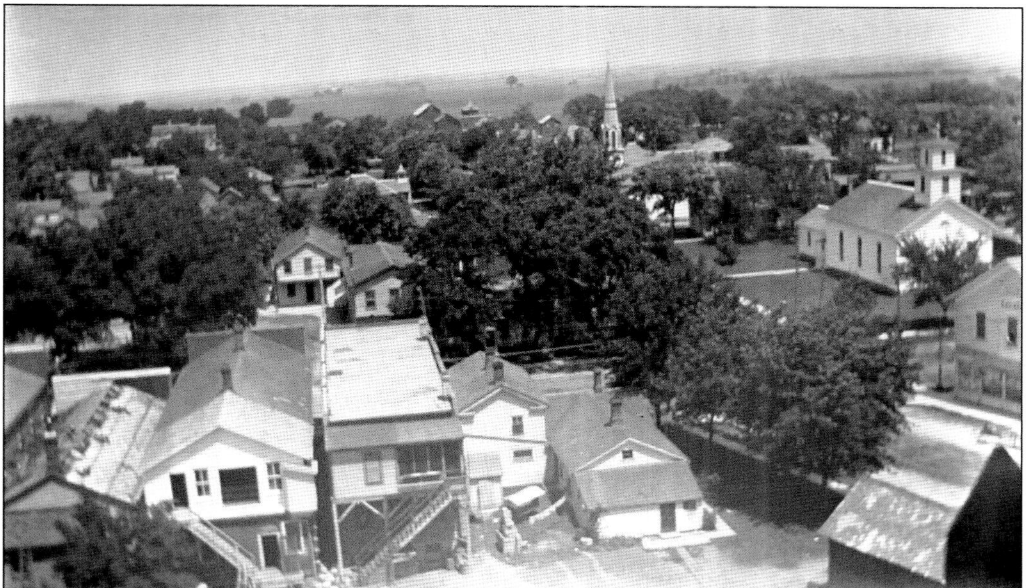

The view from the town water tower, looking to the north, shows both the First Congregational Church and Trinity Lutheran Church. In the center, two of the businesses that operated at the east end of the town square are visible. The other businesses are obscured by the trees. The photograph dates to between 1913 and 1918. (Photograph by Carl Schmalz; courtesy of Robert Schmalz.)

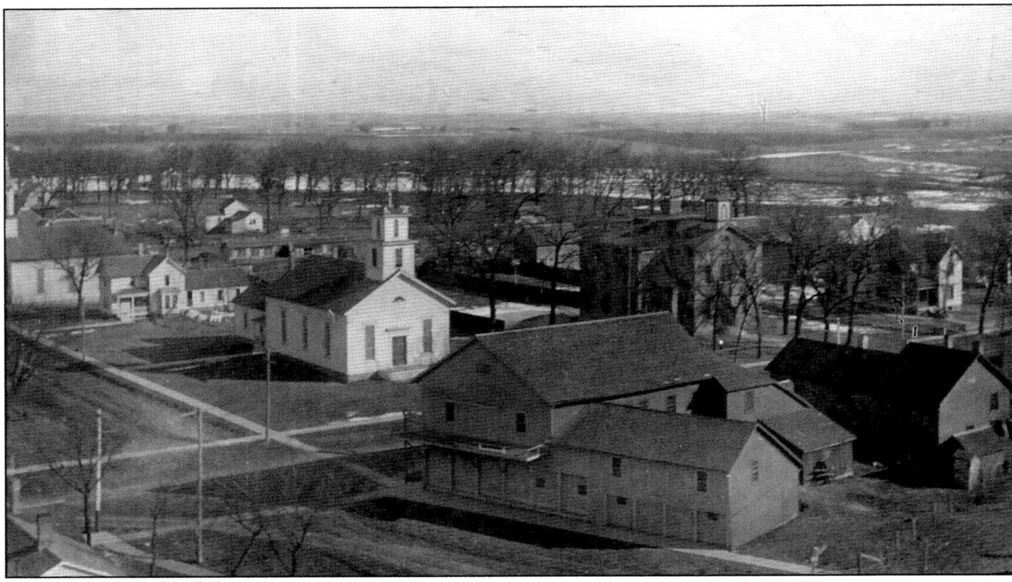

The First Congregational Church is a prominent icon on Huntley's landscape. Across Main Street in the foreground is the building housing Andrew Disbrow's harness shop and the IOOF (Independent Order of Odd Fellows). This photograph from the late 1800s shows the town school prior to its 1909 addition. To the east and north of town, the swampy land often flooded, and in the winter made for miles of great ice-skating for Huntley children. (Courtesy of Tom and Barb Conley.)

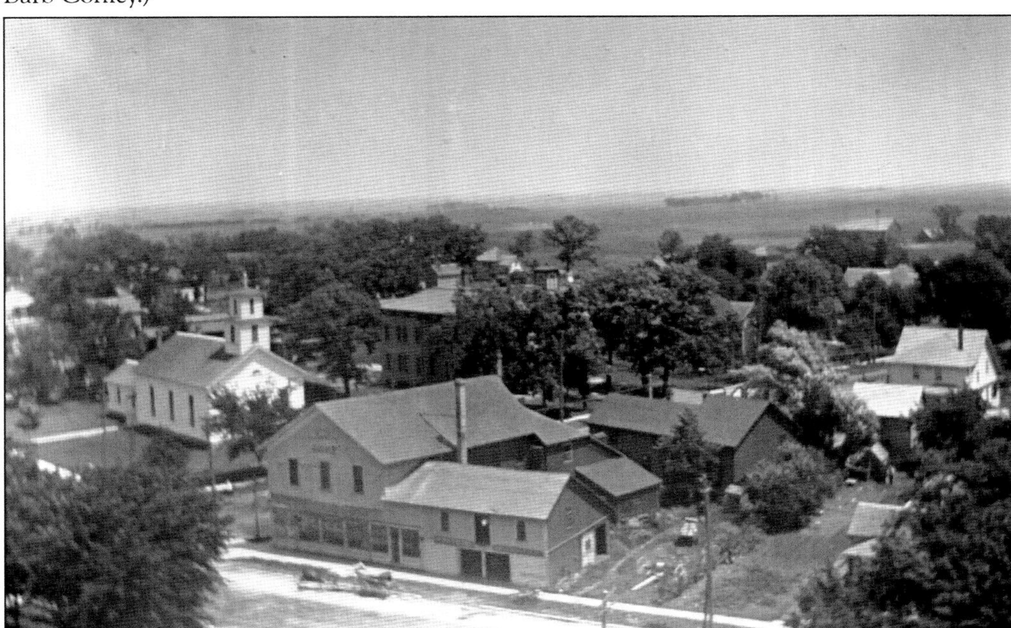

The 1909 addition to the town schoolhouse can be seen in this photograph taken about 1915. Note the changes to the Disbrow/IOOF building in the foreground, as compared to the above photograph. More of the town is built up in this later photograph. (Photograph by Carl Schmalz; courtesy of Robert Schmalz.)

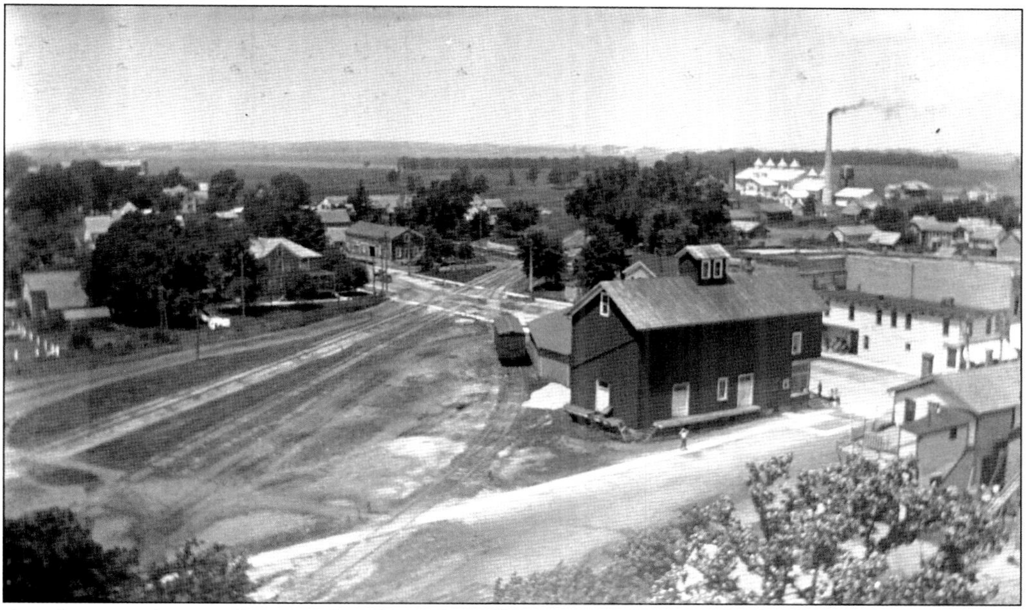

Another aerial view of town taken from the village water tower overlooks the Sawyer and Kelley Mill (the large black building). The Borden's milk condensing factory is in operation in the distance. Railroad Street runs along the side of the mill. At right, Devine and Skeels General Store can be seen across from Sawyer and Kelley Mill. (Photograph by Carl Schmalz; courtesy of Robert Schmalz.)

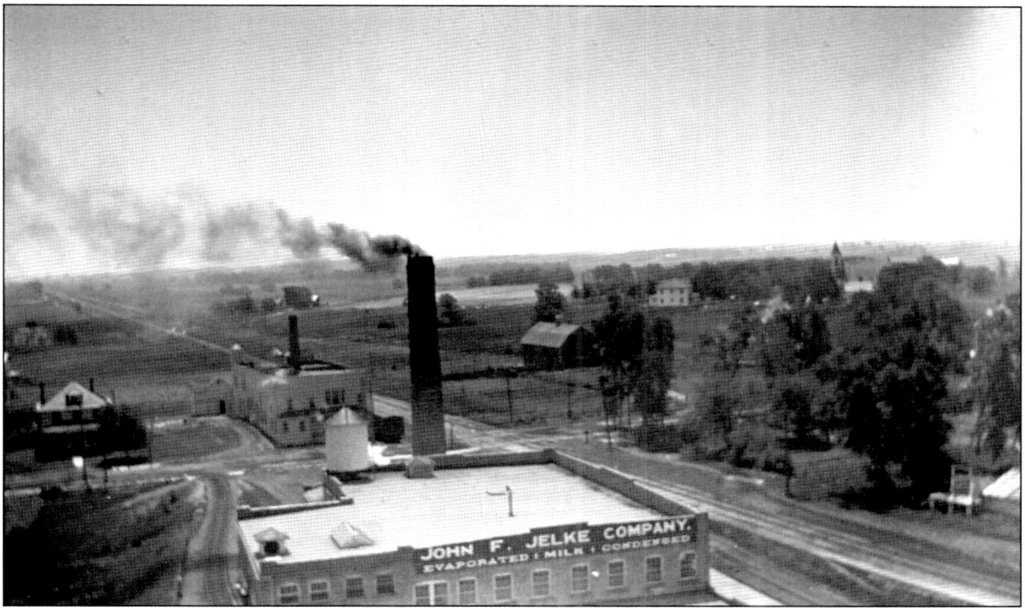

Most Huntley water tower climbers focused their cameras to the north looking into town. This rare view of Huntley is to the south. The John F. Jelke Milk Factory is shown, and behind it is the Victor Mey milk processing plant. In the distance to the far right is St. Mary Catholic Church, which was located next to the town cemetery. (Photograph by Carl Schmalz; courtesy of Robert Schmalz.)

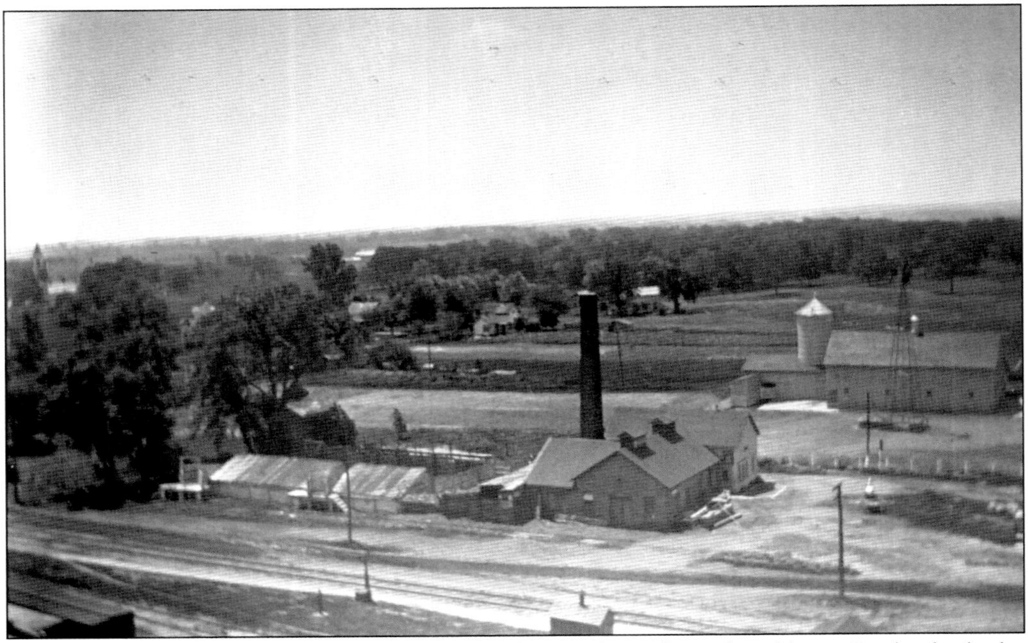

Enos Conley's feed, seed, and coal business is shown along the railroad line. Conley built the store in 1911 then added a second story in 1918. This photograph dates to sometime between those years. The Keating cattle farm and barn are to the right. The view is from the town water tower facing west. (Photograph by Carl Schmalz; courtesy of Robert Schmalz.)

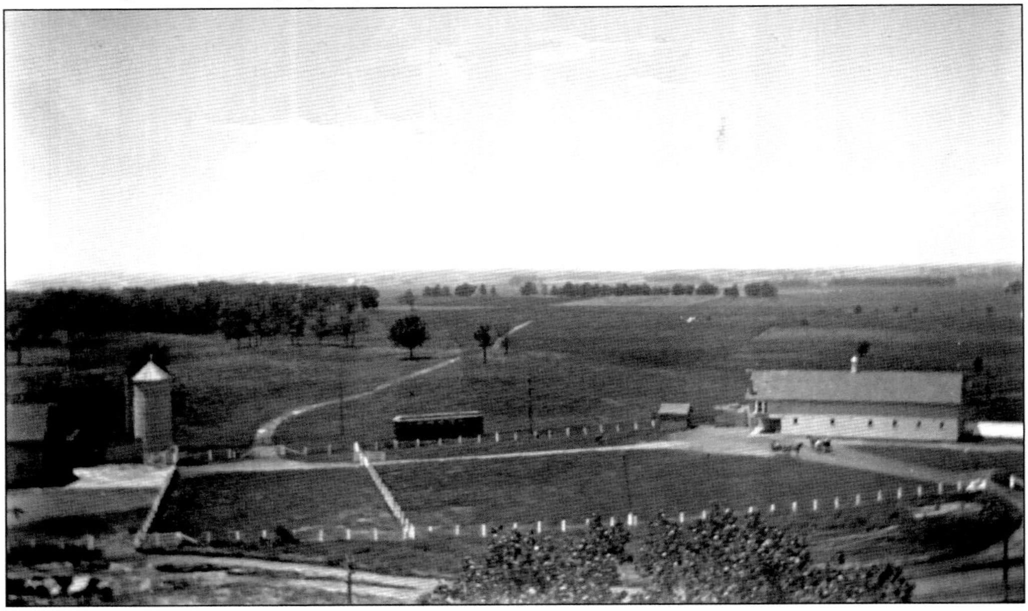

The Elgin-Belvidere interurban trolley makes its way along the west side of Huntley in this photograph that is the panoramic extension of the above shot. The Dairy Route, as the trolley line was called, operated from 1905 to 1930, making access to jobs and shopping an easy ride for Huntley commuters. See more in chapter 8. (Photograph by Carl Schmalz; courtesy of Robert Schmalz.)

Seven

HAVING FUN

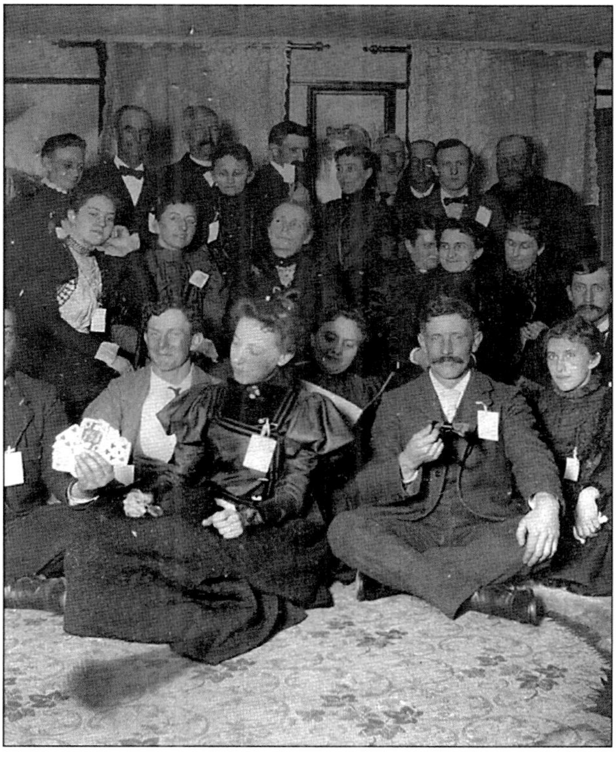

One of the many social clubs in Huntley during the late 1800s was this Card Club of 1898. The playing cards are prominently displayed at front left. This photograph was taken at the Mason home on Woodstock Street and shows the club's 1898 members. From left to right (first row) are John Hawley, Theo Shearer, Belle Kozier, Kit Weltzien, John Ellis, and Edith Burns; (second row) Louise Fisher, Maem Ellis, Ellen Parsons, Mrs. Butler, Carrie Fisher, Jennie Mason, and Fred Fisher; (third row) Mrs. Johnson, Fred Johnson, T. L. Parsons, Mina Hawley, Frank Weltzien, Anna Hadley, Henry Sinnett, M. E. Butler, Glynn Smith, and Orris Mason. (Courtesy of Tom and Barb Conley.)

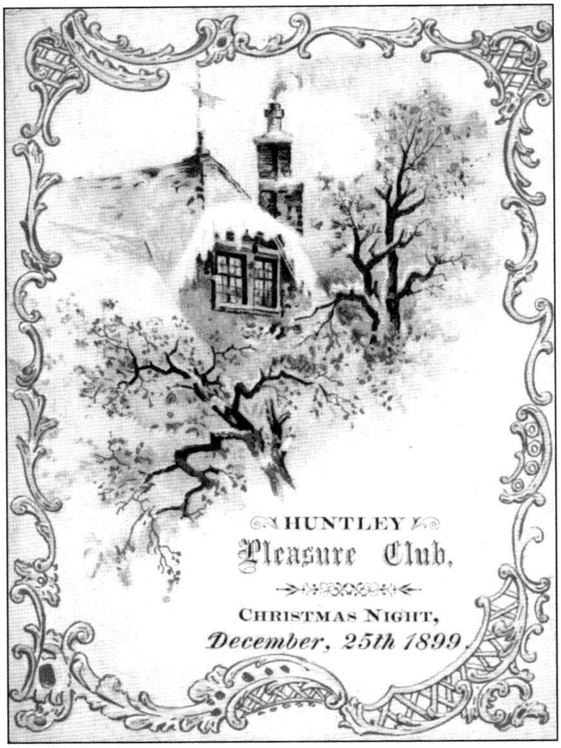

Many Huntley residents looked to social clubs to add to the holiday festivities. This invitation from the Huntley Pleasure Club was for Christmas night in 1899. Tickets were $1, and supper was extra. Brubaker Brothers Celebrated Harp Orchestra provided the music. The Huntley Pleasure Club was known over the years as the West Huntley Pleasure Club, the Merry V (five) Pleasure Club, or the Jolly Seven Pleasure Club. Events were held in Weltzien and Smith Hall upstairs at the northwest corner of Woodstock and Coral Streets. (Courtesy of Huntley Area Public Library.)

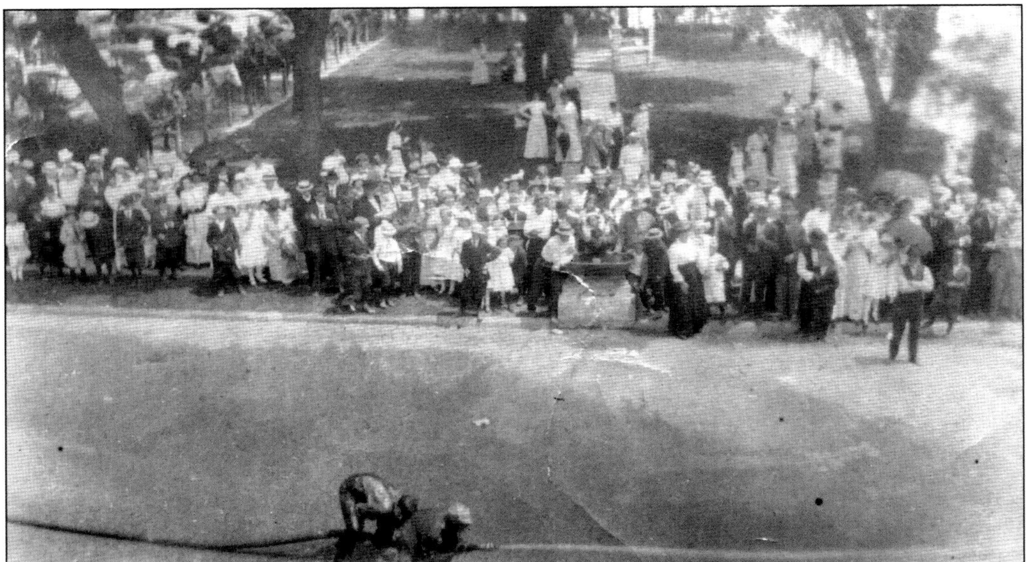

Huntley Fire Department's water fights along Woodstock Street between Coral and Main Streets were a popular entertainment. Crowds cheered to see which team would be victorious in using a water spray from a hose to push an empty barrel to the opponent's goal. This pictured event from about 1915 likely was part of the annual farmers' picnic, which also included a parade and egg races. The water fights became a tradition that continued into the 1990s. (Courtesy of Huntley Area Public Library.)

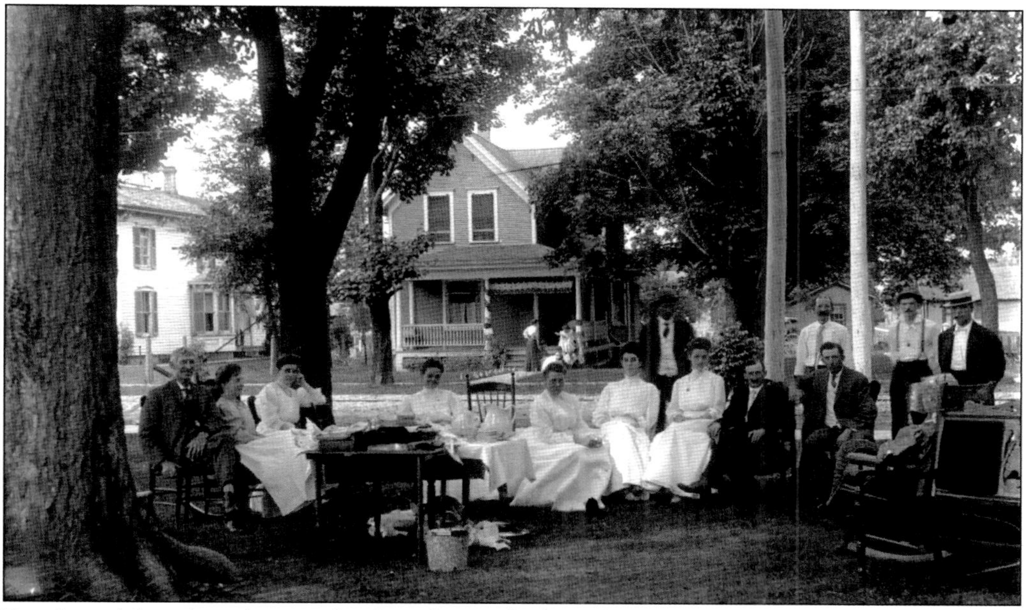

Family and friends gather on the front lawn of Ed Cook's home on Woodstock Street around 1918 to enjoy the summer shade and refreshments. The street was home to many of the town's most prominent businessmen. Cook is at the far left. His wife, Myrtle, is in the rocking chair at far right. Their guests are unidentified. The Cook house, not seen in the photograph, was built in 1893. (Courtesy of Tom and Barb Conley.)

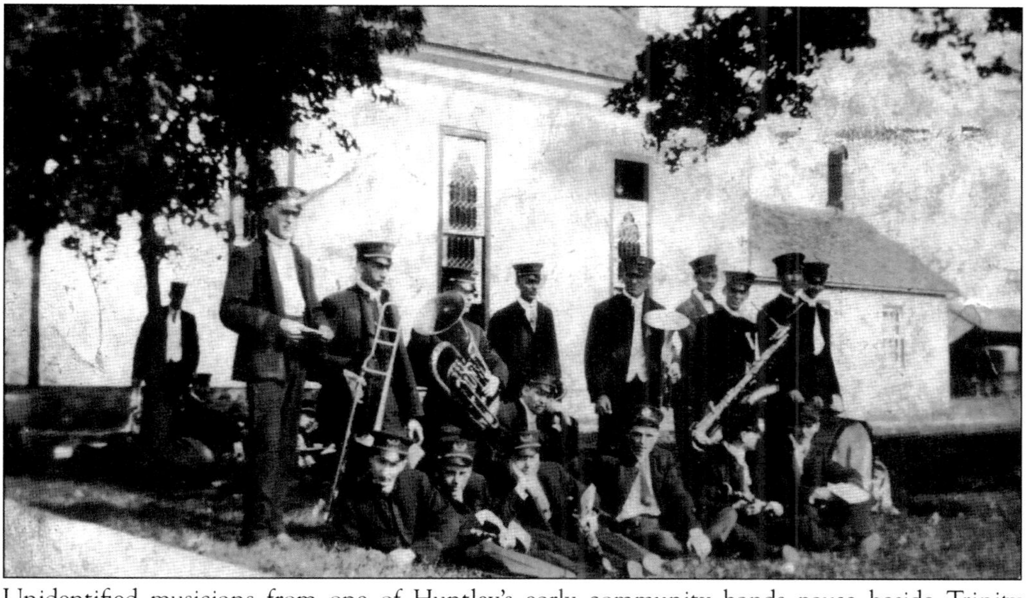

Unidentified musicians from one of Huntley's early community bands pause beside Trinity Lutheran Church around 1918. Huntley's first brass band was organized in 1859 with members T. L. Parsons, Charles Hubbard, John Cummings, Jerome Glazier, John White, James Foley, Charles Jones, and Sam Clarke. The group disbanded when most of its members joined the Civil War. Other bands organized over the years and performed in the town square bandstand. (Courtesy of Tom and Barb Conley.)

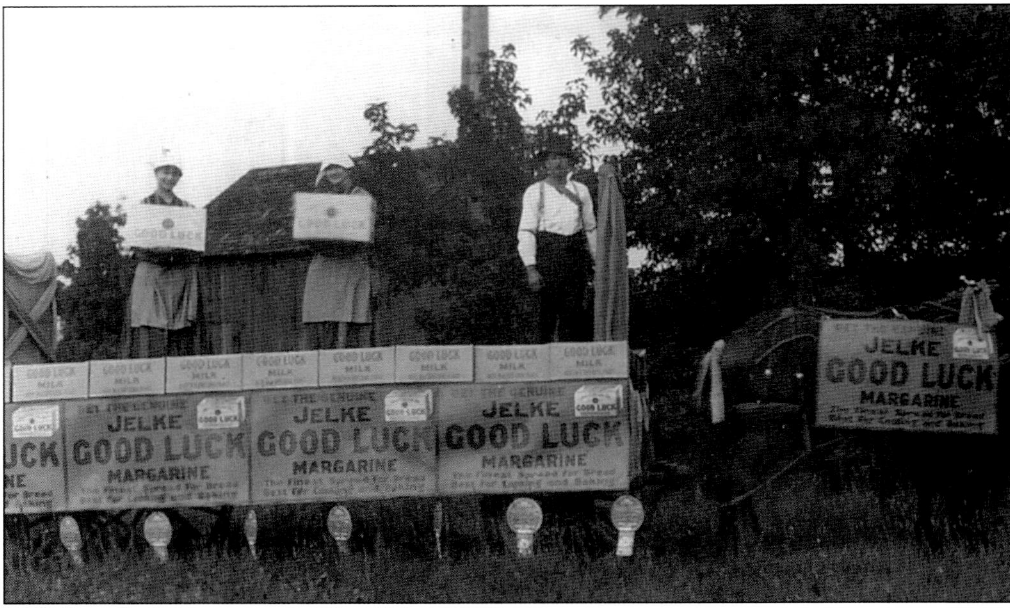

Huntley's Jelke milk factory sponsored this horse-drawn float promoting its popular Good Luck margarine in a parade around 1915. From 1890 through the 1920s, the newly marketed margarine became a family staple, as it did not turn rancid like butter. Vigorous promotional efforts made the new product a success. Although most margarine was produced by meatpacking companies, Jelke, a milk producer, was one of the largest margarine makers. Good Luck later was renamed Imperial Margarine. Borden's tower is in the background. (Courtesy of Tom Conley.)

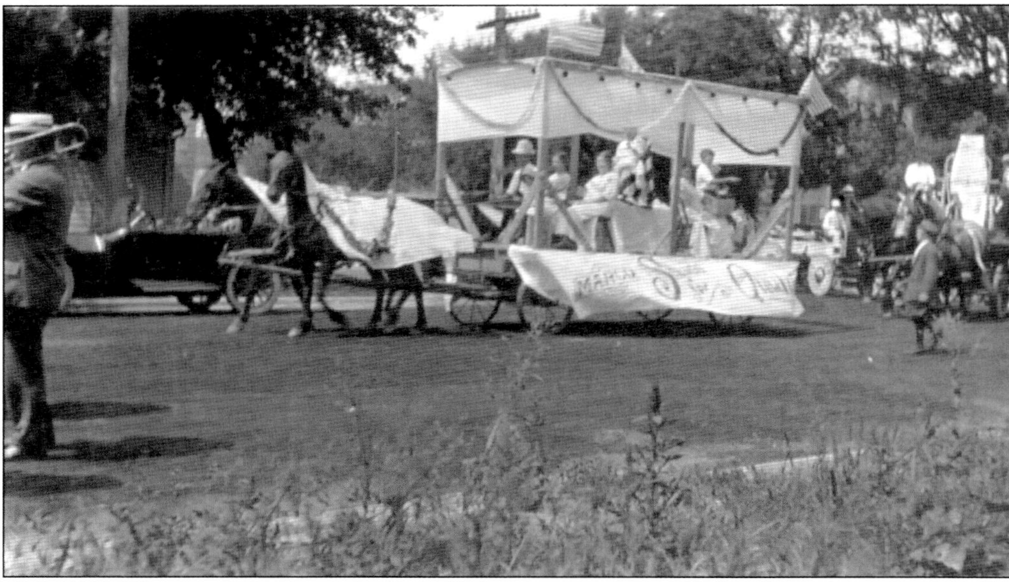

Otto Schmalz's Marco Store entered this horse-drawn float in a Huntley parade sometime between 1912 and 1915 but certainly before Schmalz closed his business in 1918. The entry may have been part of the annual farmers' picnic or possibly a Fourth of July celebration. The parade proceeded up Railroad Street and around the town square, passing in front of Schmalz's store. (Courtesy of Robert Schmalz.)

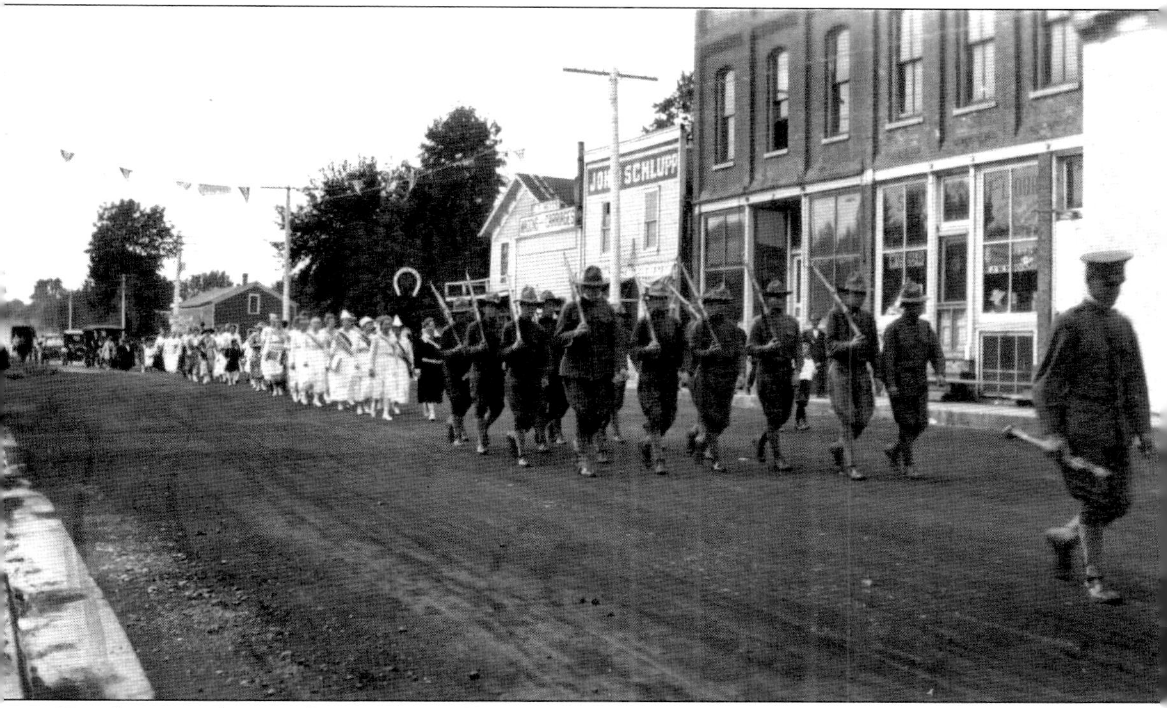

Huntley turned out to honor its World War I veterans sometime around 1918. The parade is headed east along Main Street toward the town square. Those from Huntley who served in World War I were William Amos, W. F. Bartelt, Harold Christiansen, Clyde Clanton, John Cleland, Earl Crowley, Harold Curtiss, Oscar Enstrom, Arthur Ferris, Alfred Frenck, Arthur Garbe, Arthur Graupner, Harry Gutschow, Irvy Gutschow, Charles Hadley, Edwin Heuer, William Hubbe, Clay Marsh, Theodore Michlowski, Royal Miller, Carl Schmalz, Elmer Sewell, Earl Sinnett, Dr. Oliver Statler, Harry Weltzien, Edward Williams, and William "Pat" Williams. (Courtesy of Huntley Area Public Library.)

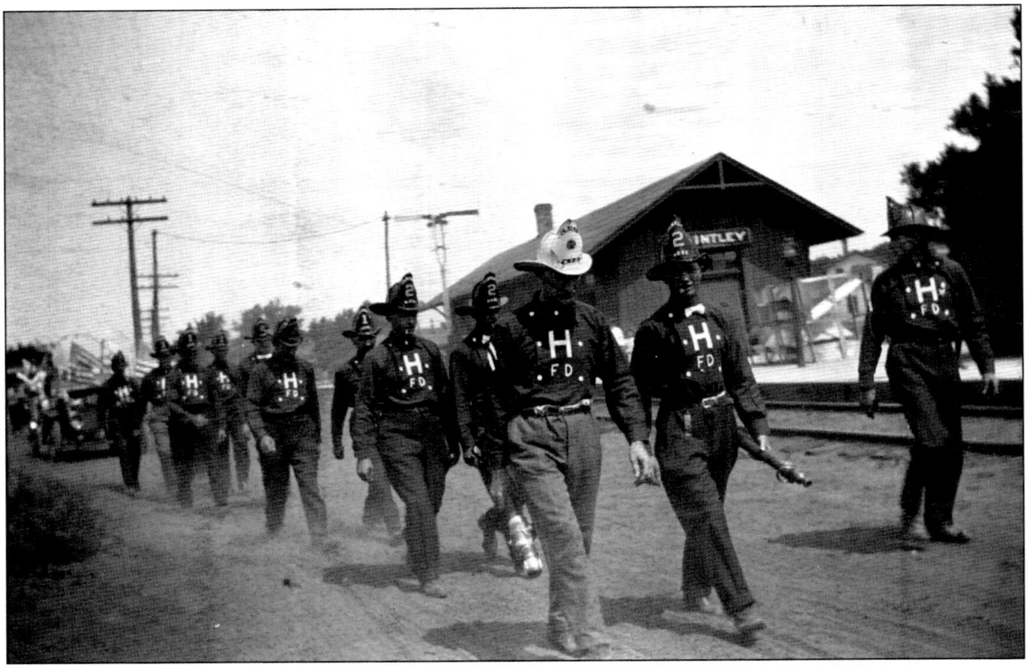

Huntley's volunteer fire department marches past the train depot on Railroad Street sometime between 1912 and 1918. Huntley businessman and fire chief Ed Cook leads the group in parade along the unpaved street. (Photograph by Carl Schmalz; courtesy of Robert Schmalz.)

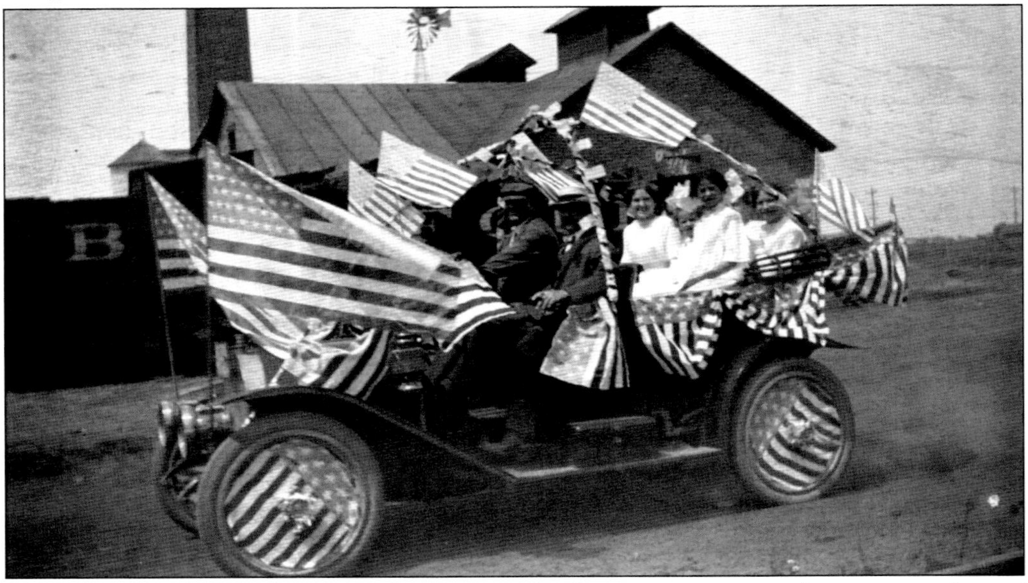

Immediately behind the firemen in the same parade, this patriotic entry makes its way in front of Enos Conley's feed store. The mustached man with the cigar in the front seat is Platt Winne Sr., a wealthy farmer who at one time had the largest dairy herd in McHenry County. The women in the back seat are believed to be his five daughters. The girl with the darkest hair is his daughter Marie. Daughter Ada is to the farthest right. (Photograph by Carl Schmalz; courtesy of Robert Schmalz.)

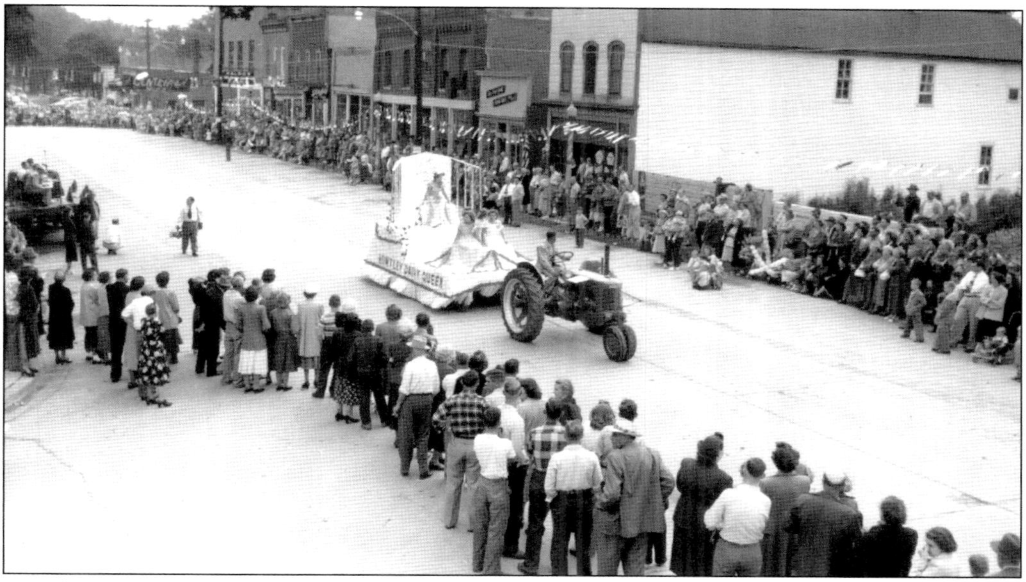

Huntley celebrated the 100th anniversary of its founding in 1951 with a variety of community events, including a parade down Main Street. Crowds flanked the street to see Huntley dairy queen Delores Reeves and her court, which included Eva Adamson, Oona Heinz, Marion Scheisher, and Maxine Korn. The dairy queen title evolved into the Miss Huntley pageant, which is sponsored each year by the Huntley Area Chamber of Commerce. (Courtesy of McHenry County Historical Society.)

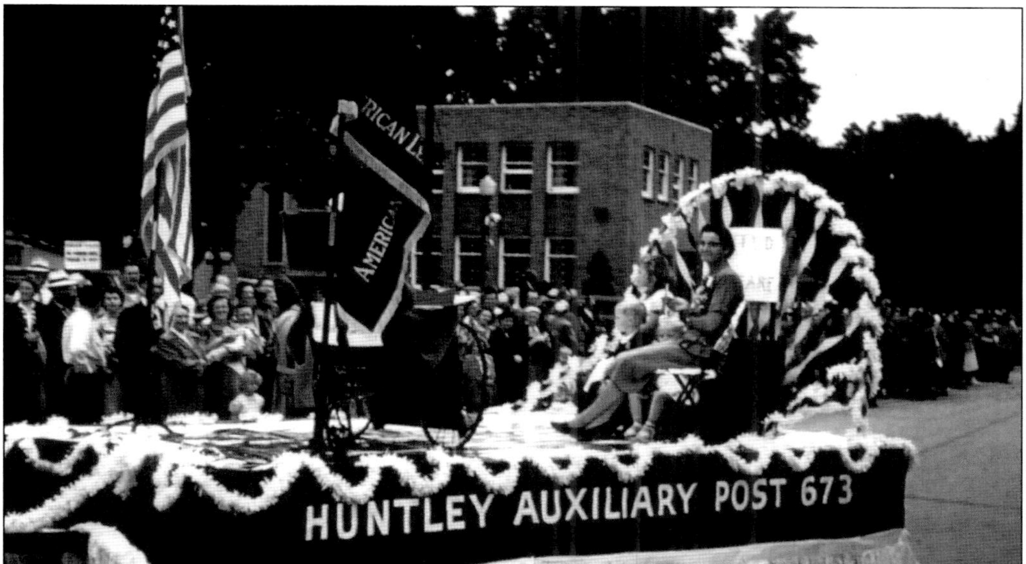

The Huntley centennial celebration parade on August 25, 1951, included the American Legion Auxiliary Post 673. Seated prominently on the float is Barbara Lohneis, a World War II Gold Star mother. Her son Andrew Lohneis, was one of three Huntley men killed in action. Morris Weltzien and Melvin Boyer also died in the conflict. A fourth Huntley man, Kenneth Darby, died of illness in a military hospital while in service during the war. (Photograph by Harley and Mabel Swanson Mackeben; courtesy of Lonni Swanson Oldham.)

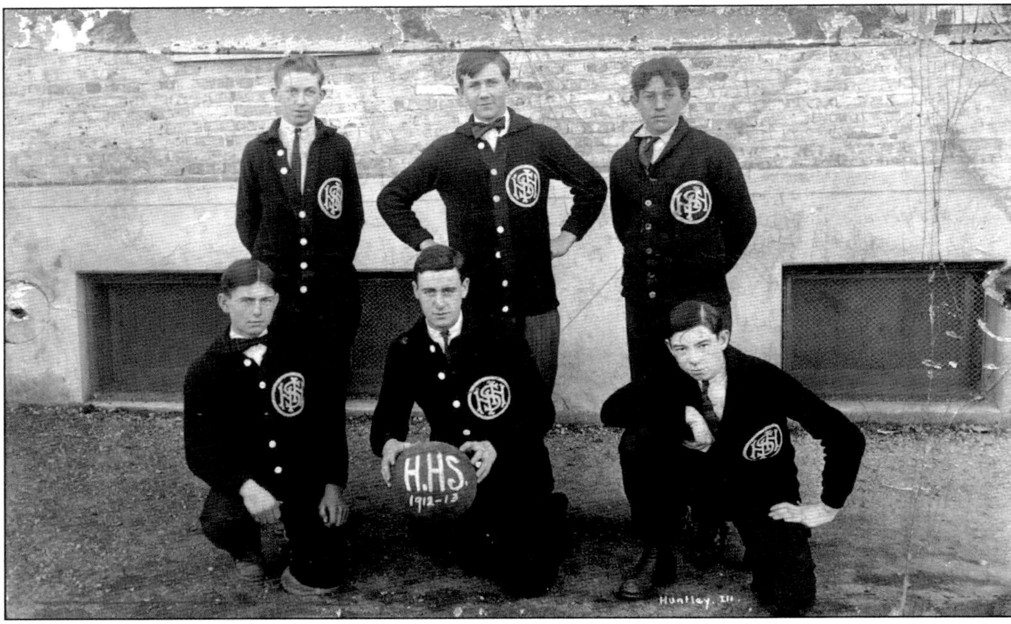

Basketball always has been a popular sport in Huntley. The high school teams provided community entertainment since before 1900. With no gym in the school, early games were played on the second floor of the general store at Woodstock and Coral Streets and later on the upper level of the Pabst building at Main and Church Streets. When a new high school was built in the early 1920s, a gymnasium was included, and games were held at school. The 1912–1913 Huntley High School team (above), from left to right, included (first row) Augie Heuer, Earl Williams, and Elmer Sewell; (second row) Gordon Stringer, Ed Weltzien, and John Rehberg. The 1913–1914 team (below) posed with coach George Sykes, at far right, and an unnamed coach at left. Team members from left to right are Gordon Kelley, Edwin Heuer, Elmer Sewell, unidentified, Harold Heuer, Earl Williams, and Gordon Stringer. Leo Dwyer holds the ball. (Above, courtesy of Jake Marino; below, courtesy of Mary Ellen Moerke.)

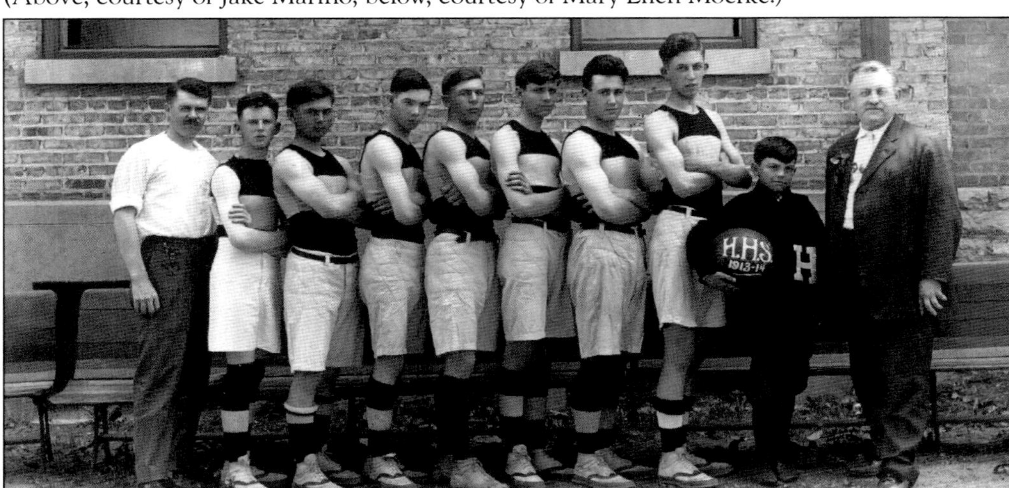

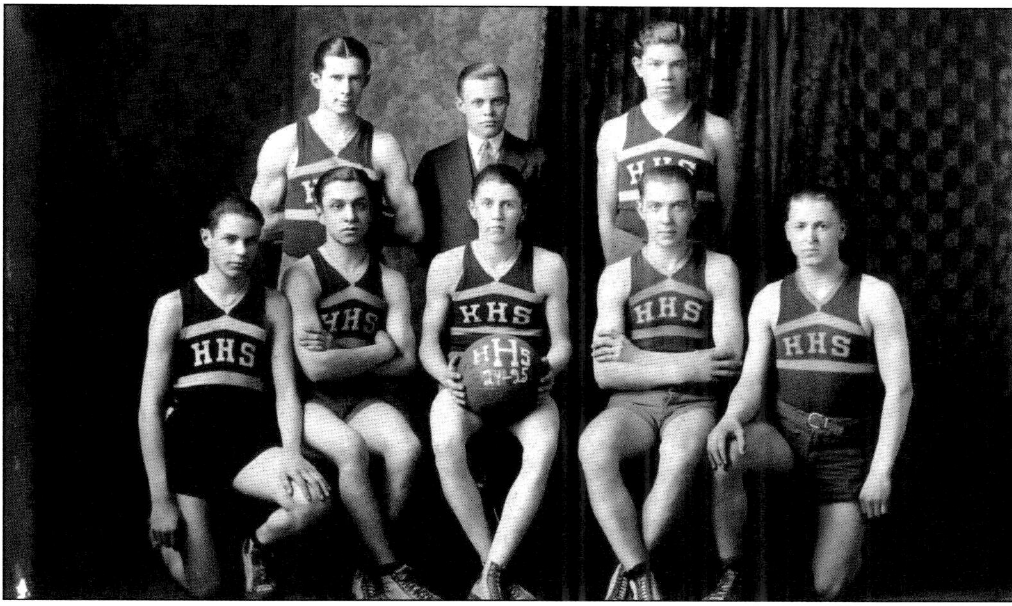

The Kalsow name has been associated with Huntley High School basketball for decades. The 1924–1925 team (above) included, from left to right, (first row) Norm Kalsow, Clarence Kunke, Robert Miller, Ernie Stading, and Bill Fyfe; (second row) Roy Williams, coach Jones, and George Rugh. Kalsow's brothers Allan and Earl played on the school team in later years. His son Tom Kalsow played basketball for Huntley High School in the 1970s, and Tom's sons Jason and Bradley were standout players in the early 2000s. In the photograph below, the 1929 team is shown, with Earl "Pete" Kalsow holding the ball. His teammates include Art Boncosky, Harold Hanes, Wilbur White, Elmer Schultze, and Howard Fyfe. At top right is coach Schroeder. (Above, courtesy of Tom and Donna Kalsow; below, courtesy of Earl Kalsow.)

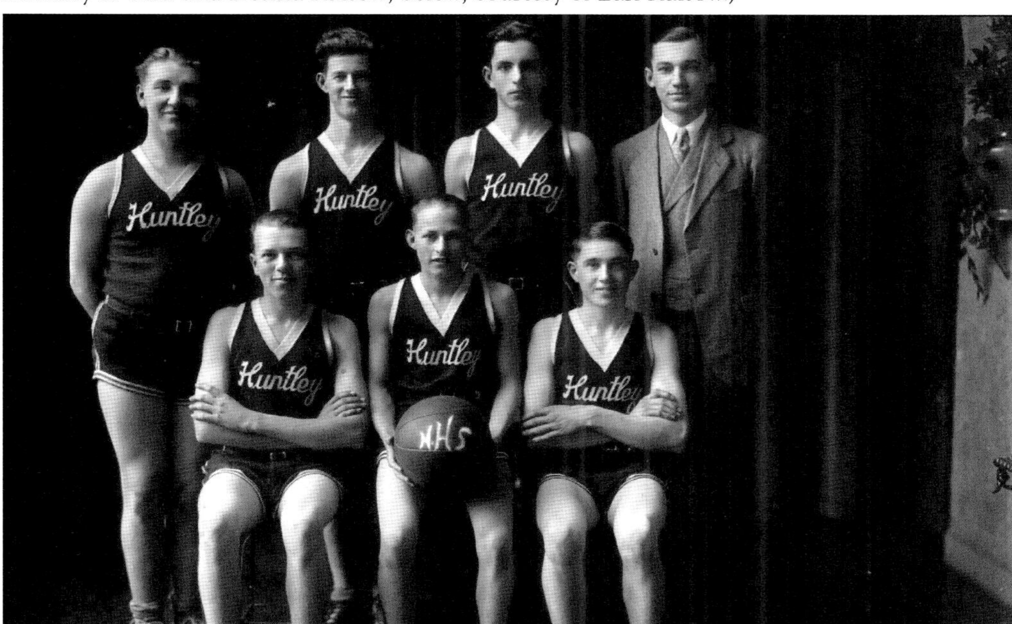

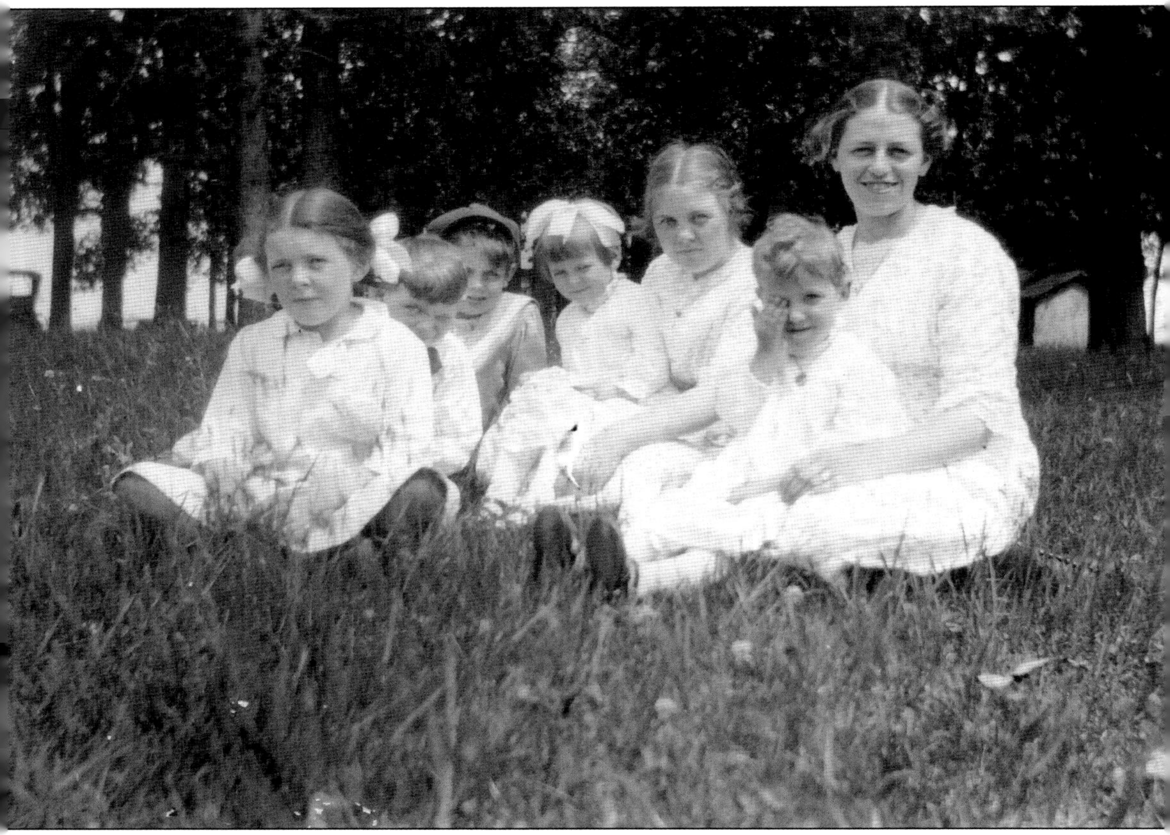

A picnic in Oakland Park was a treat for Huntley children. The park was located at the western extension of Algonquin Road across Route 47 along today's Oakcrest Drive. The park was run in the early 1900s by the Oakland Park Association, which collected dues to maintain the property. During summer months, a carousel, operated by the Skinner family, was brought in for the community's enjoyment, and a dance pavilion offered music and entertainment until the 1930s. In this 1914 photograph, Bernice Donahue (far left), Mabel Donahue (third from right), and Bernice Heinemann (far right) enjoy a day at the park. The others are unidentified. (Courtesy of Mary Beth Manning.)

Little is known about Huntley's community baseball team. Most of the players are unidentified except for Bill Ehlert, shown in the very center below the man in the suit. The team's home games were played at Oakland Park. Paul Kreutzer, who owned the only car in Huntley at the time, was paid to provide transportation for the team. This photograph dates to about 1912. (Courtesy of the Kreutzer family.)

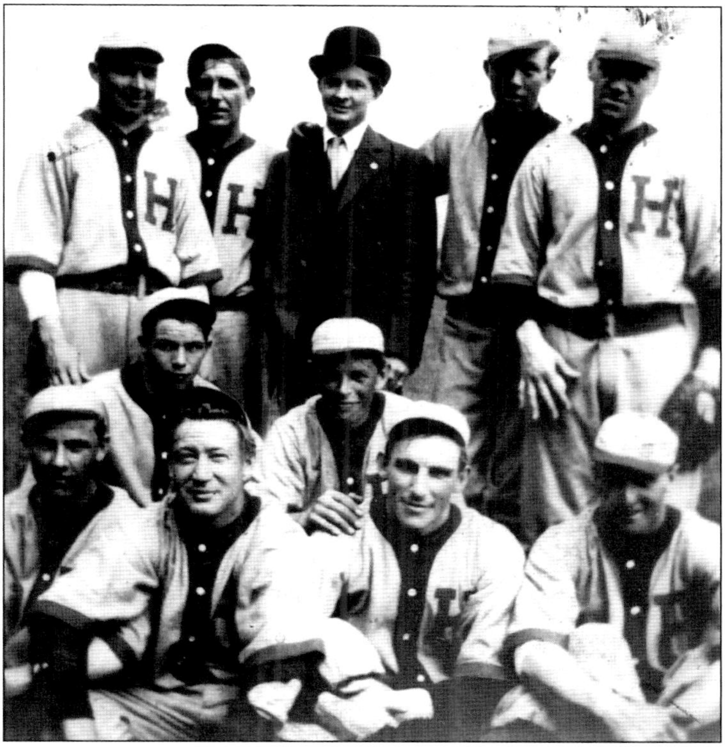

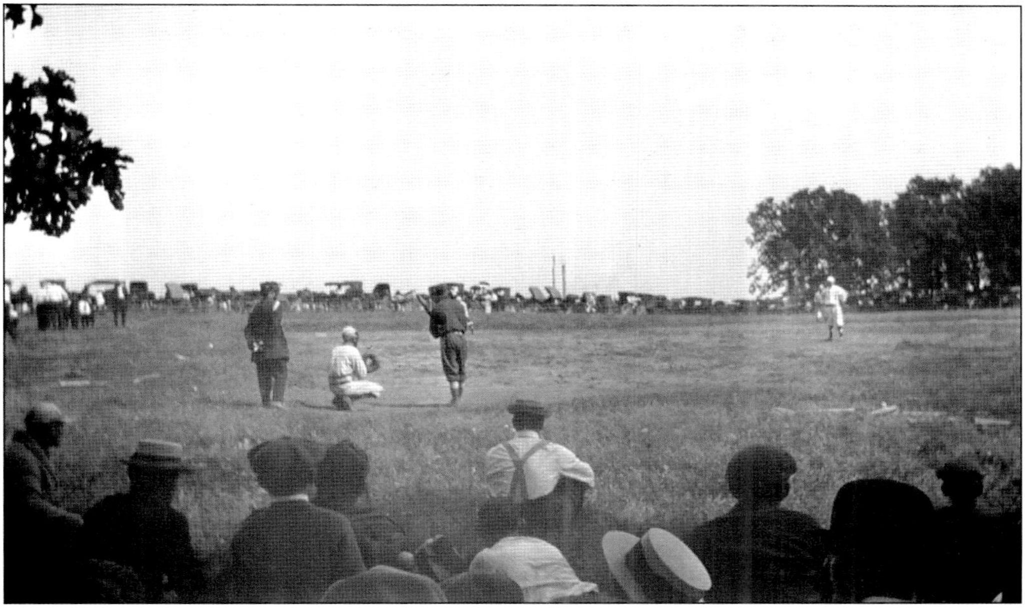

Huntley fans turned out in force to watch the local team play baseball at Oakland Park just north of town. Carts and buggies can be seen lining the edge of the field. The photograph dates to between 1912 and 1918. Charles Lazansky was known to have served as an umpire for games at Oakland Park. The Borden's milk factory smokestack can be seen in the distance. (Photograph by Carl Schmalz; courtesy of Robert Schmalz.)

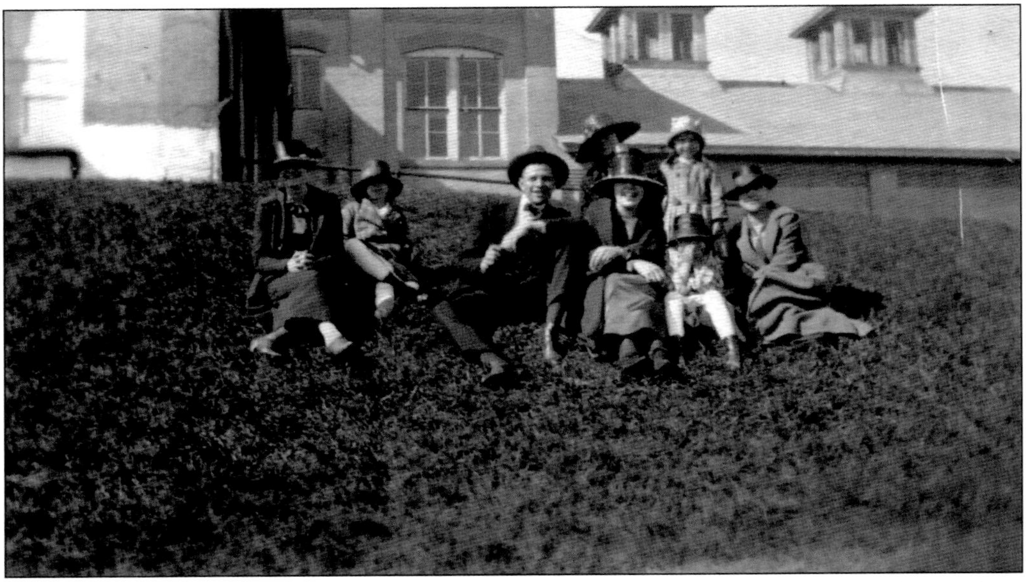

Harold Heuer (center) and his unidentified friends enjoy a sunny day in front of the Borden's milk factory around 1917. (Courtesy of Mary Ellen Moerke.)

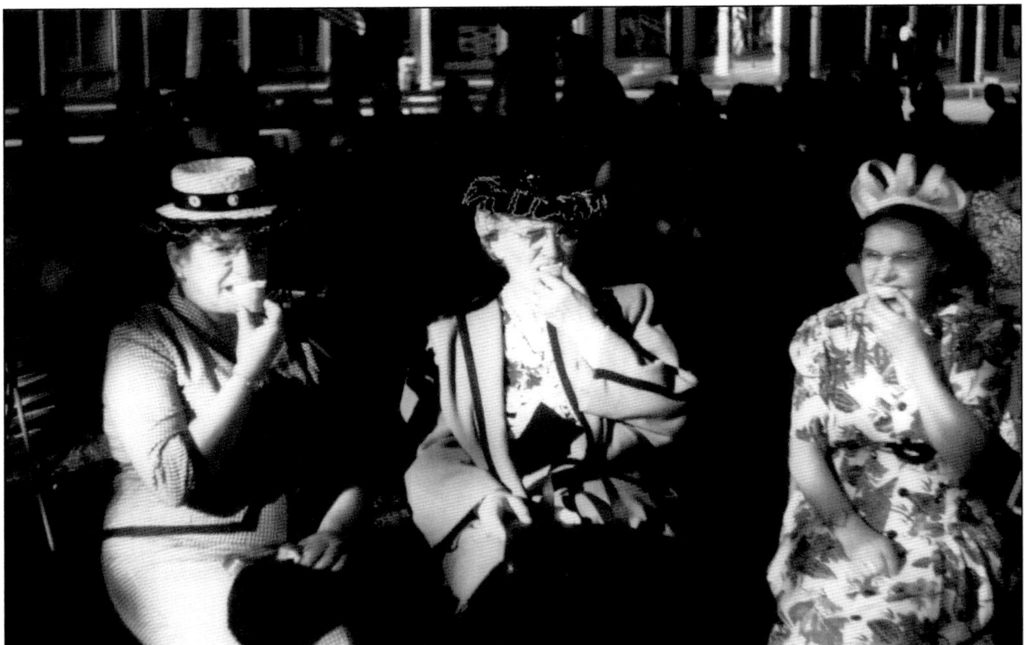

Margaret (Davis) Laue (center) and friends Louise Schoof (right) and Gladys Maushak (left) enjoy ice-cream cones in Huntley's town square park as part of Dean milk company's grand opening celebration. Dean's opened its Huntley plant on Mill Street in the summer of 1946 and provided refreshments, entertainment, and a parade for local residents on June 22 of that year. (Photograph by Harley and Mabel Swanson Mackeben; courtesy of Lonni Swanson Oldham.)

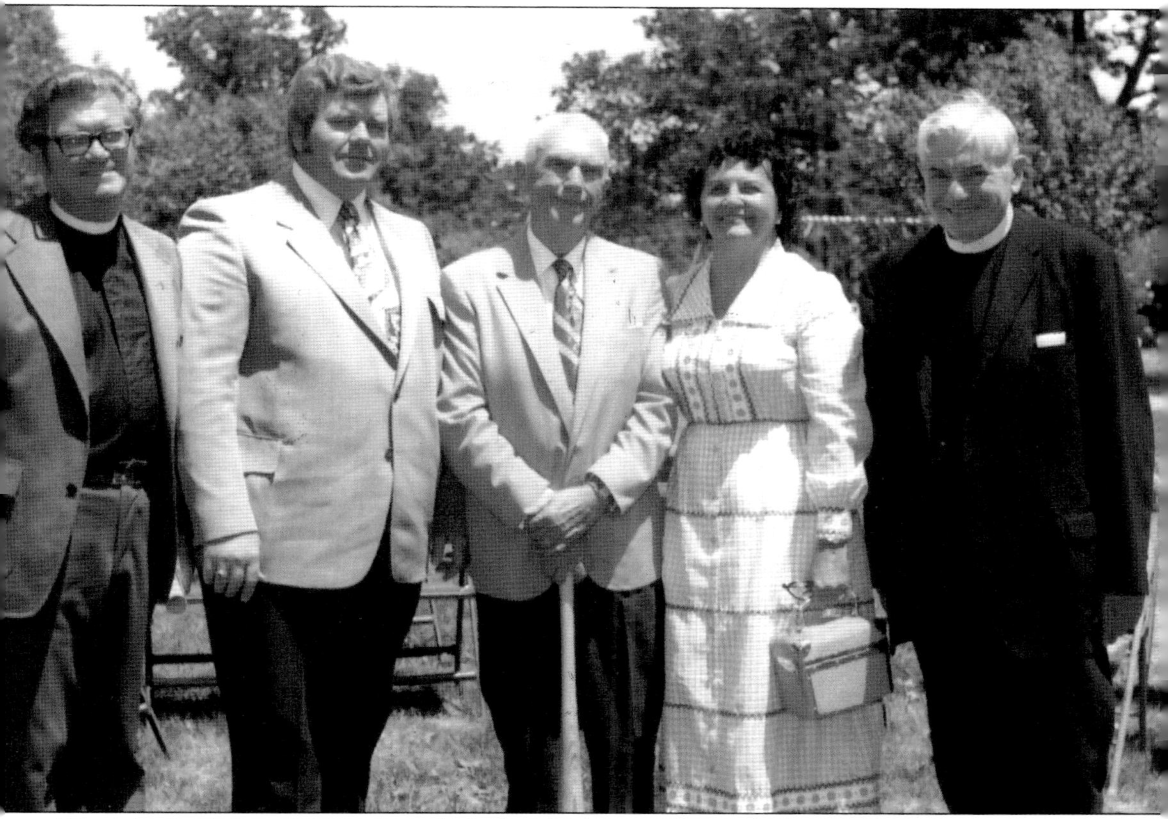

Edwin F. Deicke's name has been linked with the Huntley Park District since its inception. Deicke (1896–1984), an insurance executive, farmer, community servant, and philanthropist, was among the founders of the park district in 1965. The park board's first meeting was held at Deicke's Sun Valley Farm on West Main Street. In 1965, Deicke purchased a 28-acre tract of wooded land along Route 47 for $33,500 and presented it as a gift to the people of Huntley. The area, previously known as Donahue Woods, had been the site of carnivals and the local Boy Scout cabin. On June 4, 1972, the land Deicke and his wife, Lois, donated to the community was dedicated as Deicke Park. On hand for the ceremony were the pastors of the three original Huntley churches. From left to right are Rev. Fred Harms of Trinity Lutheran Church, Rev. Dr. Robert Frank of the First Congregational Church, the Deickes, and Rev. Fr. L. Dudley Day of St. Mary Catholic Church. (Courtesy of Huntley Park District.)

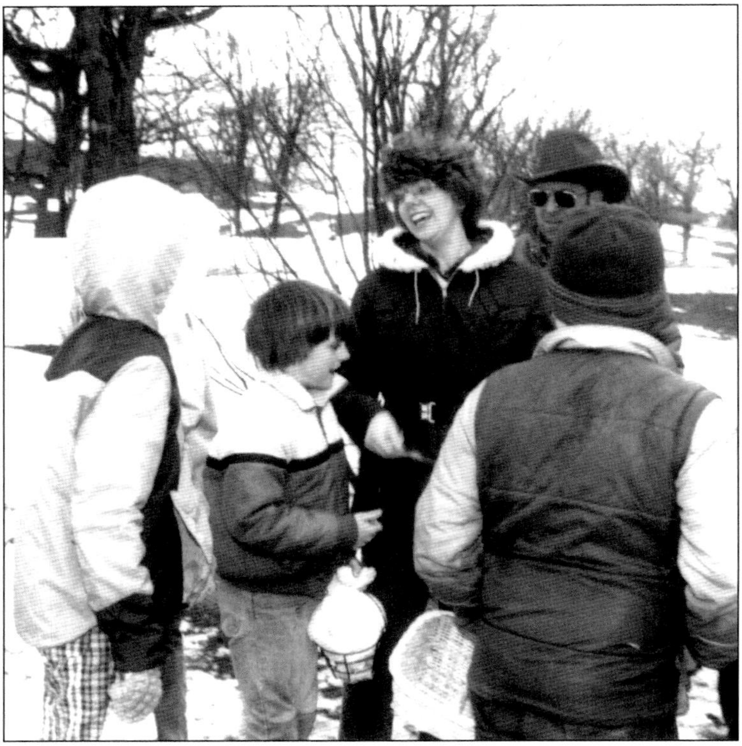

Former Huntley Park District director Betsey Warrington oversees the Easter egg hunt at Deicke Park on a cold, snowy April 10, 1982. About 70 eager children turned out to gather eggs. The egg hunt continues to be an annual park district tradition. Behind Warrington, wearing sunglasses, is her husband, Larry. Betsy served as park district director for 20 years, much of it as a one-person staff. A park is named in her honor. (Courtesy of Huntley Park District.)

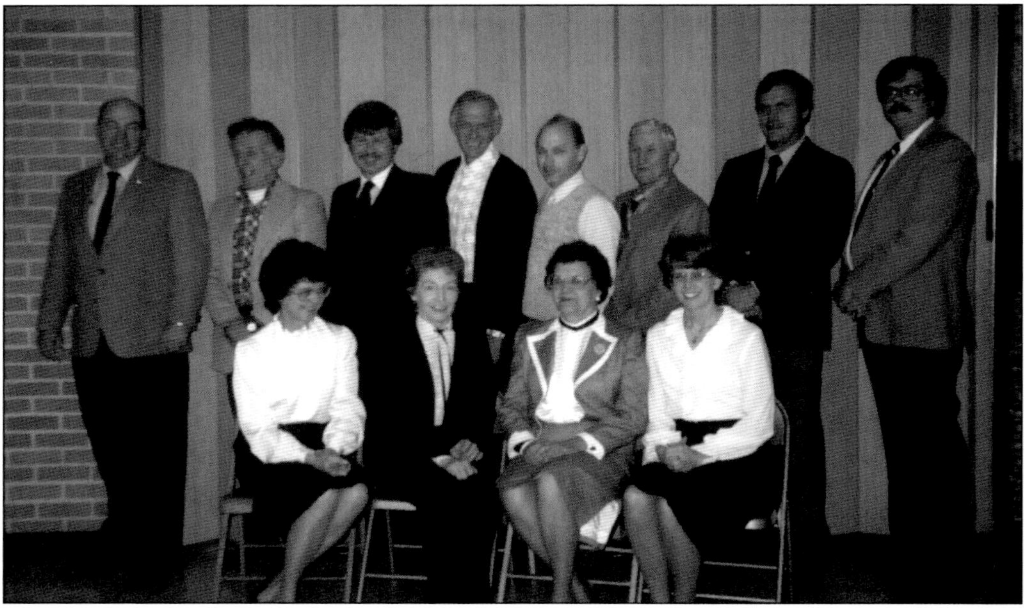

Huntley Park District commissioners and staff members were honored at a Deicke Service Recognition Day on December 5, 1984. Pictured from left to right are (first row) Mary Lou Hardy, Lois "Boots" Parisek, Lois Deicke, and Betsy Warrington; (second row) Jack Tures, Mike Kiley, Tom Jurs, Frank Parisek, Darryl Gurnett, LeRoy Wirsing, Larry Kahl, and Mark Yurs. Several of the past commissioners have parks named in their honor. (Courtesy of Huntley Park District.)

Eight

Life in Huntley

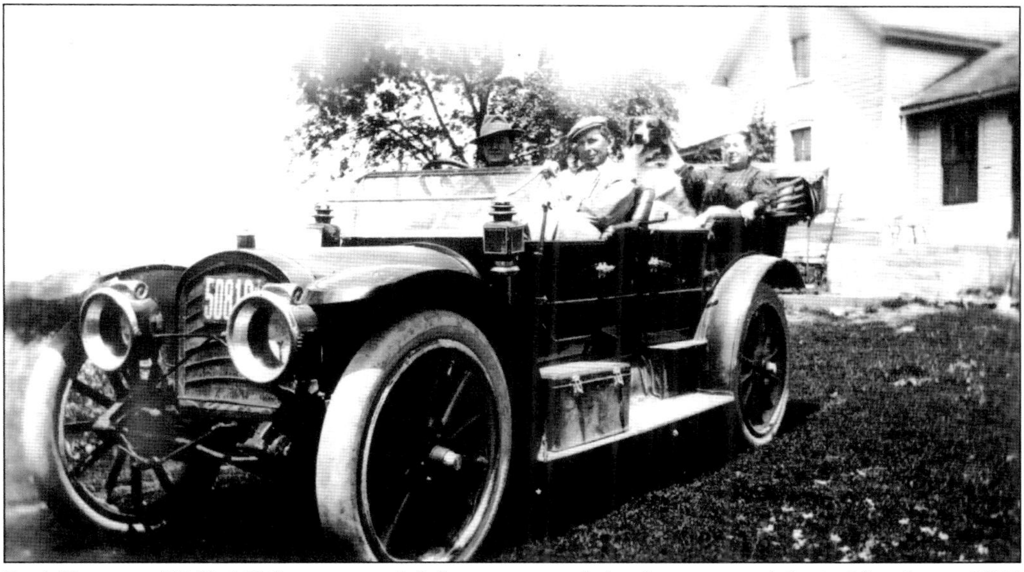

Paul Kreutzer (1848–1934), a successful farmer, owned the first automobile in Huntley, a 1906 Thomas B. Jeffrey that he purchased in Belvidere on June 2, 1906, for $1,150 cash. Here is Kreutzer's second car, a 1911 Thomas B. Jeffrey for which he paid $2,400. His son Charles G. Kreutzer is on the left in the front seat, which was the driver's side at that time. Joseph Kreutzer is at right. Paul's wife, Kunigunda, is in the back seat. (Courtesy of the Kreutzer family.)

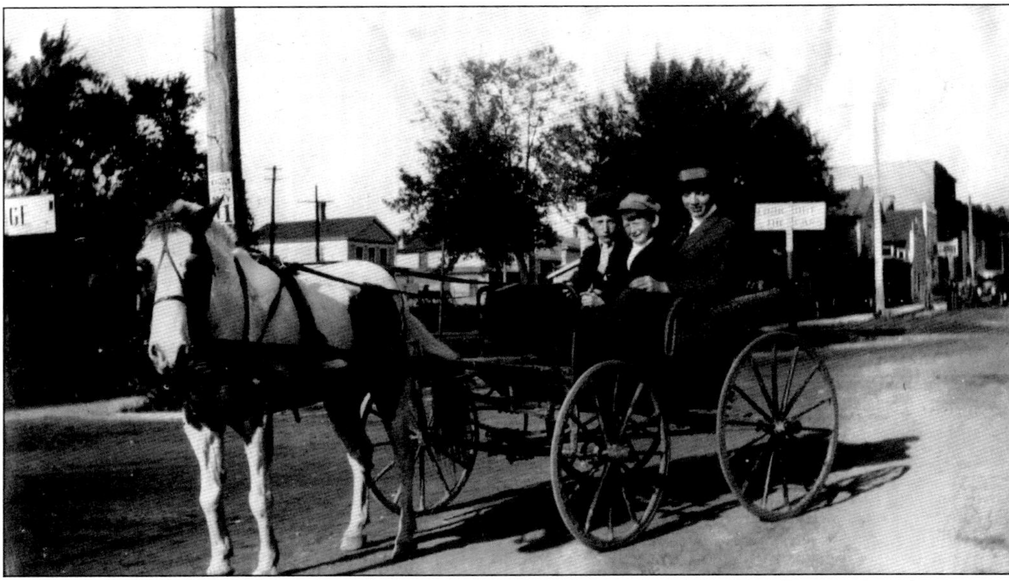

The Connor family was out for a ride with their horse Topsy on a nice day in Huntley around 1912. The horse and carriage is at Vine Street (now Route 47), and the photograph is looking east along Main Street. The sign behind them reads "Look Out for the Cars." Pictured from left to right are Will Connor, Ray Conner, and their cousin Will Ryan. (Courtesy of Mary Beth Manning.)

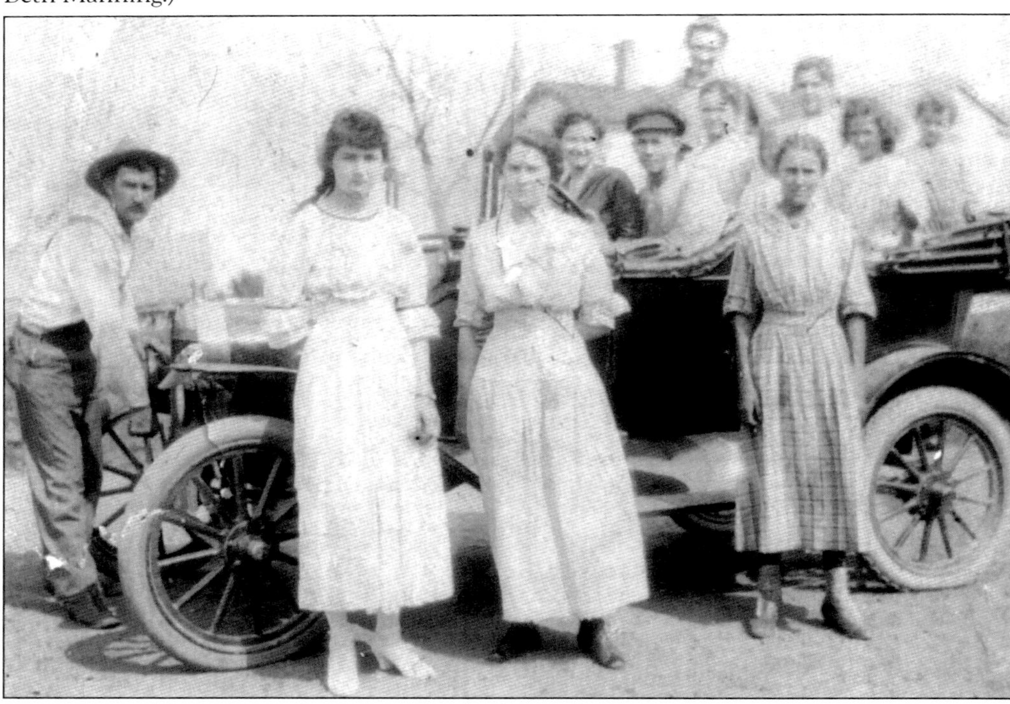

George Drendel cranks up the car to take the family for a ride. George and Mary Drendel came to Huntley in 1908. They had nine daughters and one son, Frank, shown seated at the wheel. Mary is standing at right. (Courtesy of the Vernon and Shirley Drendel family.)

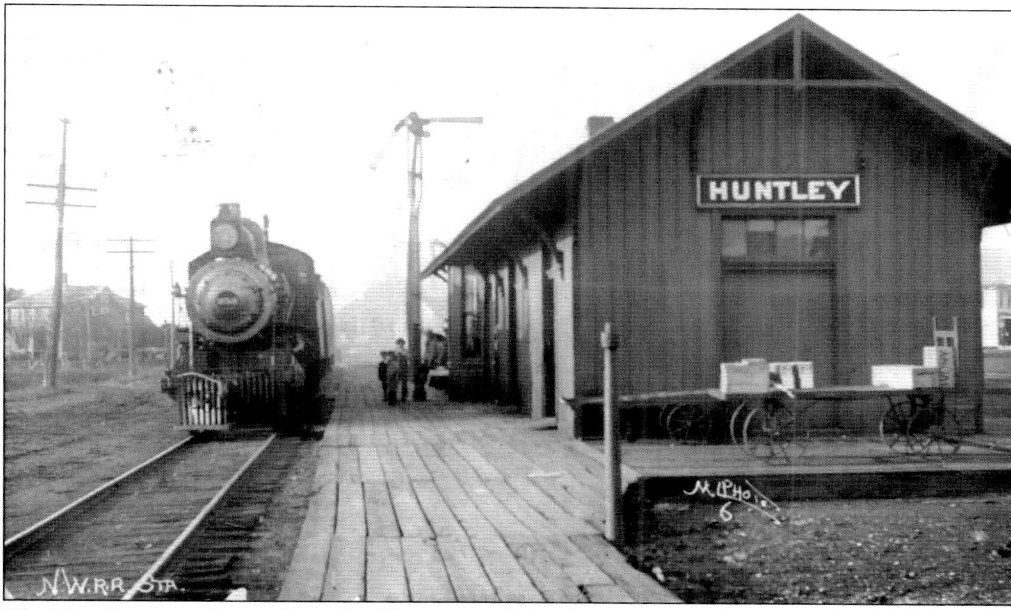

The Huntley train depot along the Chicago and North Western Railway line provided passenger and freight service. In this photograph, dated 1911, the train is facing south. The view is to the north. (Courtesy of Tom and Barb Conley.)

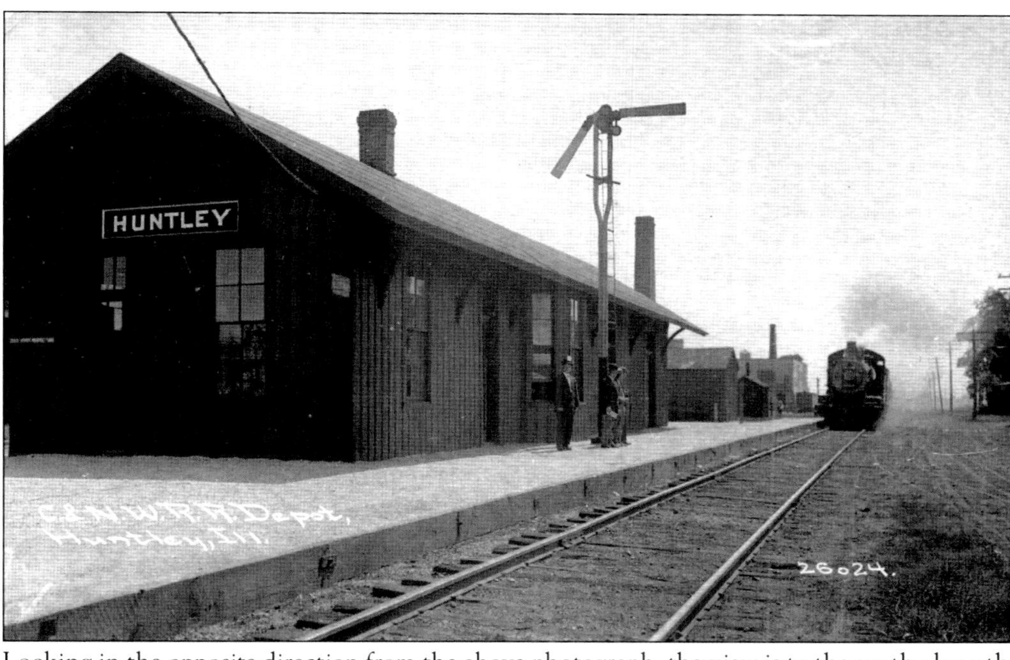

Looking in the opposite direction from the above photograph, the view is to the south along the tracks. The gentleman at left has his ticket in his hatband as he waits for the train at the Huntley depot around 1911. (Courtesy of Jake Marino.)

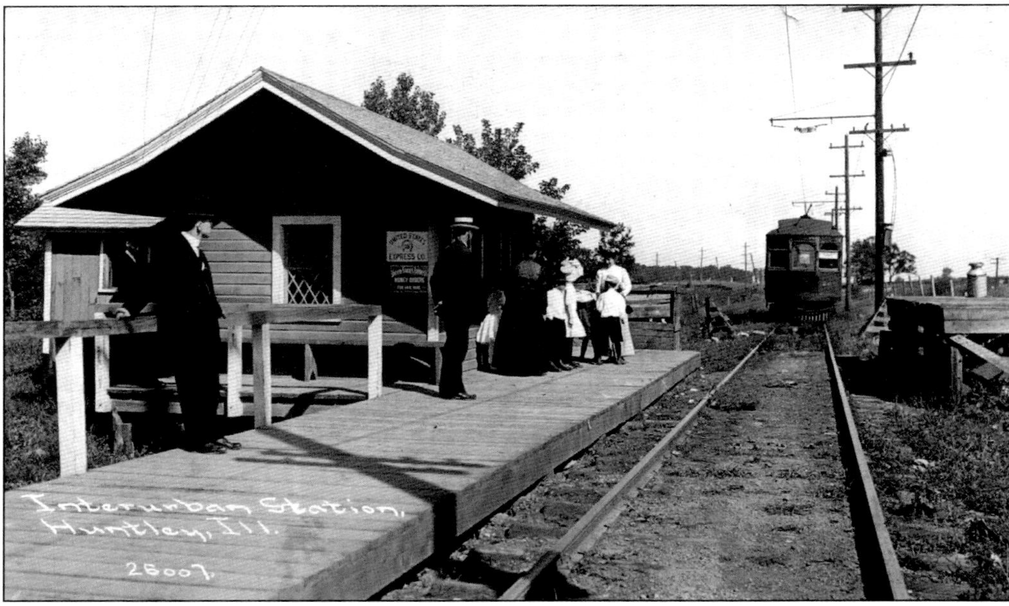

The Elgin-Belvidere electric trolley provided convenient passenger transportation for Huntley residents from 1905 to 1930. Regular service throughout the day provided easy means to jobs, shopping, and visiting. This station was located on the north side of Main Street, a half a block west of Vine Street (now Route 47). Note the milk cans on the platform to the right. (Courtesy of Mary Beth Manning.)

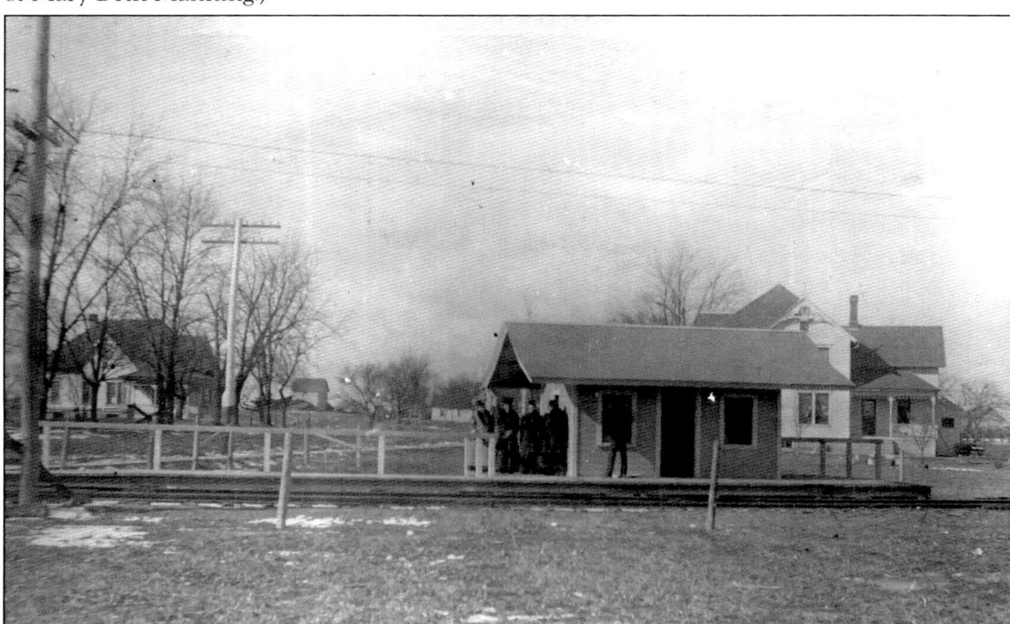

This view, looking to the west, shows the Elgin-Belvidere interurban trolley ticket station and depot located at Main Street just west of Vine Street. Rural riders could flag the trolley to stop for them in the countryside. Here in town, businessman Fred Fenwick's house is behind the station. Charlie Stevens's house is to the left. (Courtesy of Tom and Barb Conley.)

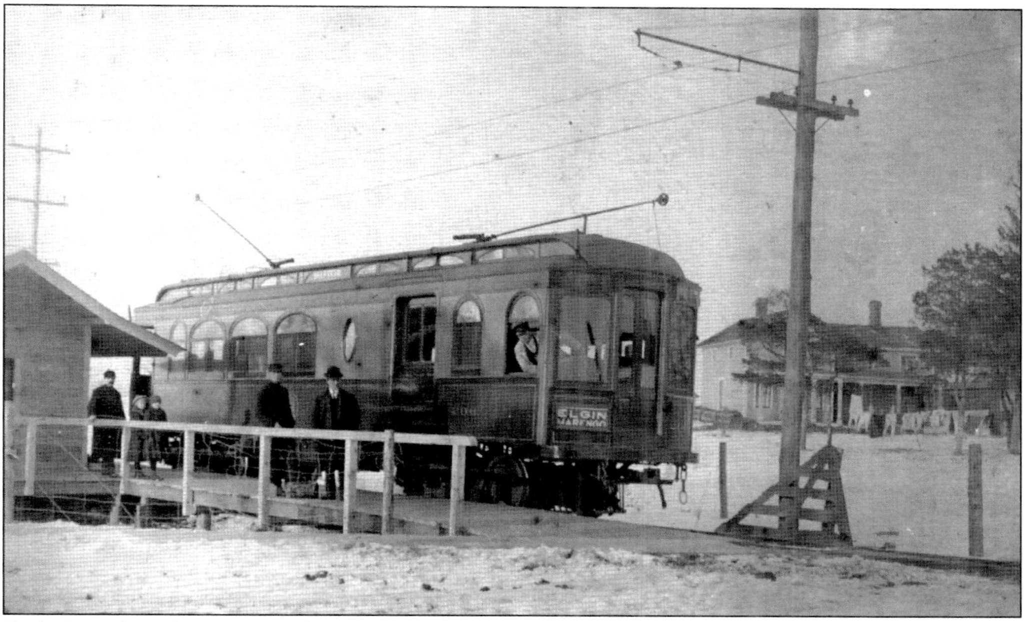

Early Huntley pharmacist Ed Cook took this photograph of the interurban trolley that provided stops in Union and Marengo on its way to Belvidere. The trolley operated from 1905 to 1930. (Courtesy of Tom and Barb Conley.)

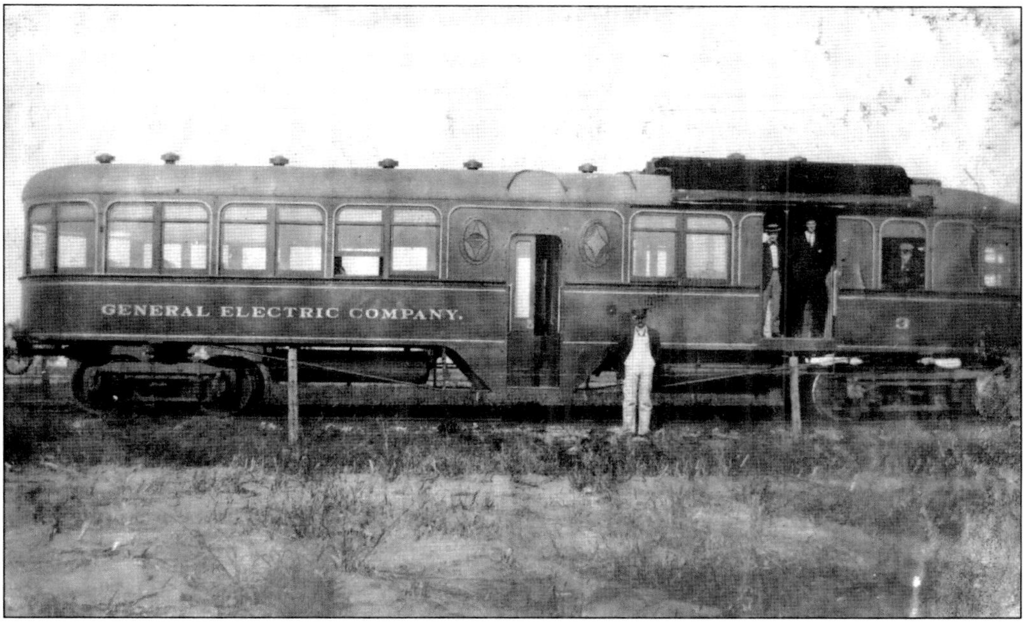

A car from the interurban trolley line sits near Huntley along the route between Elgin and Belvidere. The trolley made stops at Gilberts, Union, and Marengo. Although a convenience for local residents, the service could boast of only three profitable years in 25 years of operation. (Courtesy of Tom and Barb Conley.)

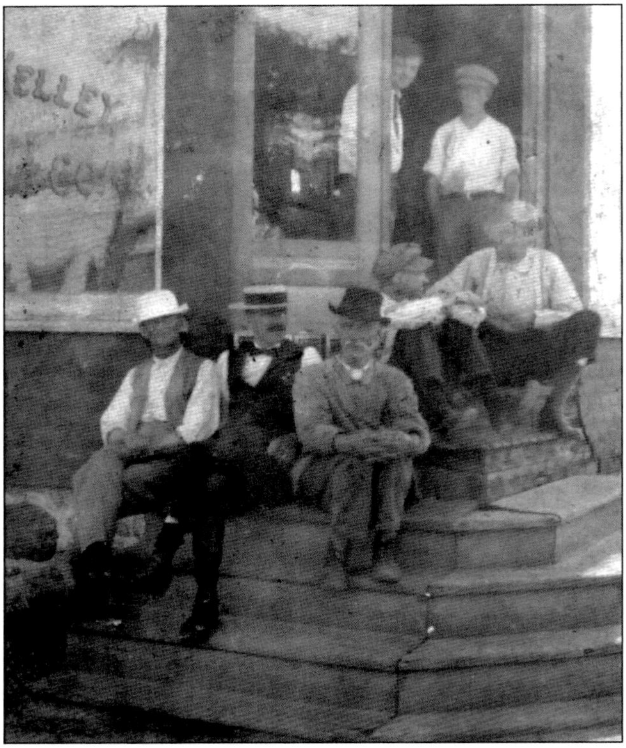

Town businessmen gather to chat on the steps of Sawyer and Kelley Mill on the southwest corner of Main Street and what was then known as Railroad Street, now a parking lot at the southern extension of Woodstock Street. The building and corner entrance still can be seen at that location. The photograph is undated and the men's names are unknown. (Courtesy of Tom and Barb Conley.)

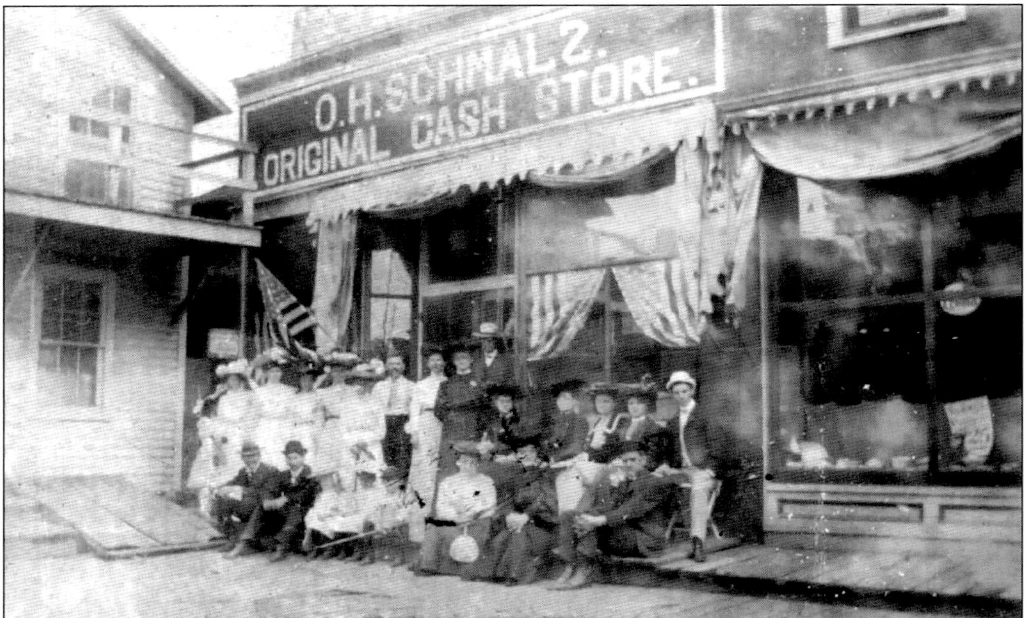

A patriotic group of Huntley residents gather in front of Schmalz General Store at what is now the corner of Coral and Church Streets. The photograph is undated and unidentified. Otto Schmalz's store was in operation from 1894 to 1918 after which time the buildings at this location on the town square where taken down. (Courtesy of Robert Schmalz.)

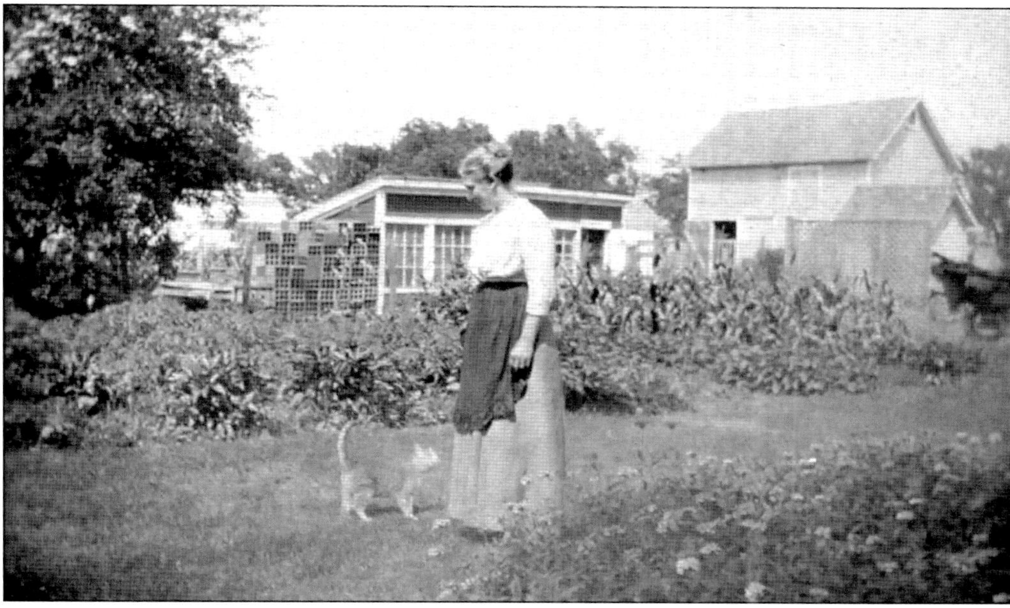

Hattie Schmalz (1868–1953), wife of general store owner Otto Schmalz, plays with her cat in the yard of their Church Street home. Many homes in the village limits at that time had small barns, chicken houses, and other small outbuildings. This photograph was taken around 1908, the same year she addressed the eighth-grade graduates at Huntley School. Her topic was "Why Women Should have the Vote." (Courtesy of Robert Schmalz.)

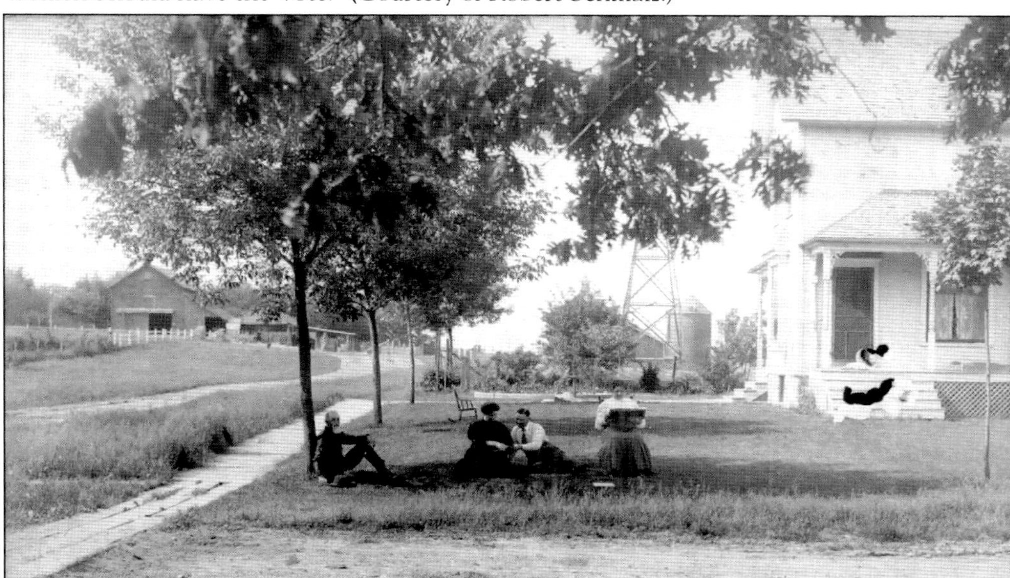

A group gathers on the lawn at the Schmalz home at the corner of Church and Second Streets around 1908. The view is looking to the north. Although the scenery is much changed, the home, built in 1900 and remodeled in 1928, still remains. Pictured from left to right are George Nelson Howe (Hattie Schmalz's father), Henrietta Schmalz, Otto Schmalz, and Addie Morris. (Courtesy of Robert Schmalz.)

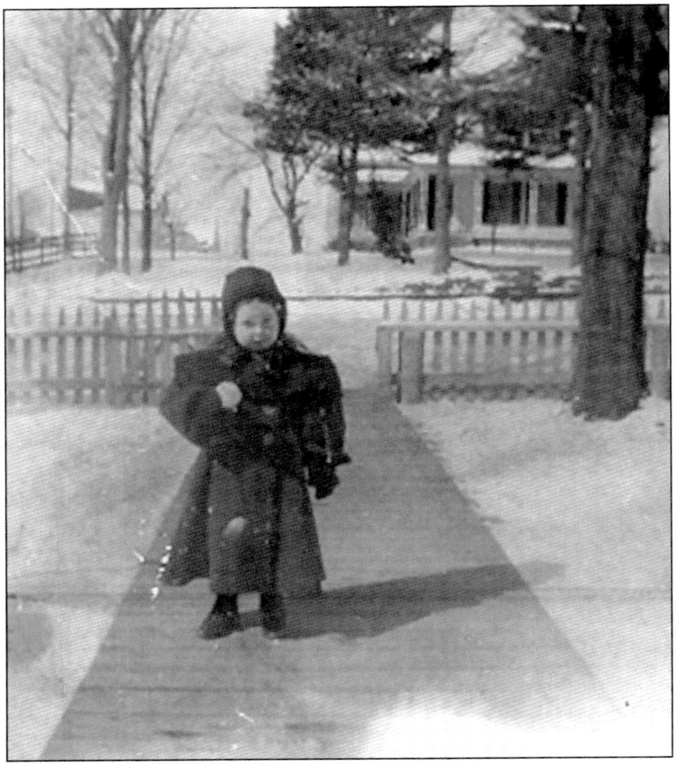

Mildred Devine (1893–1974) is shown in front of her Woodstock Street home in 1896 or 1897. Her father, William Devine, was a partner with John P. Skeels in the Devine and Skeels General Store, which operated from 1876 to 1917. Her mother, Minnie, a professionally trained musician, was president of the Huntley Musical Club. (Courtesy of Jaye Powers.)

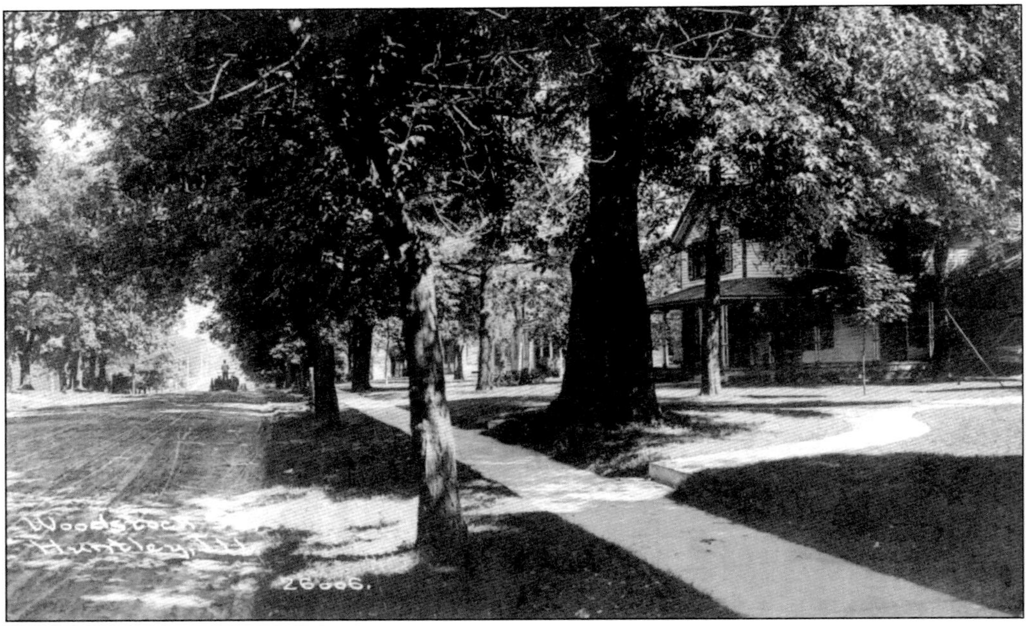

The beautiful tree-lined Woodstock Street was unpaved when this postcard, dated October 1, 1916, was sent. Today the street is covered in paving bricks, as it has been for decades. The view is looking toward the north. (Courtesy of Noel and Lillian Hansmann.)

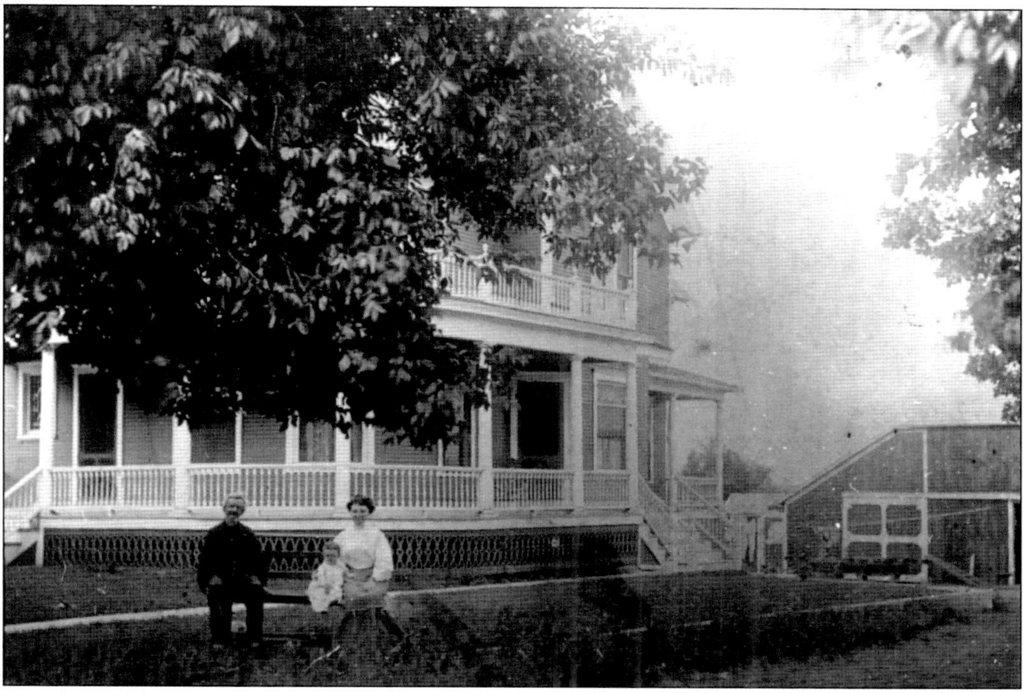

Members of the Conley family relax in front of their north Woodstock Street home around 1907. Tom Conley is at left. His daughter-in-law Margaret holds baby Tom "Glenn" Conley, who was born in October 1906. (Courtesy of Tom and Barb Conley.)

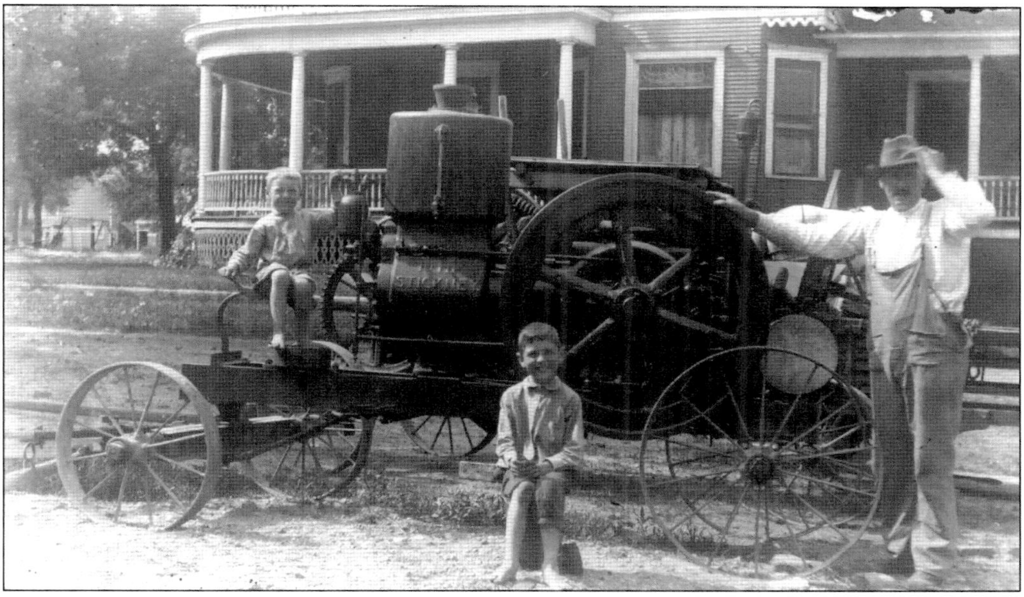

The Conley family shows off their prized steam engine with wire tie baler behind it in this photograph from about 1918. Father Enos Conley is at right. Son Earl Conley is at left, and older son Tom "Glenn" Conley is in front. The photograph was taken in front of the Conley home at 10706 North Woodstock Street. (Courtesy of Tom and Barb Conley.)

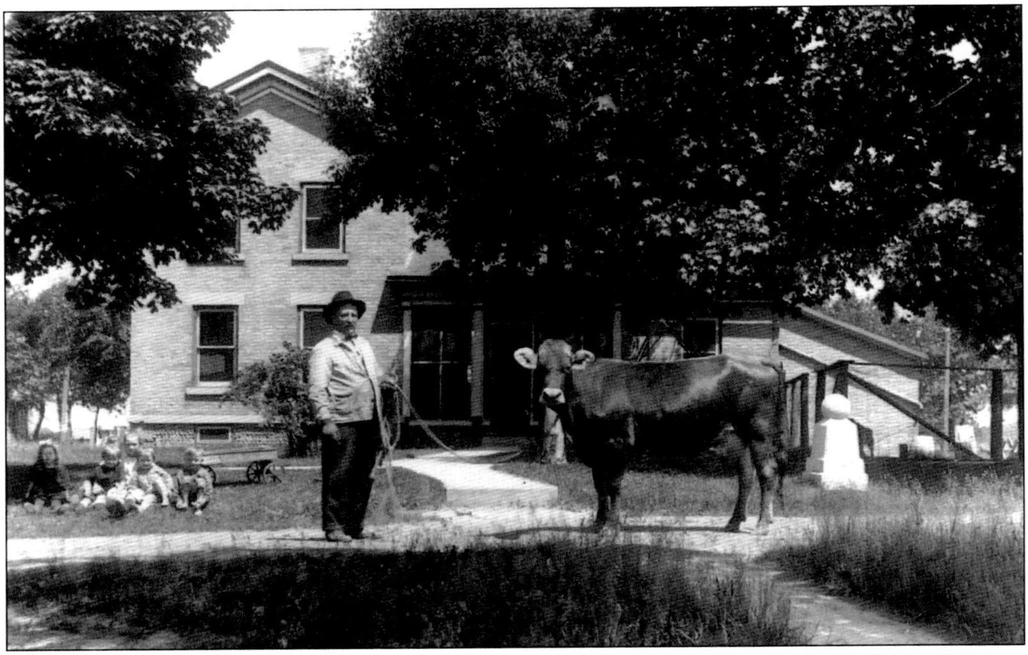

Local butcher Frank Lawson poses with his cow in front of his home on Grove Street. Lawson purchased the home in 1906, about one year after he opened his Main Street meat market. The Lawson children are seated on the lawn at left. The Lawsons' sons James and Frank Jr. served in World War II. (Courtesy of Huntley Area Public Library.)

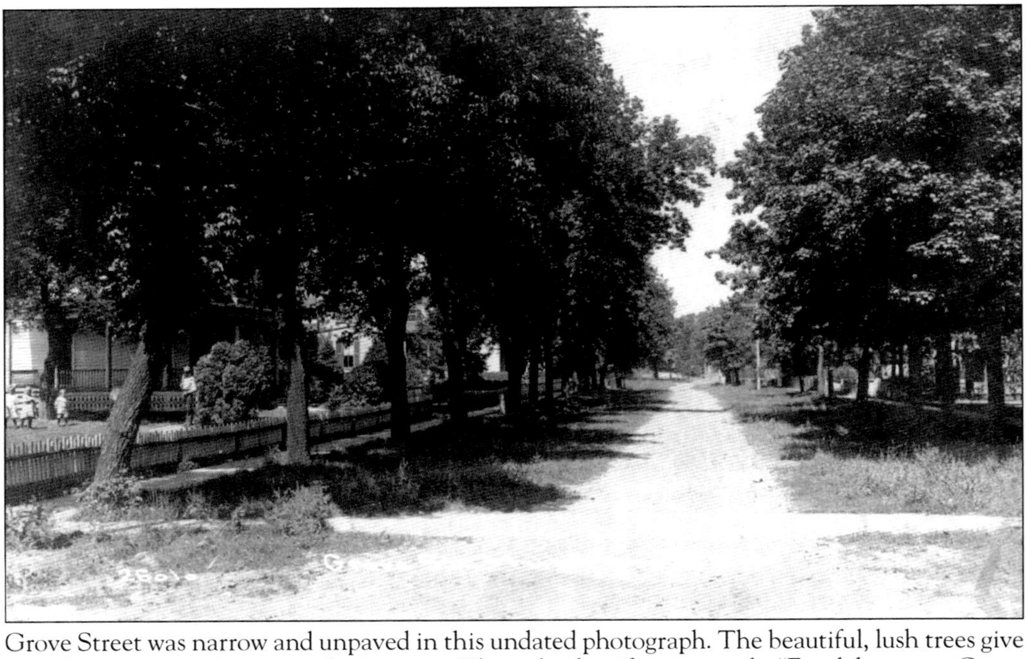

Grove Street was narrow and unpaved in this undated photograph. The beautiful, lush trees give an indication as to the reason for its name. The only identification reads, "Frank house on Grove Street." (Courtesy of Noel and Lillian Hansmann.)

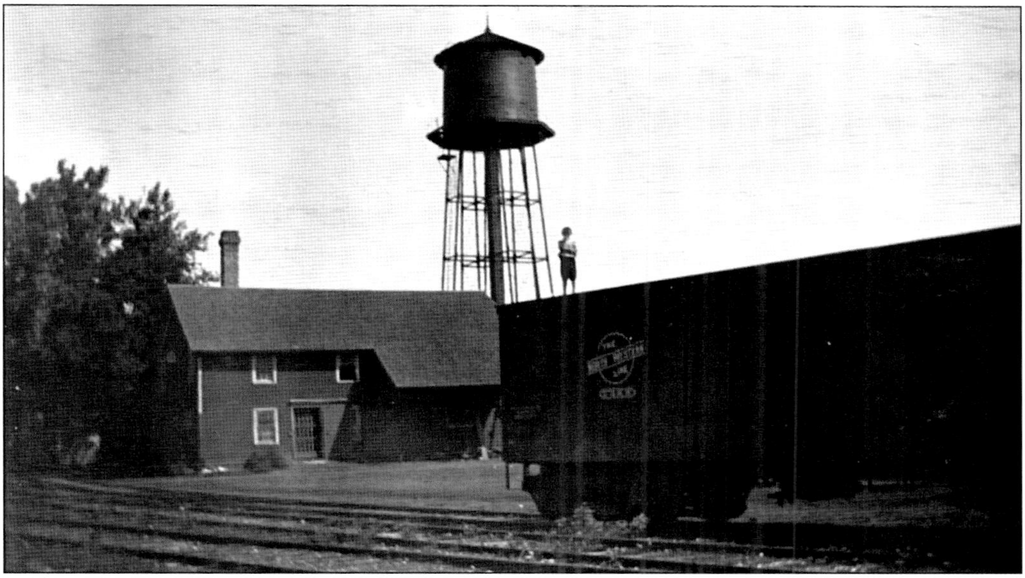

Huntley boys were active climbers in the early 1900s, scaling everything from train cars to smoke stacks to rooftops. But the favorite climbing spot was the town water tower (now gone), seen in the background. Although the individual on the train is unidentified, it is known that Arthur and Harry Heineman, Carl Schmalz, Ed Cook, and John Hawley were avid photographers of their time and took many of the wonderful aerial shots of Huntley. (Photograph by Carl Schmalz; courtesy of Robert Schmalz.)

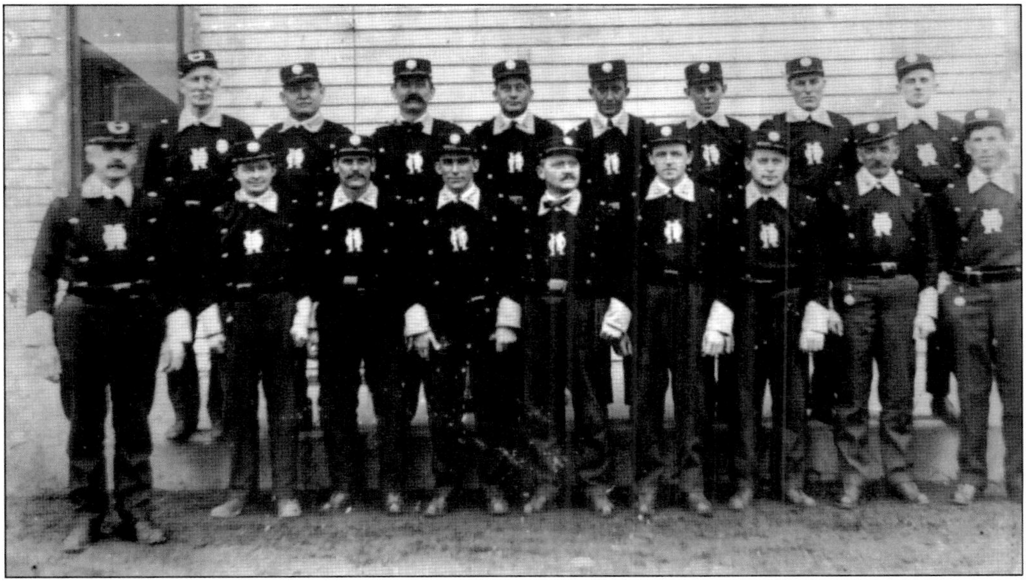

When the fire bell in the town square rang, volunteers hurried to action from their various locations around town. The 1910 squad includes (first row) marshal John Frenck, Harry Hilbert, Martin Simonsen, Ben Graupner, Otto Schmalz, Chris Ahrens, John Rammien, Herman Elsholtz, and Henry Ackman; (second row) Edward Cook, Ernest Daehn, Louis Schnelle, Leo Hennig, John Tarnow, Bill Ehlert, Bert Ehlert, and Charlie Weltzien. (Courtesy of Huntley Area Public Library.)

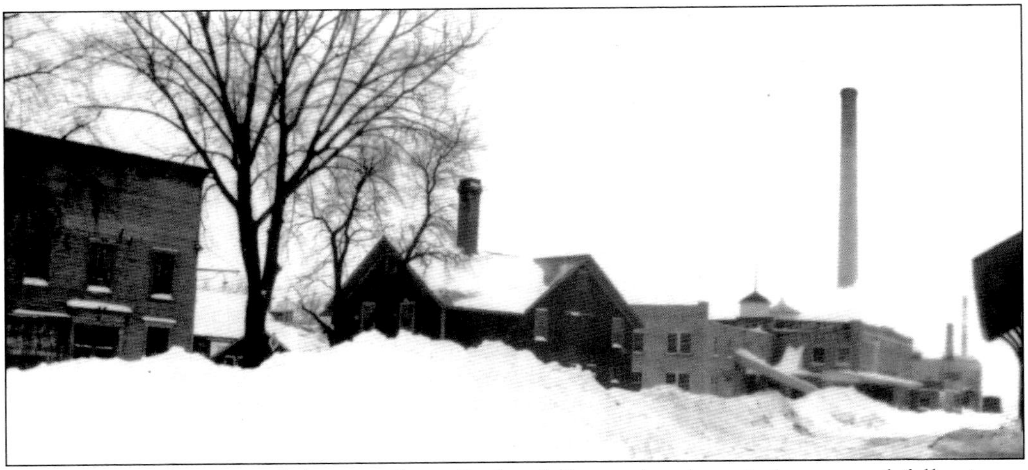

Few photographs exist of the once-busy Railroad Street, but here it is captured following a snowstorm, possibly in the late 1920s. At far left is the first village hall building, conveniently situated across from the train tracks and south of the busy town square. This facility served the community until 1939. Jelke Company, a milk processing plant, can be seen at right with its smokestack. (Courtesy of Huntley Area Public Library.)

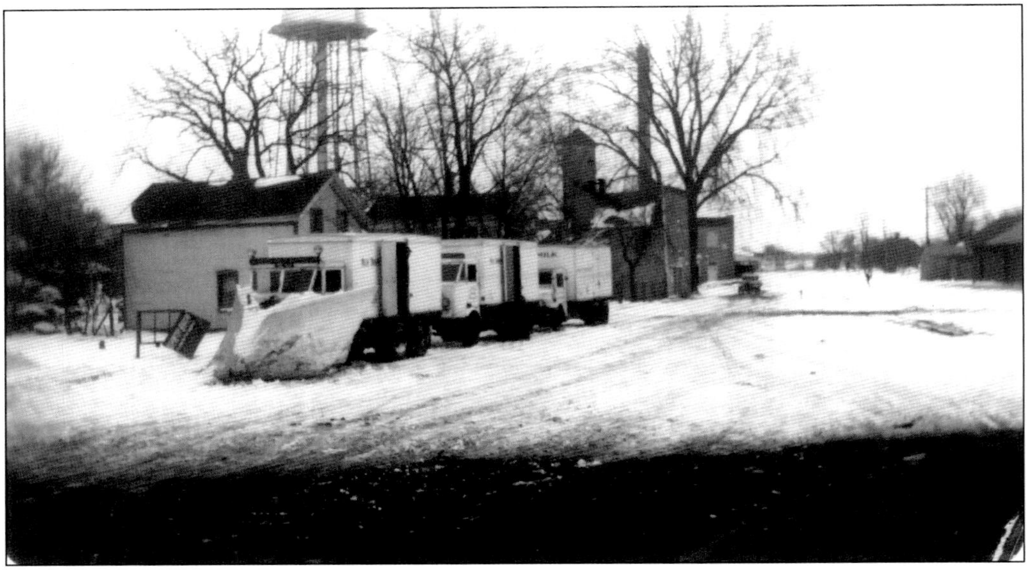

A rare view of Railroad Street looking toward the south shows milk transfer trucks equipped with snowplows. The tower to the left of the tall chimney was used by the fire department to hang their cotton hoses to dry. The once-busy street now exists only as a parking lot on the south side of Main Street at the extension of Woodstock Street. (Courtesy of Tom and Barb Conley.)

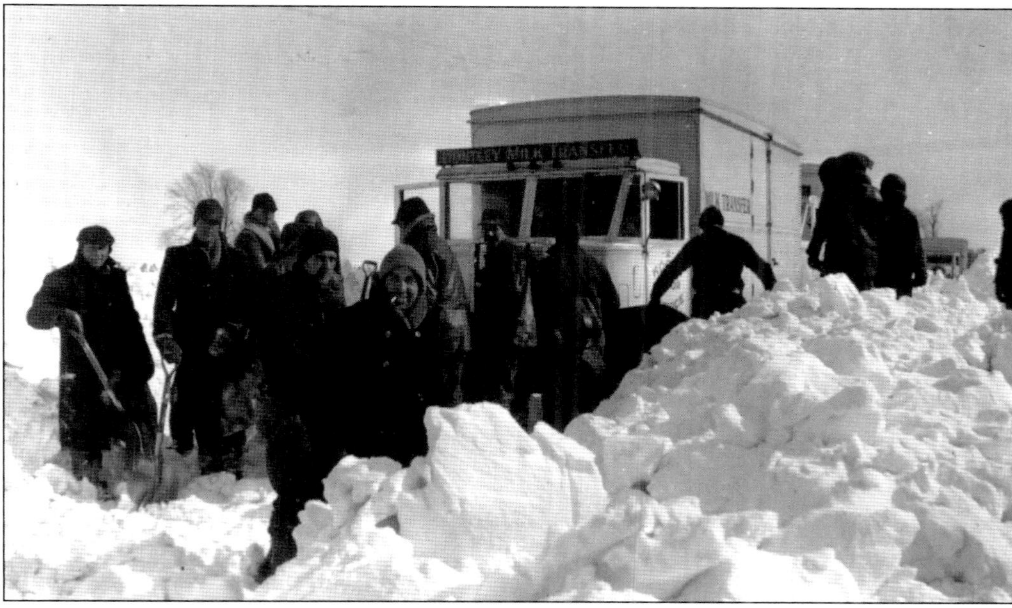

The winter of 1935–1936 was the worst of the past century in Huntley. Snow fell for weeks, ultimately bringing the town to a standstill. Schools were closed for six weeks because rural students were unable to get into town, but the milk could not wait. Huntley men shoveled mountains of snow to open the roads for the milk transfer trucks. Donald Ehorn is the driver of the truck in the foreground. Others wait along Dundee Road. (Courtesy of Earl Kalsow.)

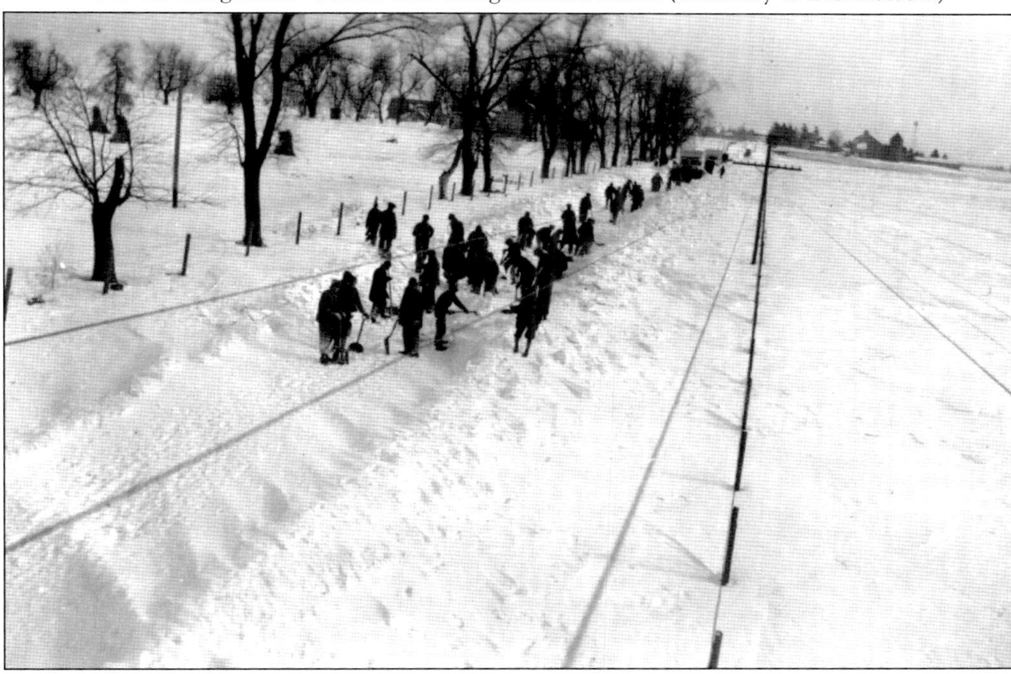

Dozens of shovelers attempted to open a snow-packed Dundee Road east of Huntley in February 1936. Snowplows from Carpentersville took two days to get through to Huntley. (Courtesy of Earl Kalsow.)

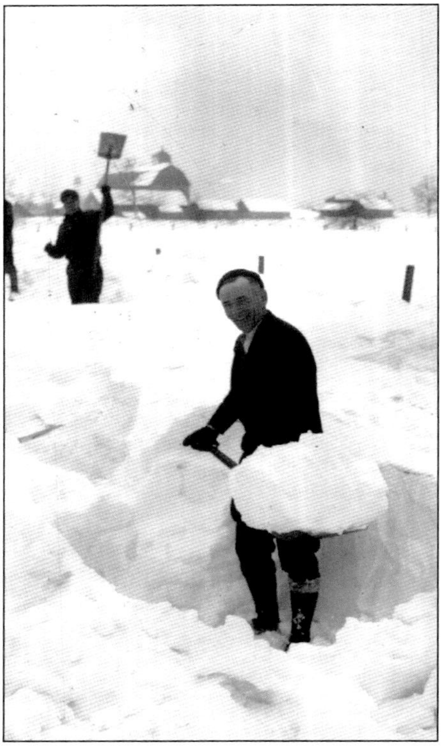

Huntley's rural postal deliveryman Charles Lazansky did not let a little snow stop him from getting through his route. This photograph, taken in January 1936, shows just the beginning of a snowstorm that continued for weeks. By February, Huntley was buried several feet deep in snow. School was closed for six weeks because buses were unable to reach many of the rural students. (Courtesy of Huntley Area Public Library.)

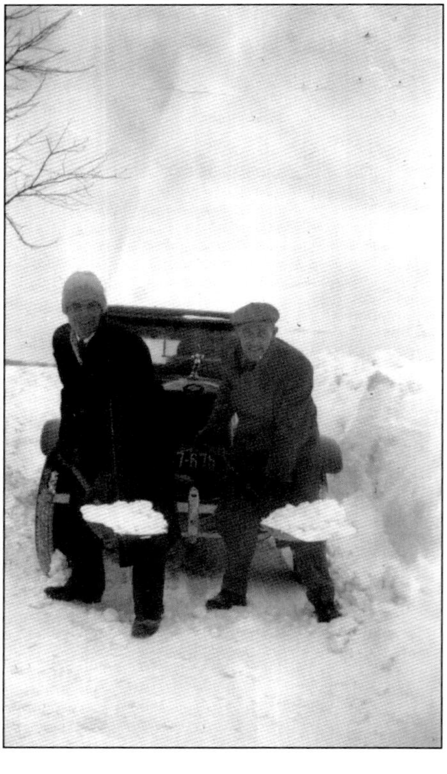

Shoveling snow was a common site in Huntley during the snowy winter of 1935–1936. Here Mary Ellen Moerke's father, Lawrence Rugg (left) and her uncle Ivan Bandlow attempt to make a path for their car. (Courtesy of Mary Ellen Moerke.)

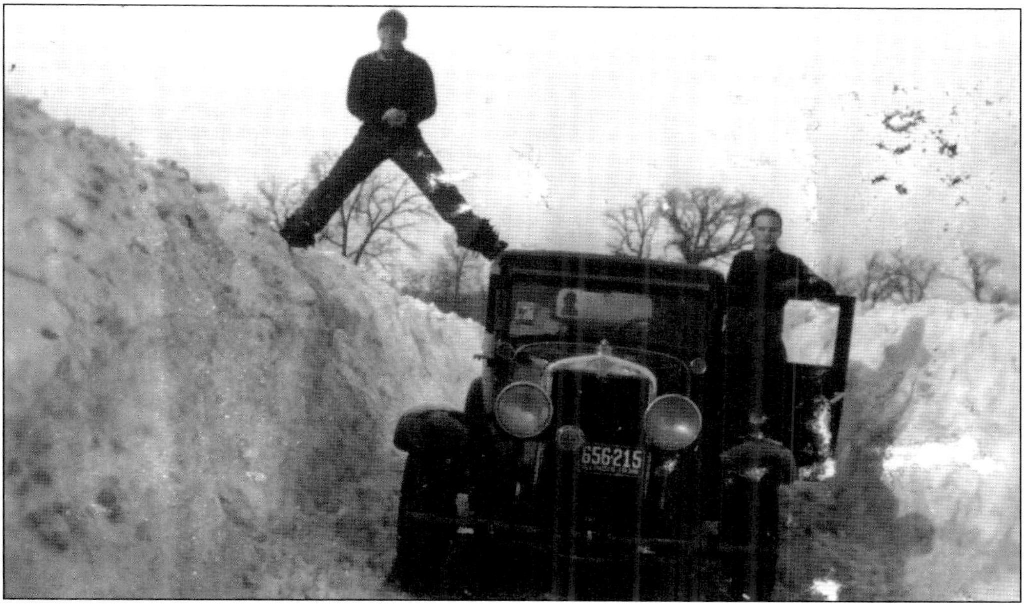

Robert Kalsow, age 17, stands atop one of the many mountains of snow on Ruth Road in February 1936. The other man in the photograph is believed to be Russell Hurd. Kalsow was a polio victim who missed most of his senior year at school. Through diligent physical therapy by his family at their Myrtle Street home, Kalsow was able to go on to college and eventually open his own business. (Courtesy of Earl Kalsow.)

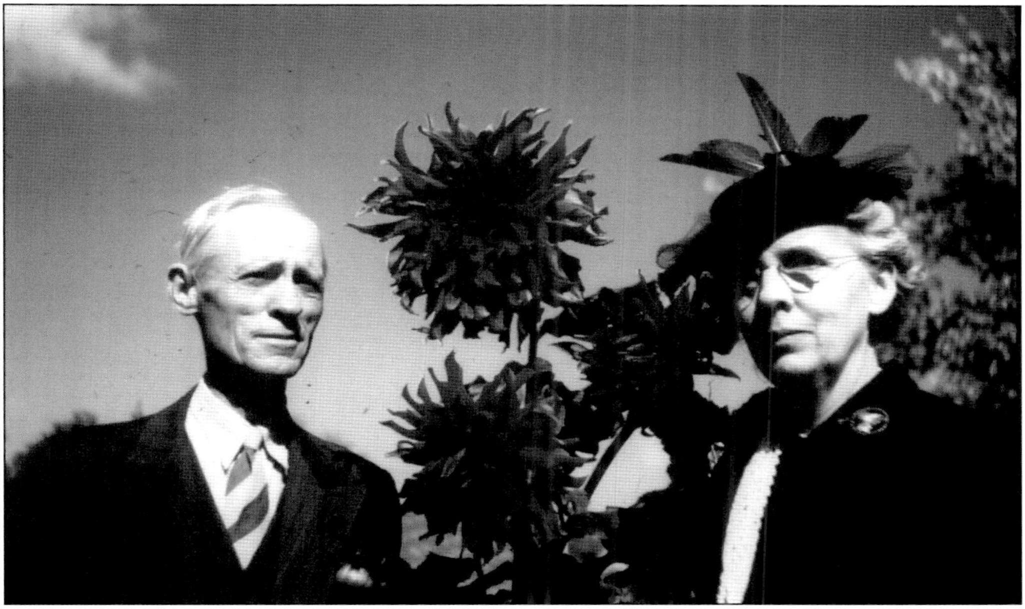

Dr. Oliver and Mae Statler pose with their prized dahlias at their Woodstock Street home in the early 1940s. The doctor graduated college in 1906, came to Huntley in 1908, and married Mae Hadley, a descendant of early Huntley settlers, in 1911. He was the Huntley doctor for more than 40 years. His office was in his home. Their son Oliver Hadley Statler is featured in chapter 5. (Photograph by Harley and Mabel Swanson Mackeben; courtesy of Lonni Swanson Oldham.)

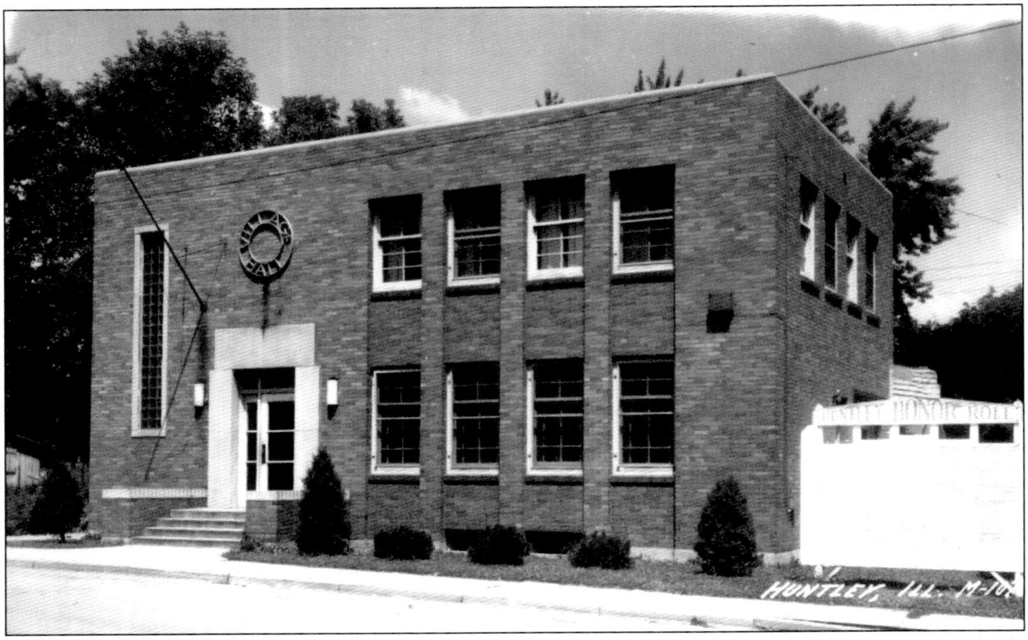

This second village hall, situated on Coral Street on the north side of the town square, was built in 1939 at a cost of $8,500. To the right of the building is the World War II honor roll, listing the names of all those from Huntley who served during the war. (Courtesy of Earl Kalsow.)

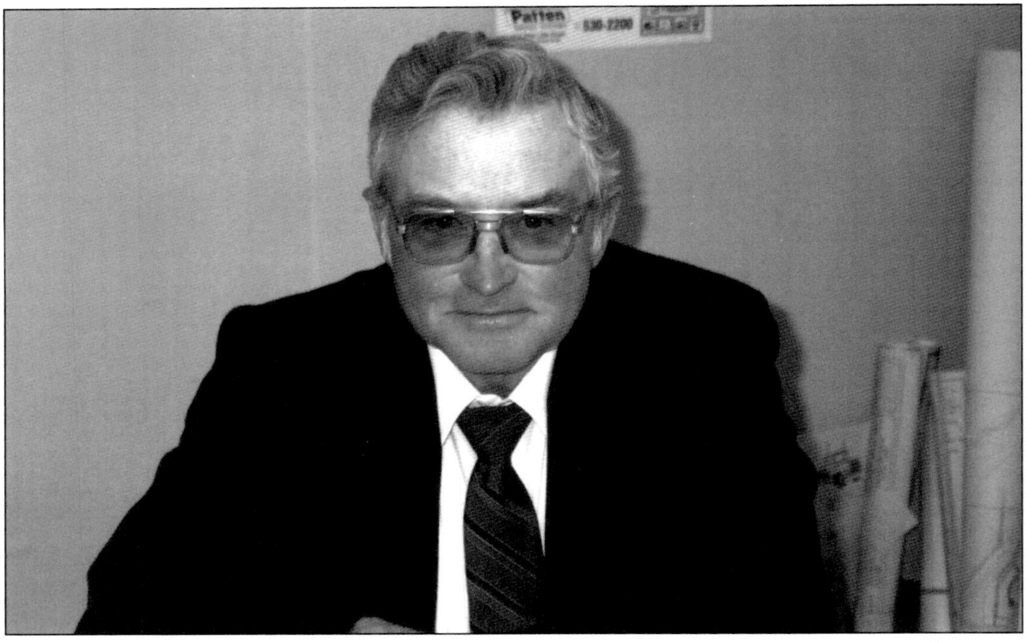

James C. Dhamer was a popular Huntley village president who died in office in November 1999 at age 69. Dhamer had been a member of the village planning commission and then a village trustee before serving 14 years as village president. When he ran for the office in 1985 against incumbent Don Enstrom, the vote was tied. A coin toss decided the result in Dhamer's favor. The town square park has been named in Dhamer's honor. (Courtesy of Rita McMahon.)

Nine

Doing Business

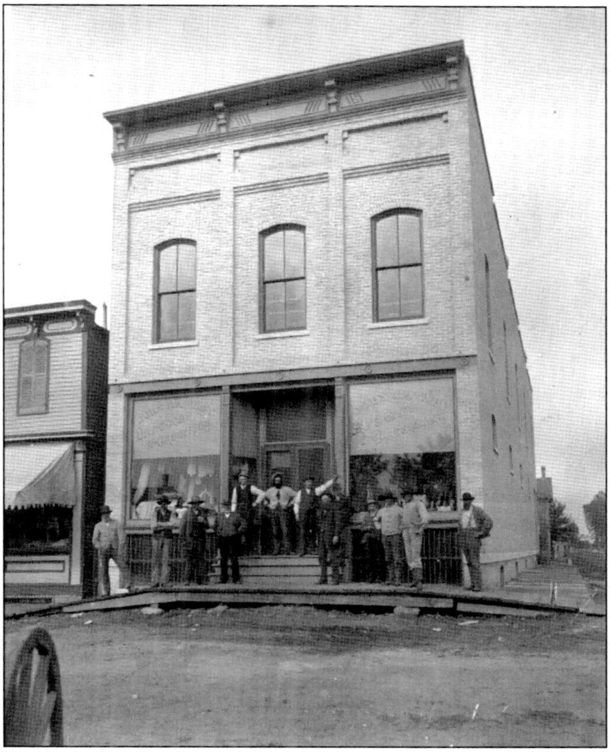

This building has been a fixture on the west side of the town square since it was built in 1879 to house John Hawley's general store. Annual sales at that time averaged $30,000. In 1881, Hawley bought out John G. Weltzien and operated as a sole owner until his retirement in 1893. Pictured here around 1880 is James "Deacon" Williams at the left of the stairs. On the steps are Frank Weltzien and Hawley and an unidentified man in the center. Orris Mason is to the right of the steps. Harry Hart is the short man to the right with the straw hat. (Courtesy of Huntley Area Public Library.)

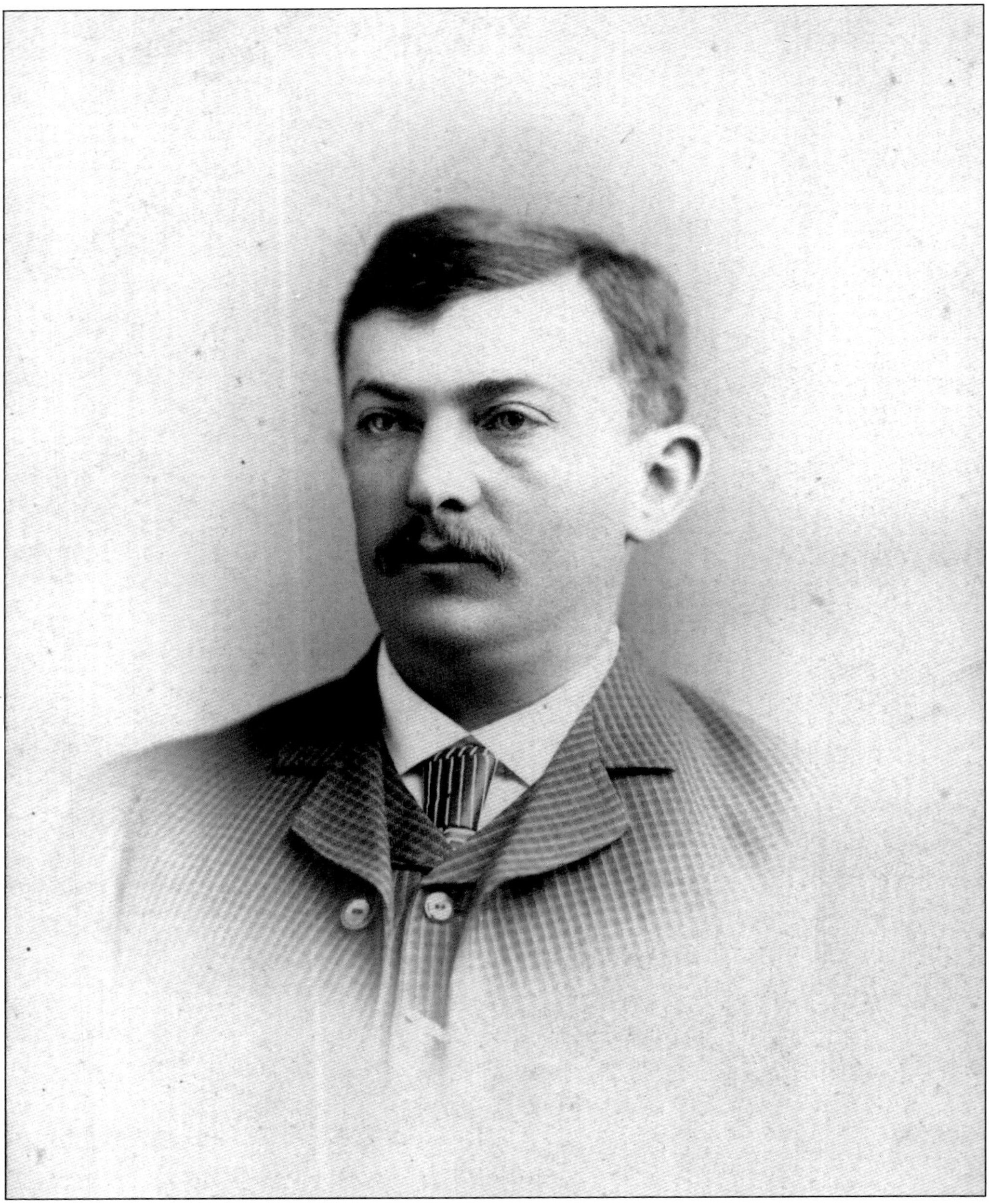

General store owner John Hawley (1855–1944) began in the mercantile business in Huntley in 1876 with his brother-in-law John G. Weltzien. Hawley bought out his partner in 1881 and operated as a sole proprietor until his retirement in 1893. Other members of the family carried on the business, and later, the building was rented to various individuals until it was sold. Hawley and his wife, Mina Weltzien, were prominent members of the Woodstock Street community. Their three daughters, Edith, Neva, and Lillian, were well known even into their later years as "the Hawley girls." (Courtesy of Huntley Area Public Library.)

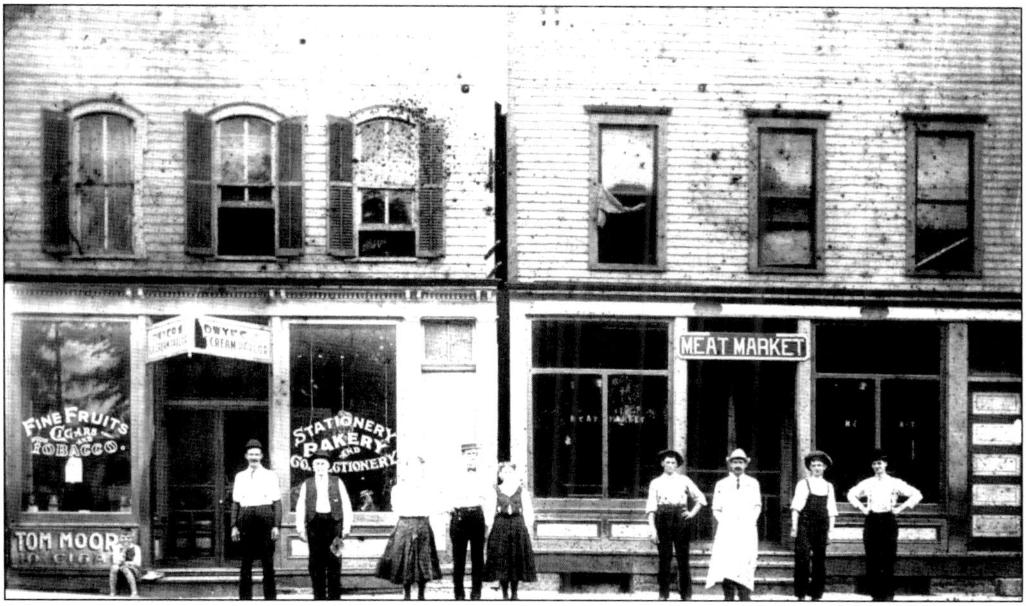

The south side of Main Street is featured in this panoramic view of the businesses in operation at the end of the 1800s. Dwyer's Confectionary and Tobacco store is at left, and Lawson's Meat Market is to the right. Edward Dwyer is at far left in the derby. Pat Keating is to his right in the vest. Frank Lawson stands in front of his store, wearing the white apron. (Courtesy of Huntley Area Public Library.)

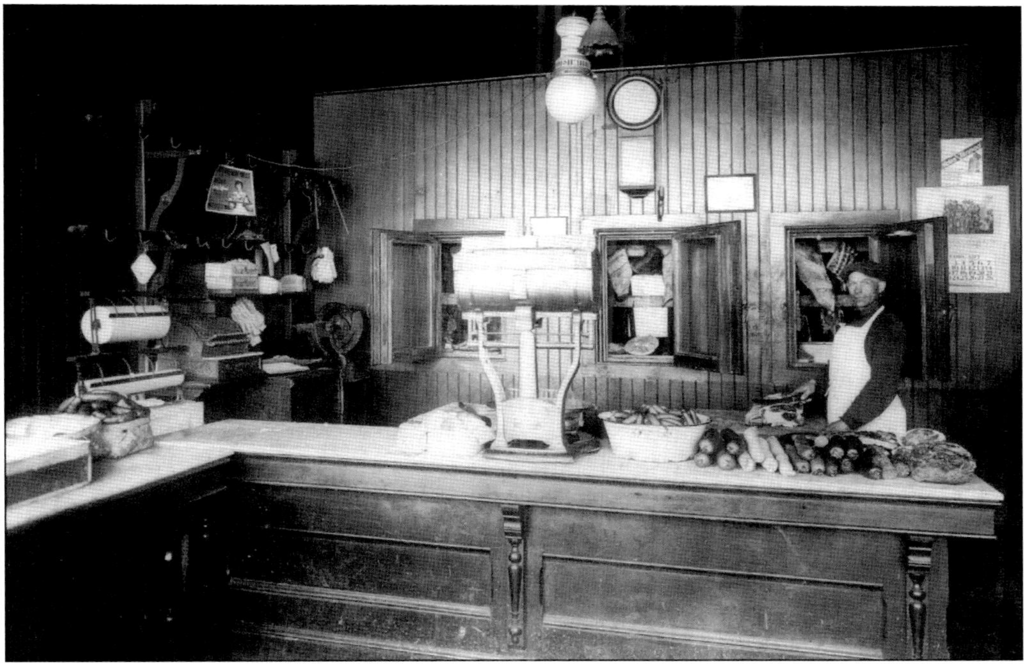

Butcher John Kalsow is shown inside Frank Lawson's meat market on Main Street in 1918. The market was in business from 1905 until Lawson's death in 1942. Longtime residents recall sawdust on the floor and jars of herring and oysters in the store. (Courtesy of Earl Kalsow.)

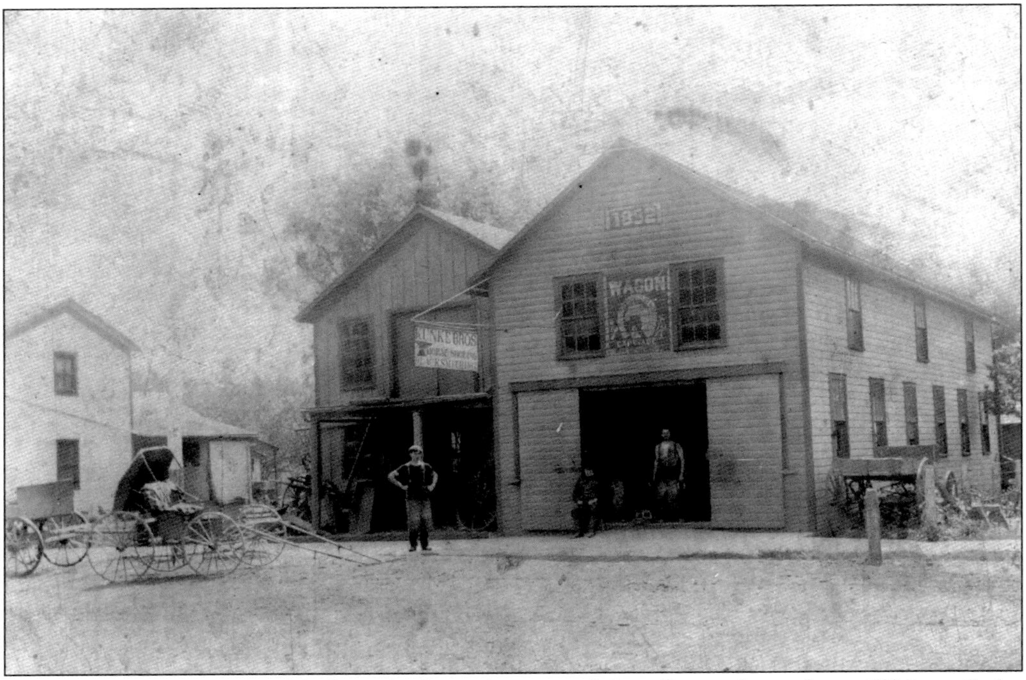

Max Kunke operated his blacksmith shop along east Main Street from about 1900 until the late 1930s, when horses no longer were the main means of transportation. Later, the Huntley school district used the building for several years to store its buses. (Courtesy of Huntley Area Public Library.)

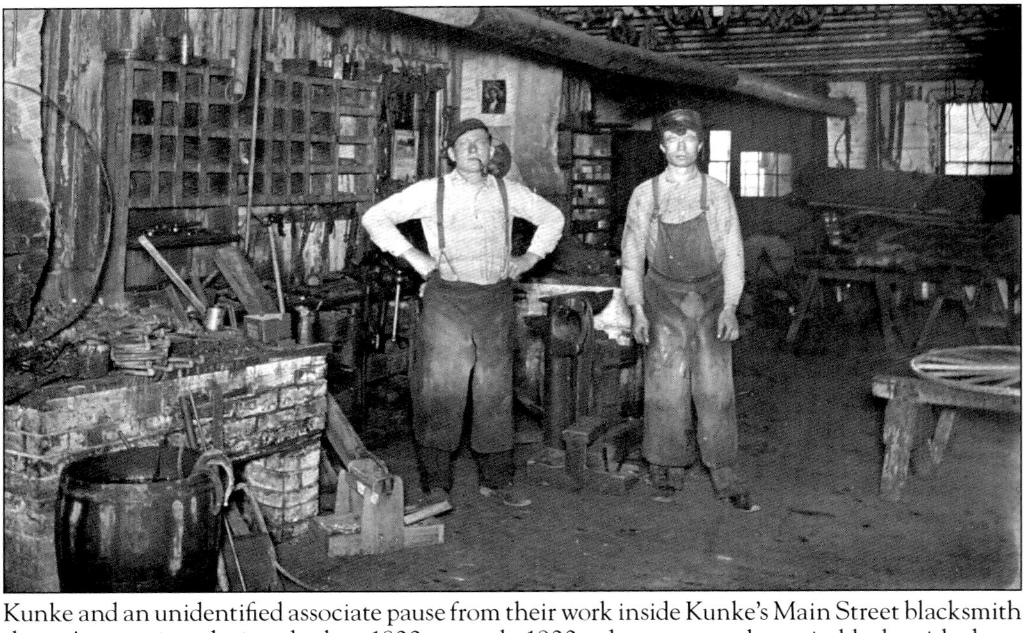

Kunke and an unidentified associate pause from their work inside Kunke's Main Street blacksmith shop. At one time during the late 1800s or early 1900s, there were at least six blacksmith shops in operation in Huntley. (Courtesy of McHenry County Historical Society.)

Ed Cook (1863–1951) was a Huntley businessman, serving as town druggist and undertaker. His brother Charles was the town doctor, who worked from the building he owned on Main Street across from the village square. When Charles died, Ed managed the building, which included his pharmacy and the local bank. Ed served for many years as the chief of Huntley's volunteer fire department and as the McHenry County coroner. (Courtesy of Tom and Barb Conley.)

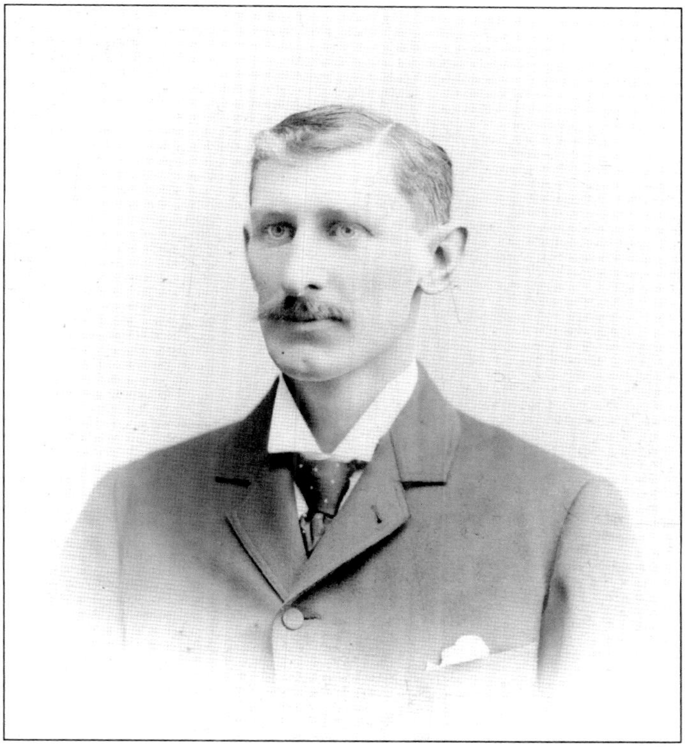

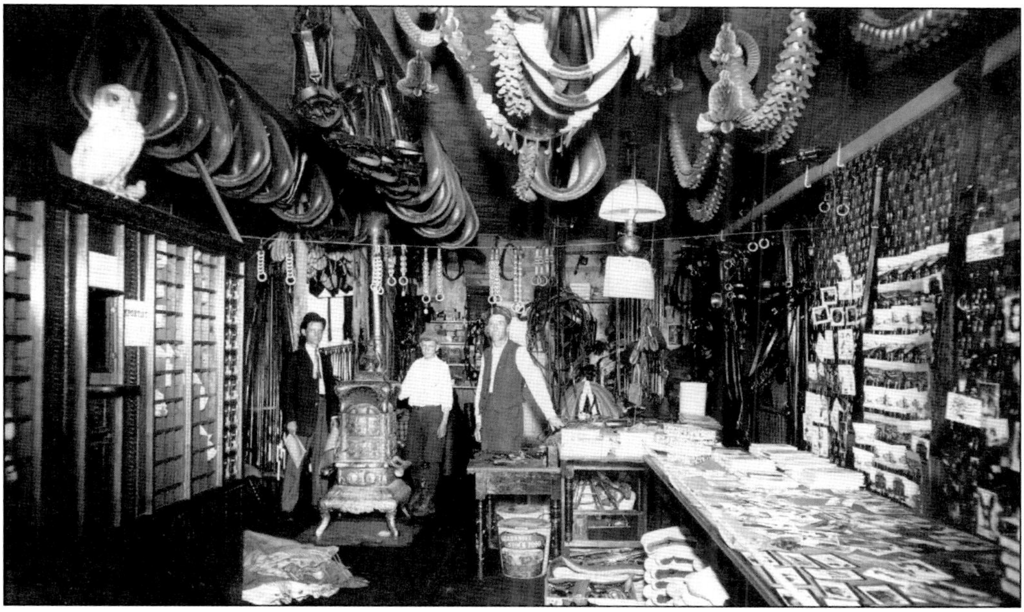

Once inside Cook's Drug Store on Main Street, customers could find a variety of dry goods for animals and humans available for sale. The ceiling of the store, although barely visible from the goods hanging there, is elaborately stenciled. Dr. Charles Cook built the building in 1893. His brother Ed continued ownership and management of the building into the 1940s. The men in the photograph are unidentified. (Courtesy McHenry County Historical Society.)

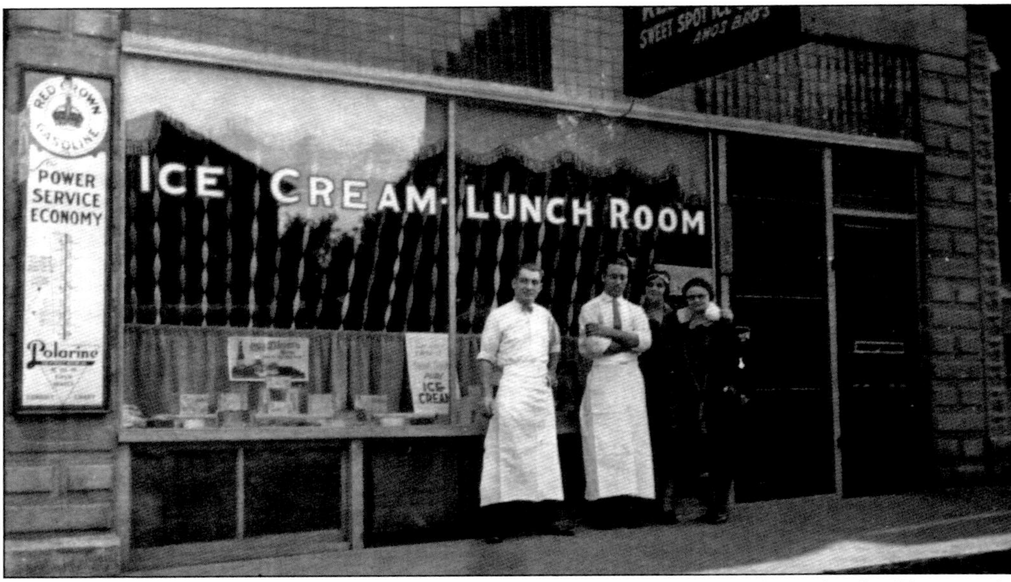

Over the years, several restaurants found a home in the west side of the Pabst building at the southeast corner of Main and Church Streets. When William Amos returned home to Huntley from service in World War I, he and his brother Franklin Amos opened their restaurant, the Sweet Spot, at that location. Dolby's Garage occupied the east end of the building. The Amos brothers are shown in front of their business. The women are unidentified. (Courtesy of Huntley Area Public Library.)

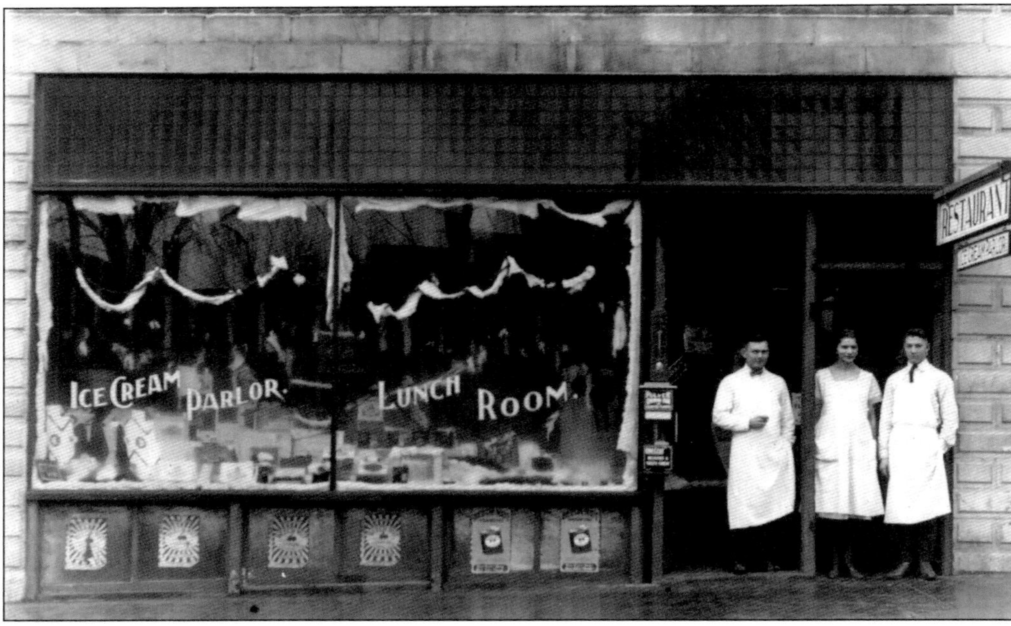

Heuer brothers Edwin (left) and Harold (right) ran their restaurant in the Pabst building next to Dolby's Garage after the Amos brothers gave up the Sweet Spot. The Heuers' sister Marie Heuer is pictured at center. The photograph dates to about 1925. (Courtesy of Mary Ellen Moerke.)

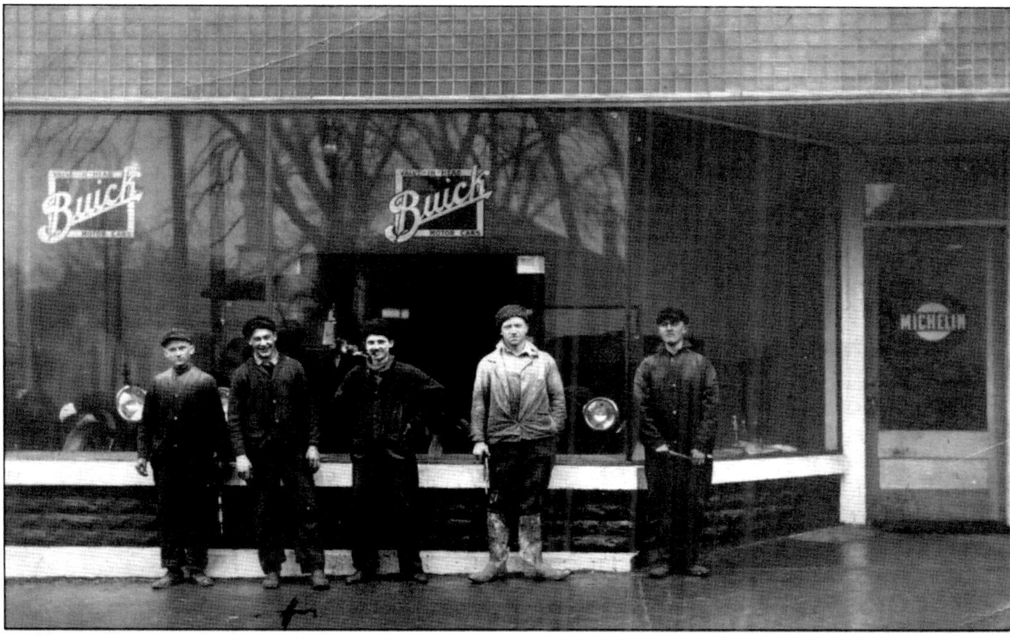

Dolby's Garage operated in the east side of the Pabst building on the southwest corner of Main and Church Streets from the time the building was built in 1916 until 1955. The garage door where cars entered for service still can be seen on the east side of the building. Sophus "Butch" Michelsen was in partnership with George Dolby for a time. Michelsen, born in 1892, is pictured second from left. (Courtesy of Dick Michelsen.)

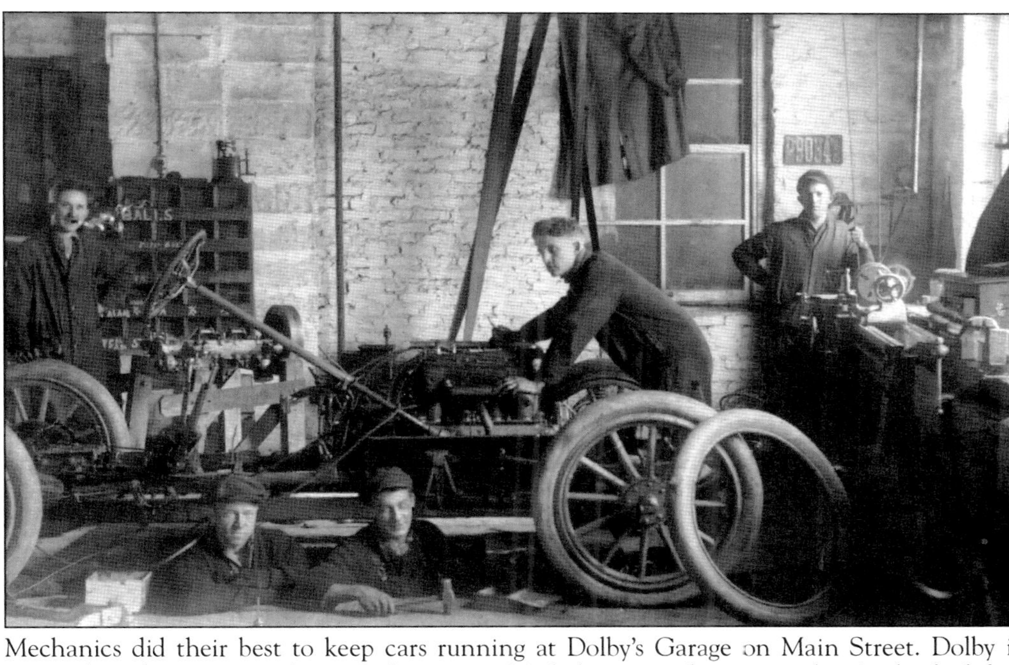

Mechanics did their best to keep cars running at Dolby's Garage on Main Street. Dolby is pictured in about 1916 working on the engine. Michelsen is in the pit at right. At the far left is Alfred Jordi Sr. The other men are unidentified. (Courtesy of Dick Michelsen.)

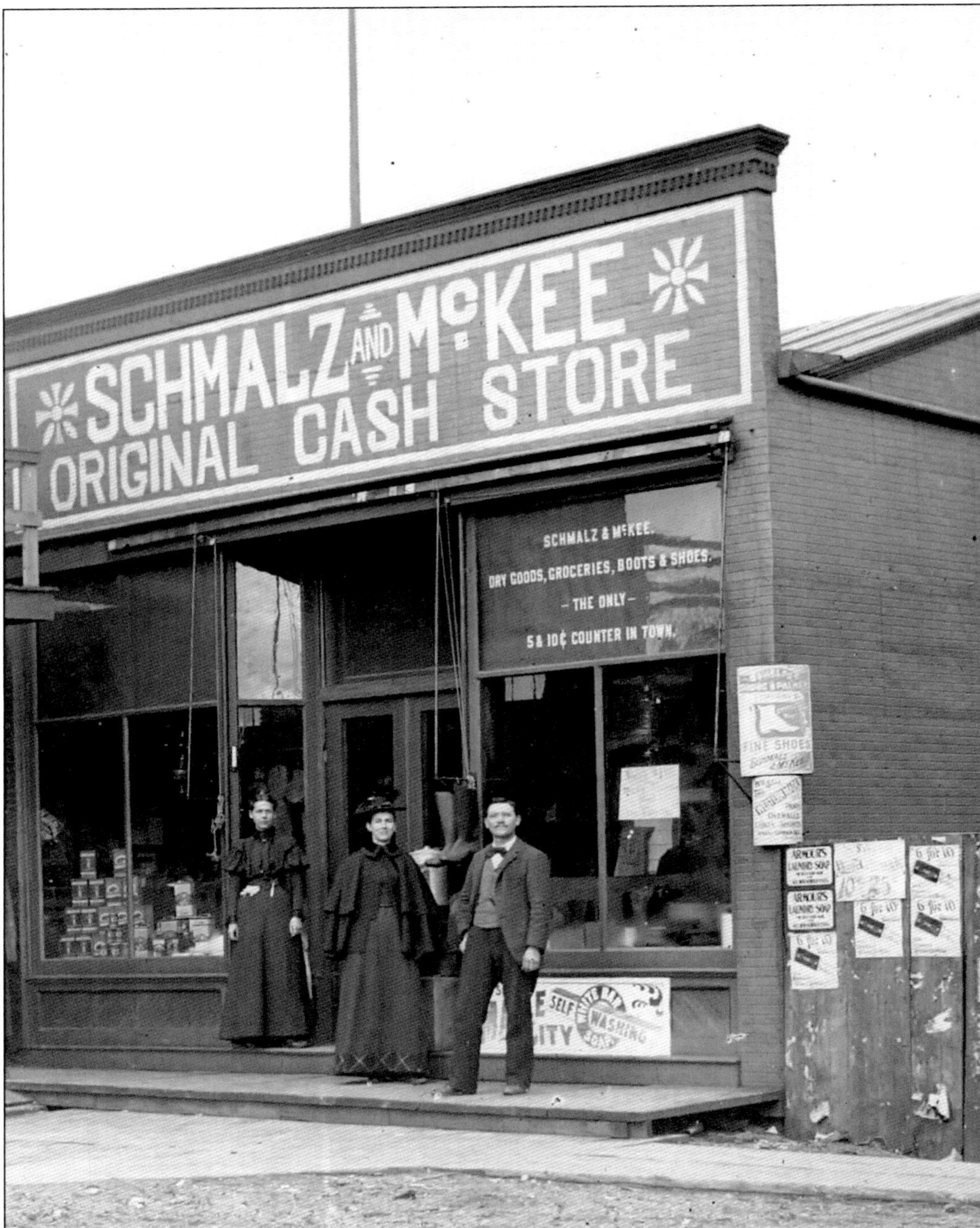

Otto Schmalz (1865–1947) and his partner Frank McKee opened Schmalz and McKee Original Cash Store at the east end of Coral Street facing west on the village square in 1894. The business featured the only five-and-dime counter in town. In 1897, Schmalz bought out McKee and operated the store independently as part of the Marco chain until September 1918. Schmalz was a popular and active member of the community. This photograph, taken about 1895, shows Schmalz and wife, Hattie, at center. The other woman is unidentified. (Courtesy of Robert Schmalz.)

Yuletide Memories

Comes again the Christmas season--
Vivid memories wake once more
Of a small, mid-western village
And a place called "Schmalz's Store"
Brave in all its Christmas trapping,
Gaily decked with dolls and toys,
Once a year supreme attractions
For the village girls and boys.
How we hurried from the school house,
Soon as study hours were o'er,
Flocked like noisy, chattering magpies,
To the thrills of "Schmalz's Store!"
Oh! the dolls so truly gorgeous,
Satin skirted, teeth like pearls,
Sleeping eyes and flaxen tresses,
Made to torture little girls.
"Old Maid" games and ribbon candy,
Peanut brittle, balky mules,
Picture books and "Christmas mixture,"
Toy pianos, mimic tools,
Dolly buggies, cunning flat irons,
Marbles, tops and dominoes,
Everything to help old Santa
Stuff the stockings to the toes.
Candy bead strings, rainbow candles,
Fruits ne'er seen on land or sea,
Striped canes and tinsel garlands,
Glistening angels for the tree.
Ropes of green and bells of scarlet,
"Live forever"--wreaths of holly,
Nothing lacking one might wish for
To make your Christmas bright and jolly.
Years have passed and time in passing
Changes brings to me and you,
Cities fall and kingdoms tumble--
The little store has vanished too--
But could anyone who knew it
Thirty years ago or more
Ever half forget the splendors
Christmas brought to "Schmalz's Store?"

By Marion Lawson Voss

This charming poem, written by a Huntley resident years ago, gives a glimpse of Christmas past and the holiday delights that could be found at Schmalz's store. Marion Lawson Voss (1896–1976), the daughter of meat market owner Frank Lawson, wrote the poem "Yuletide Memories" in the 1940s. Voss grew up in Huntley and distinctly recalled the thrill of Schmalz's General Store at Christmastime. The store was located near the intersection of Coral and Church Streets near where the old village hall sits on the town square today. The school Voss mentions still exists on East Main Street. It would not have been far from Schmalz's store.

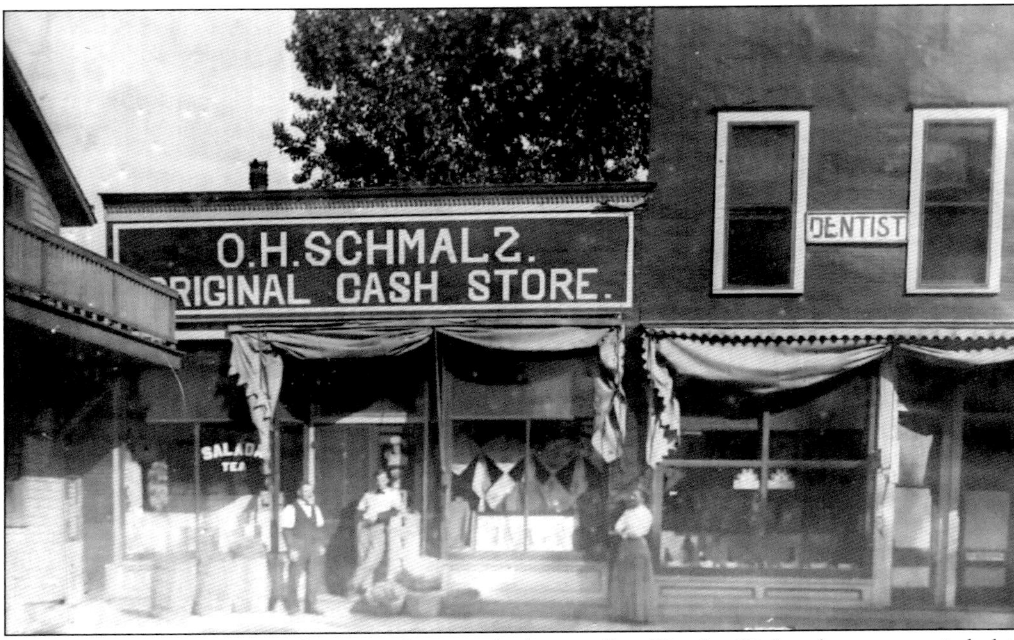

The Otto Schmalz General Store, along with dentist Dr. Charles Richardson, occupied this northeast corner of the town square where Coral Street came east then turned to the south around the square. Church Street is behind these buildings. Those pictured are unidentified. (Courtesy of Robert Schmalz.)

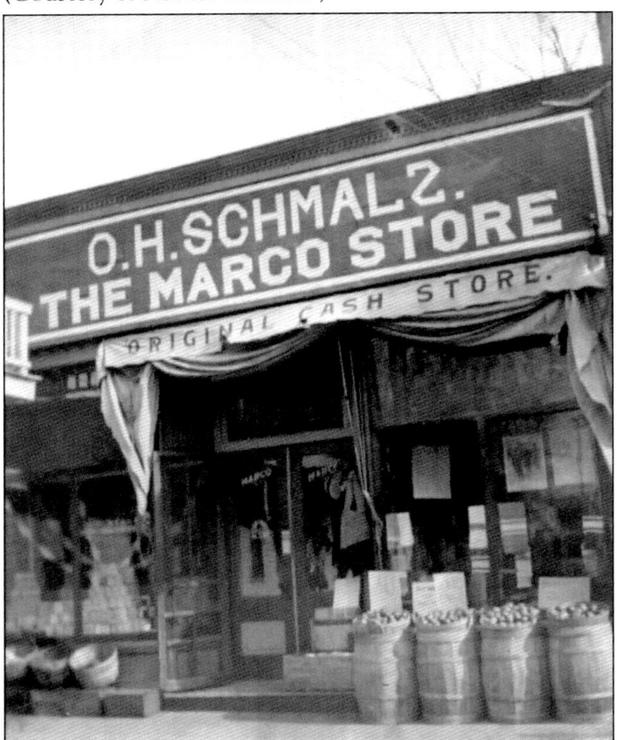

Fresh produce outside of Schmalz's Marco Store tempts shoppers along the town square in this photograph from the early 1900s. From this small-town beginning, owner Otto Schmalz's son Carl went on to a successful retailing career as chairman and chief executive officer of a major Boston department store (see chapter 5). (Courtesy of Robert Schmalz.)

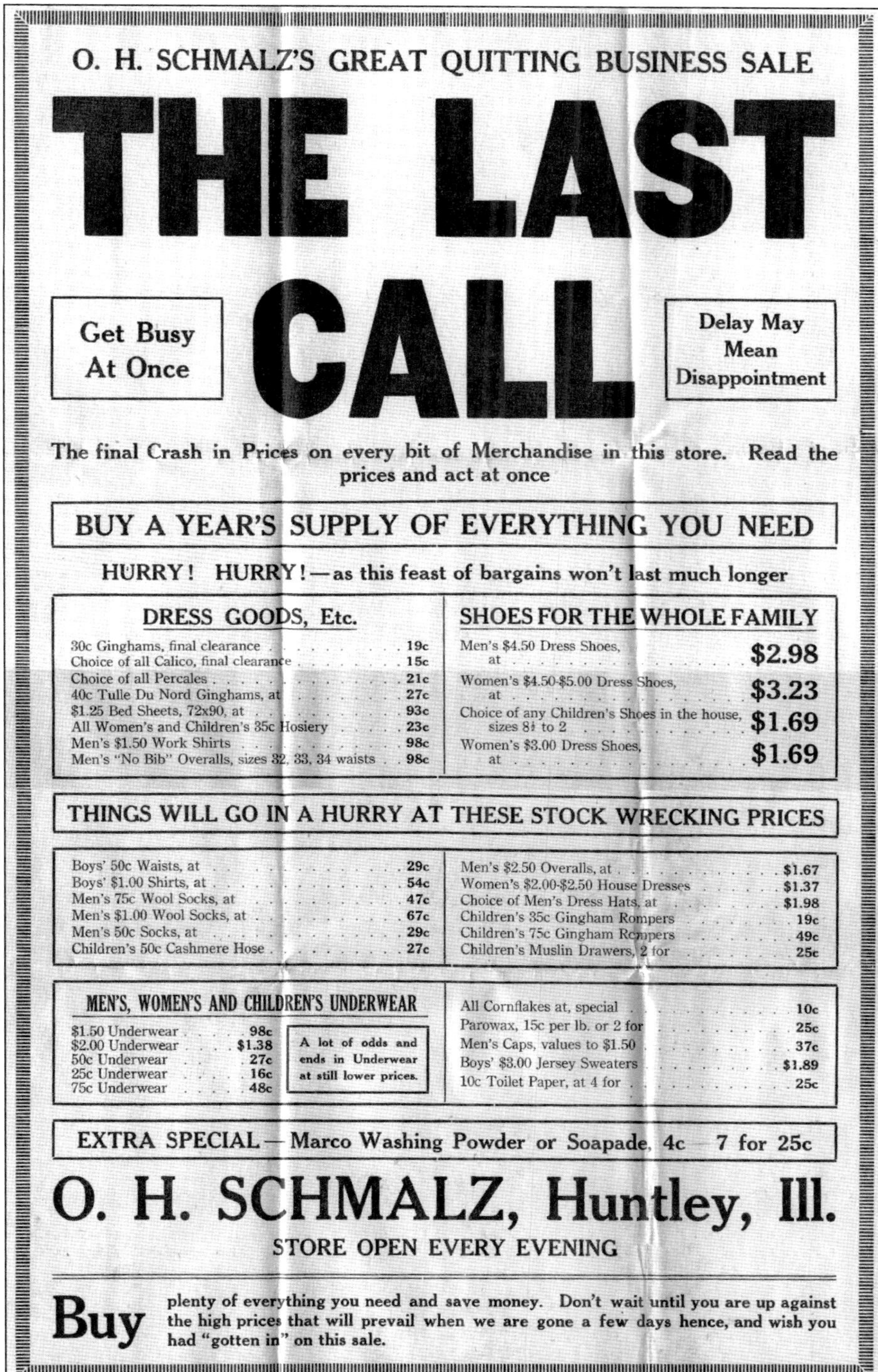

Schmalz closed his Marco Store in September 1918. His going-out-of-business advertisement featured rock-bottom prices. Men's wool socks were 47¢, and overalls were on sale for $1.67. All boxes of cornflakes were on special for 10¢ each. (Courtesy of Robert Schmalz.)

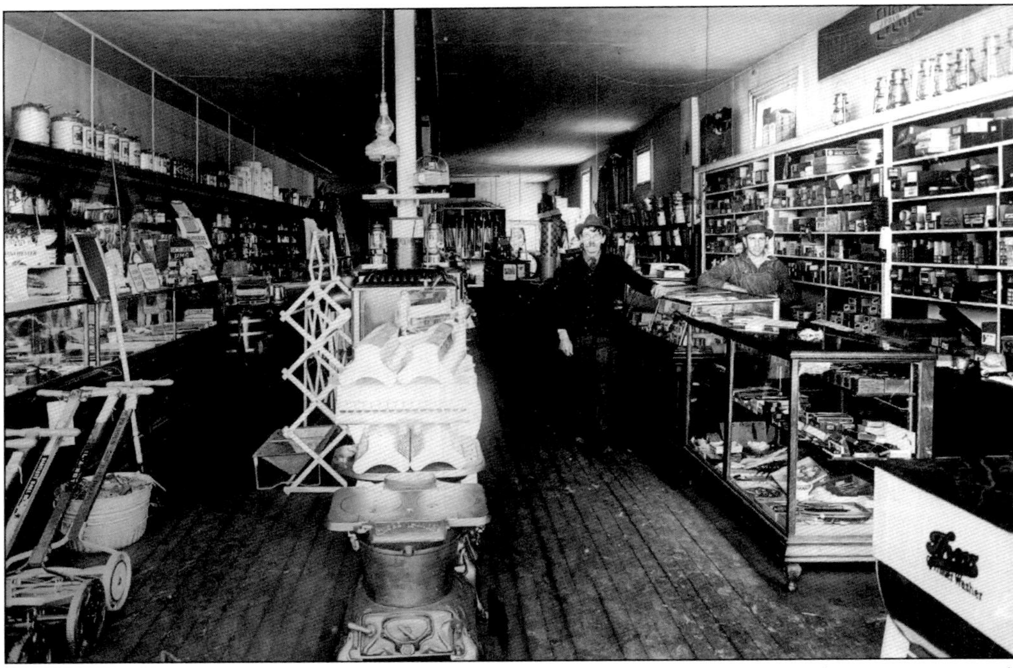

In the 1920s, Henry Heineman operated his popular hardware business in what was commonly known as the Hawley building on the west side of the town square. Pictured inside the store are Heineman (left) and his son Earl. (Courtesy of Mary Beth Manning.)

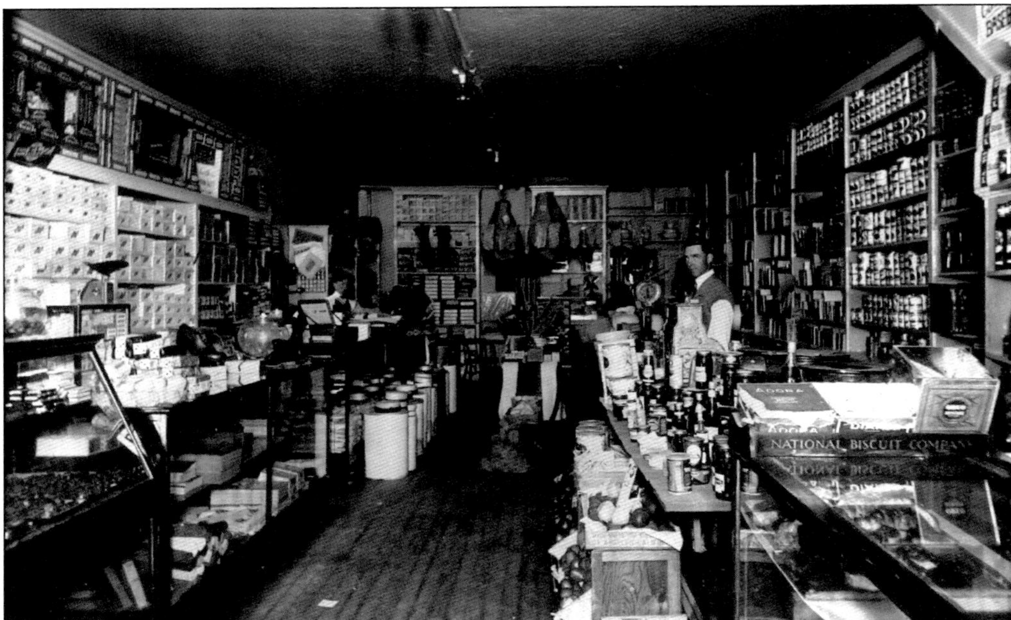

Walter Farley (1881–1966), pictured at right, apprenticed in the O. H. Schmalz General Store before going on to establish a grocery store of his own. Here he is pictured inside his Main Street store between 1910 and 1920. The clerk, barely visibly at the left rear, is Edwin Heuer. The store, later sold to Leo Dwyer, still was known as Farley's Store. (Courtesy of Mary Ellen Moerke.)

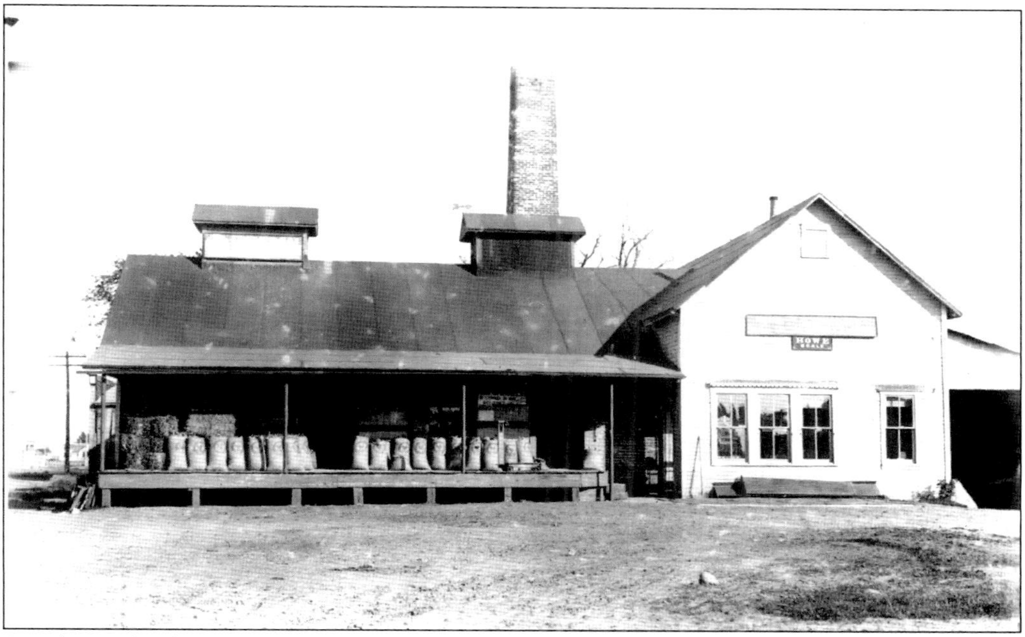

Supplying the farmer was a necessary endeavor in Huntley's early years. Enos Conley began operation of his store in 1911, selling feed, seed, and coal. This photograph was taken some time before a second story was added to the building in 1918. The business was located near the railroad tracks. (Courtesy of Tom and Barb Conley.)

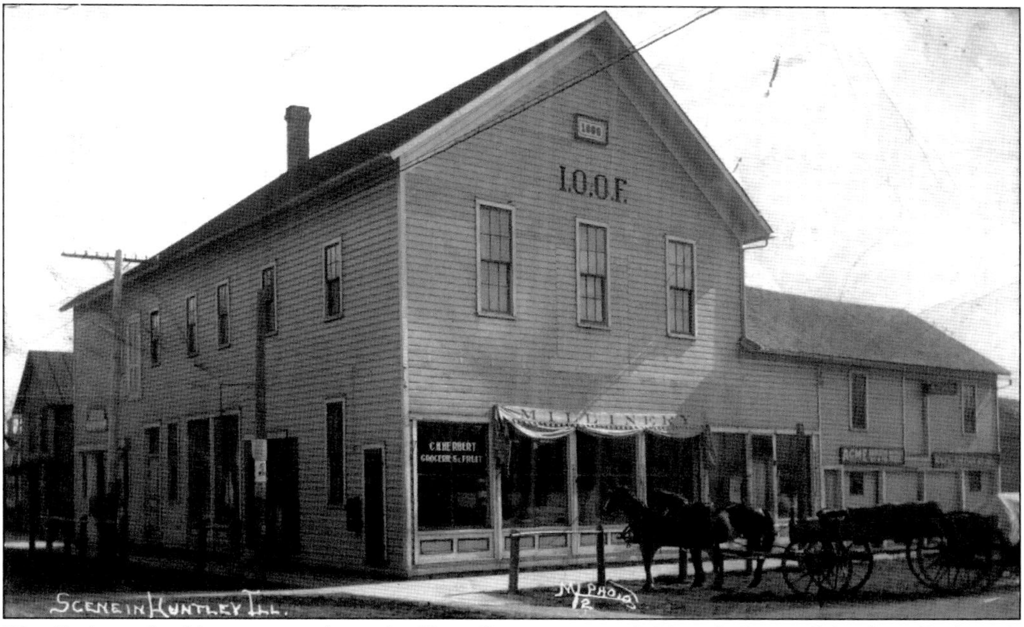

The Disbrow building, across from the First Congregational Church, housed Andrew Disbrow's wagon-making business along the Main Street side. C. H. Herbert Groceries and Fruit and a millinery shop operated at the Church Street entrance. The IOOF met in the building, which was built in 1882. The photograph dates to about 1910. (Courtesy of Noel and Lillian Hansmann.)

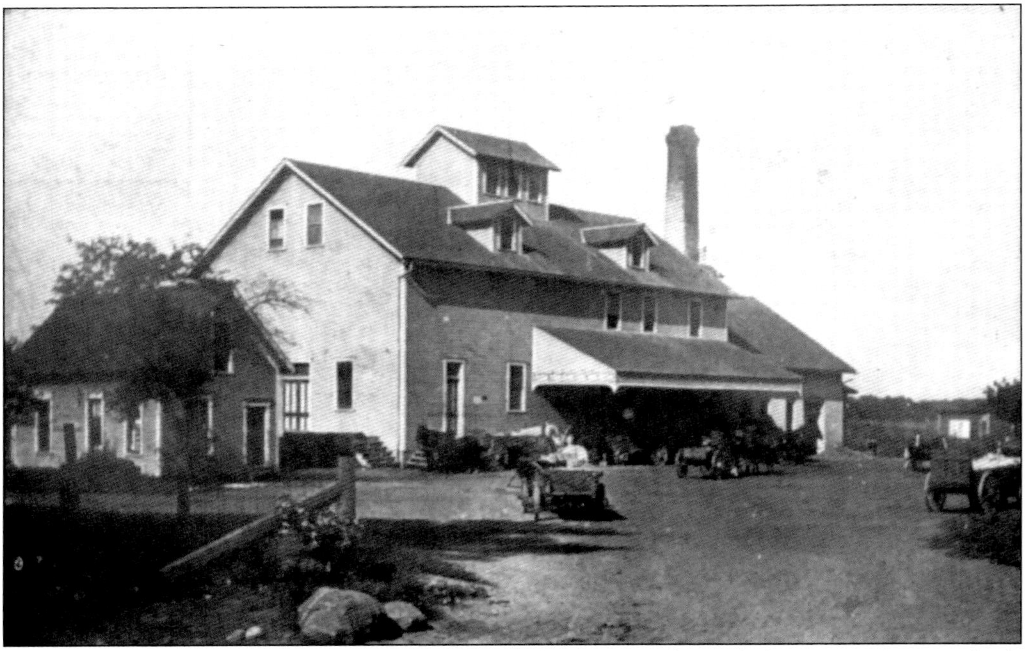

One of two mills operated by Sawyer and Kelley, this one was located along Vine Street, which is part of Route 47 today. The second mill was in town at the southwest corner of Main and Woodstock Streets. The mill processed grain brought in by local farmers. The small building on the left became part of B and B Service Station. (Courtesy of Tom and Barb Conley.)

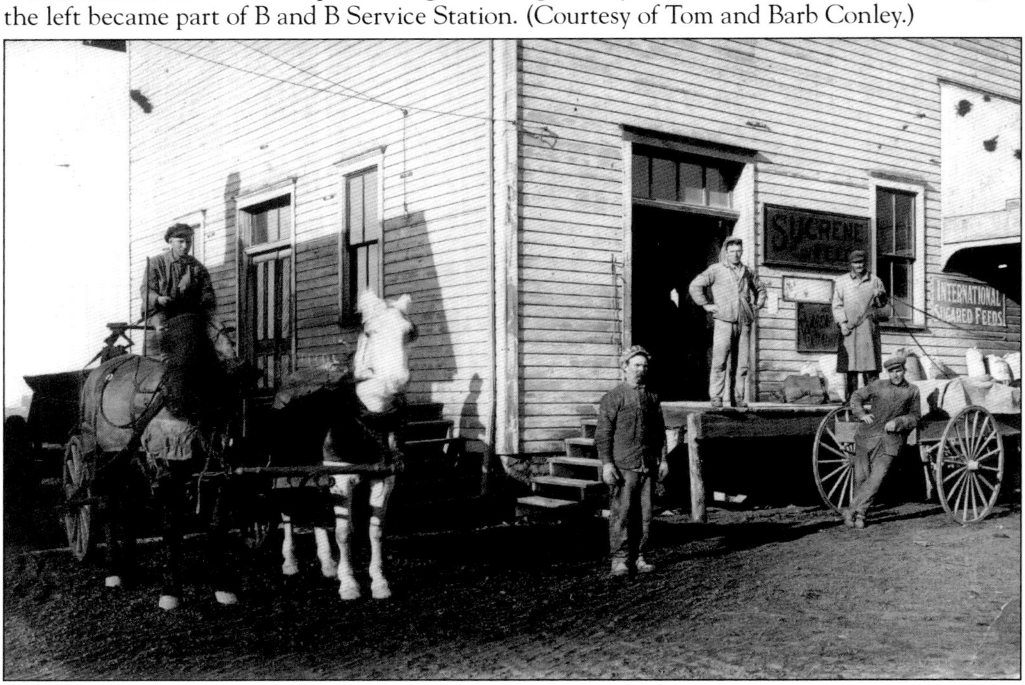

Farmers take a break from their workday around 1900 at the Sawyer and Kelley Mill, earlier known as Kelley and Hilberts Mill, on Main Street. Daniel Donahue is pictured at center in the foreground. (Courtesy of Mary Beth Manning.)

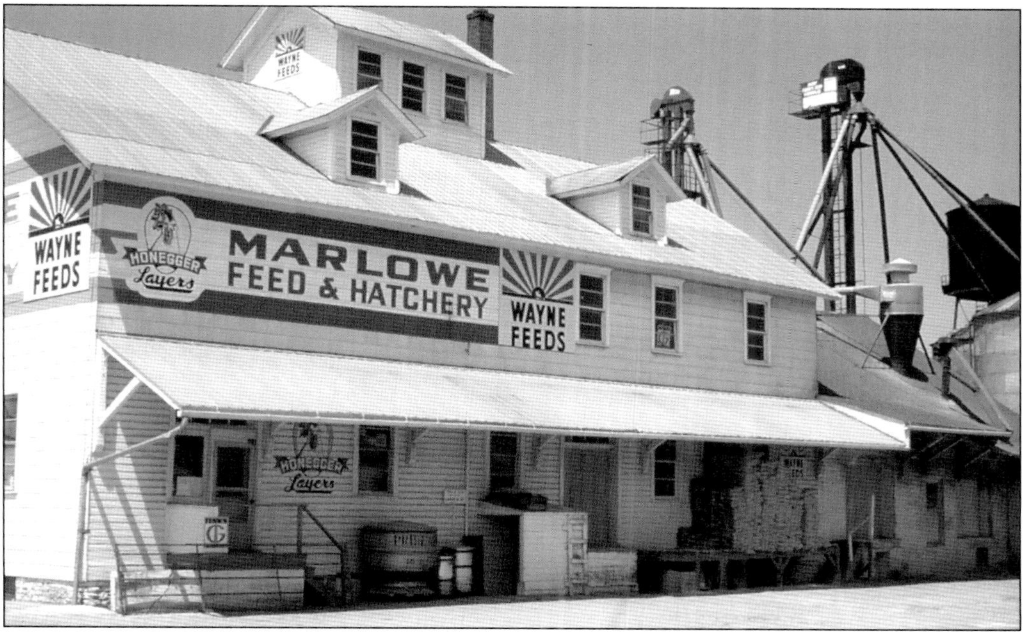

In 1945, Henry Marlowe purchased the original Sawyer and Kelley Mill on Route 47 to house his growing feed and hatchery business. Marlowe came to Huntley in 1931 as Huntley High School's first agriculture teacher. Later, because of his low salary and growing family, Marlowe started a hatchery and feed business to supplement his income. (Courtesy of Gene and Norma Lindsey.)

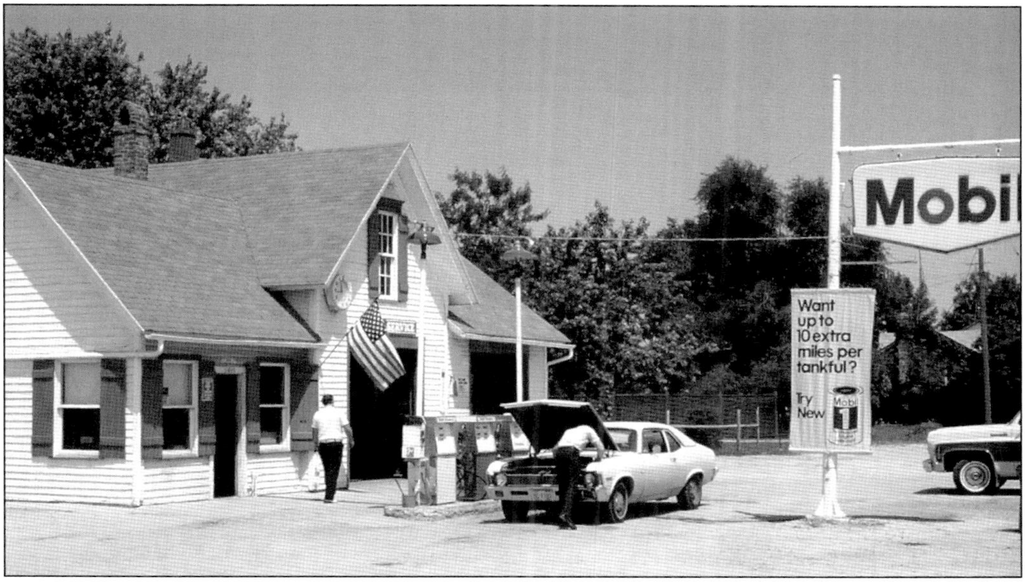

B and B Service Station operated in front of Marlowe Feed for many years. The building, seen at left in the picture of Sawyer and Kelley Mill on the previous page, was a small outbuilding that was moved in front of the mill. In the 1940s, Bill Seiler and Lyle Rubash ran the service station. Seiler recalled the difficulties in keeping cars and especially milk trucks in good running order during World War II because of the shortage of new parts and tires. (Courtesy of Gene and Norma Lindsey.)

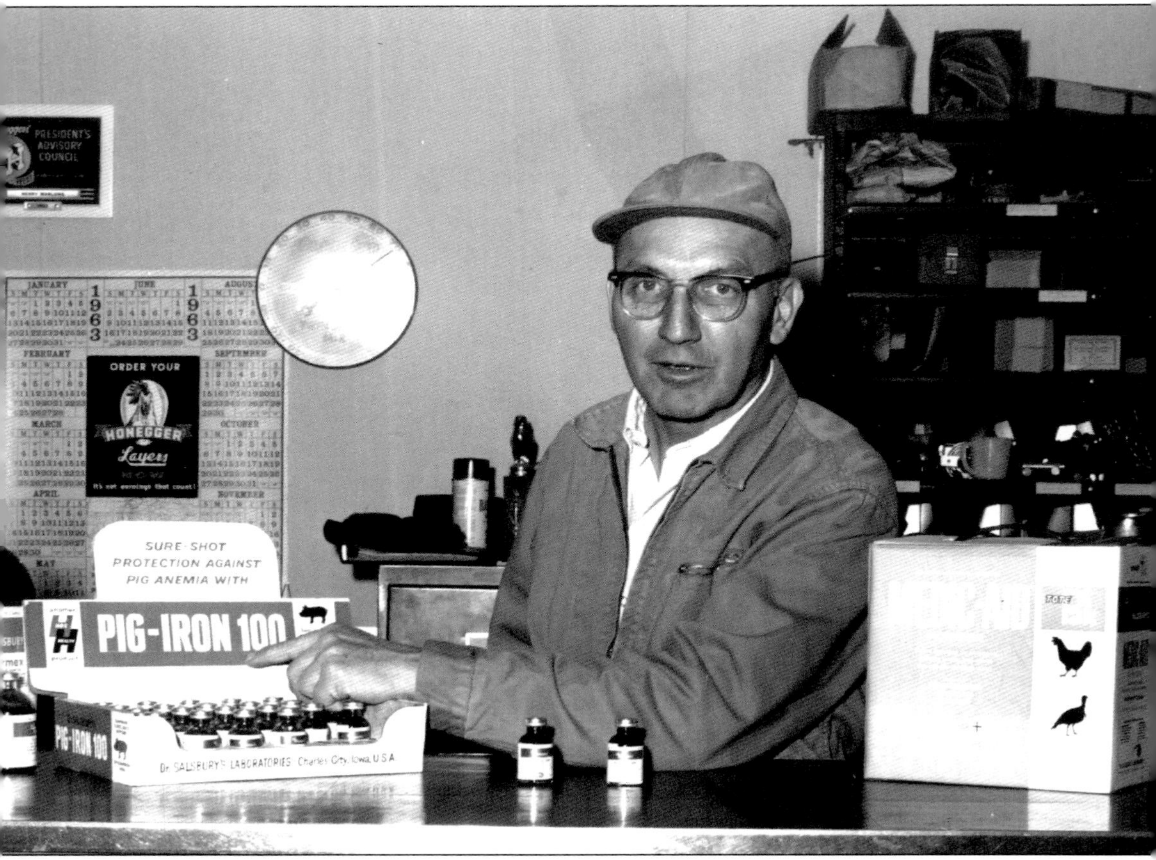

Henry Marlowe sold a variety of farm supplies at his feed and hatchery business on Route 47. Marlowe was an agriculture teacher at Huntley High School and served as a 4-H leader for 25 years. He was the director of the McHenry County Fair for 14 years and also served as president of the Illinois Poultry Hatchery Association. He and his wife, Helen, raised some 200,000 pullets a year. Marlowe also served on the Huntley Zoning Board and was active in the Lions Club and the First Congregational Church. When he died in 1984, his wife carried on the business until 2001. A School District 158 middle school is named in his honor. (Courtesy of Helen Marlowe.)

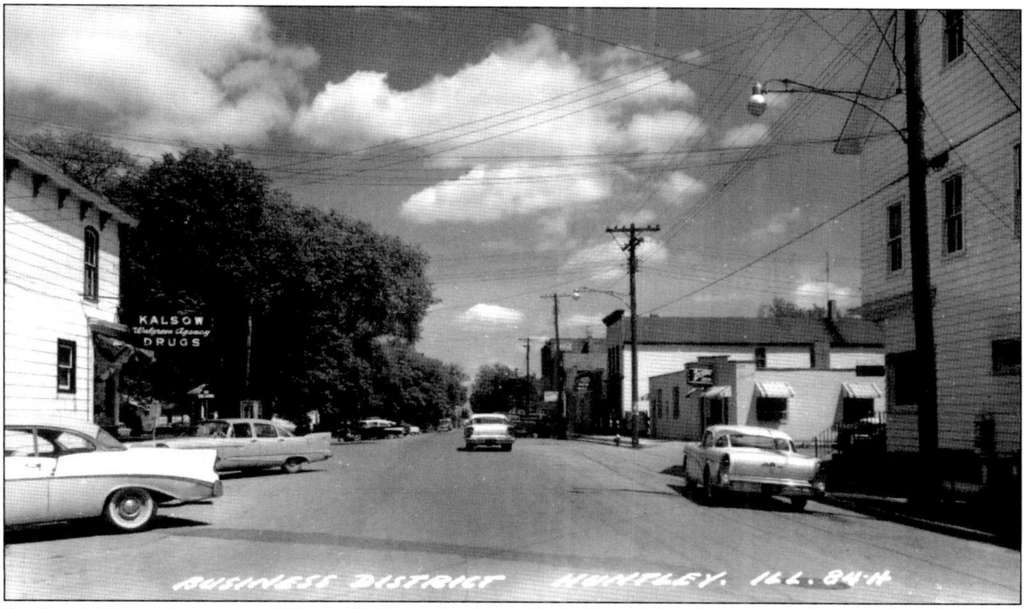

In the 1950s, pharmacist Norm Kalsow (1909–1978) moved his Walgreen's franchise drugstore to the northwest corner of Main and Woodstock Streets. At the far right corner, a barber pole is visible in the basement of what at this time was the local post office. Sam Fabri was the Huntley barber for more than 40 years. Leon Olhaber's tavern (with the awnings), the Parkside Pub, is at the right. (Courtesy of Tom and Donna Kalsow.)

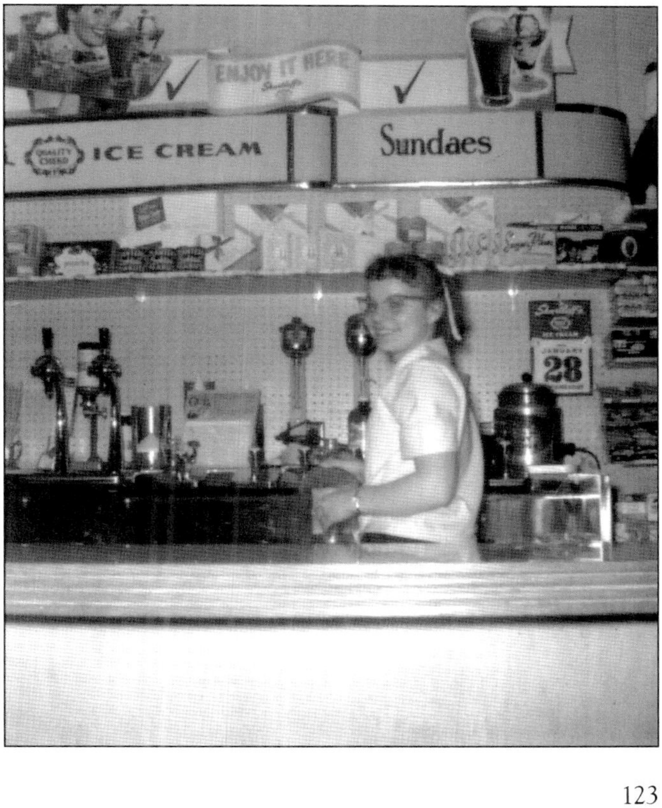

Nancy Urbach works the soda fountain at Kalsow's Drug Store in January 1959. At this time, the store was located at the west end of the town square along Woodstock Street. Advertisements for the store claimed they served "Shurtleff"s Quality Checked Ice Cream." (Courtesy of Tom and Donna Kalsow.)

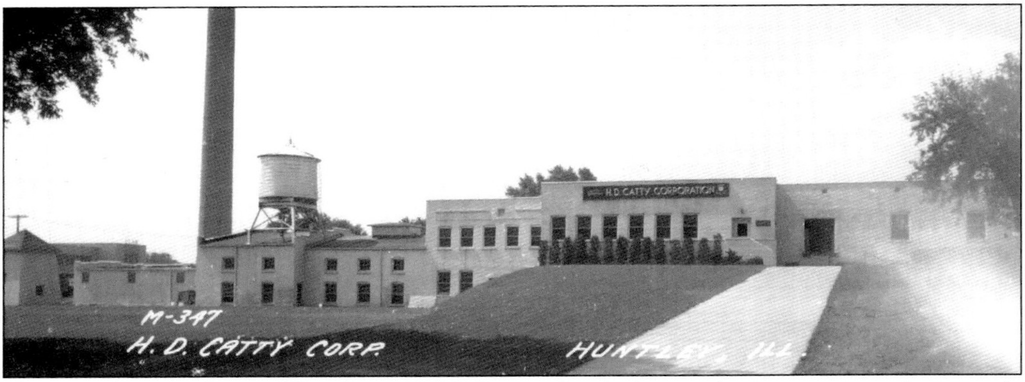

The sprawling facility at Church and Mill Streets has had several reincarnations. In its early years, it served as home to the Cornell brothers' and later Jelke's milk processing plants. In the 1930s, the Huntley Brewing Company made Bel Boy and Indian Maid beer. The William Fencil Gasket Company operated here during the early 1940s. Its last use, for more than 50 years until about 2006, was as the site of H. D. Catty Corporation, a producer of cellophane and foils for product packaging. (Courtesy of McHenry County Historical Society.)

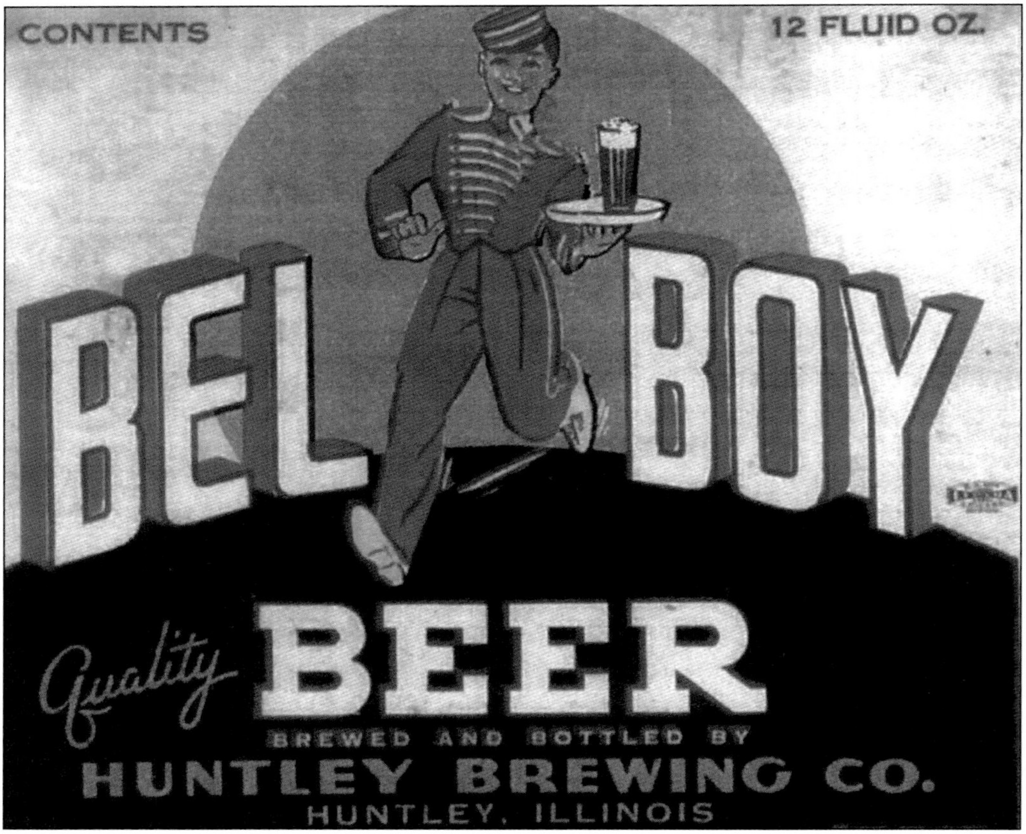

The building that once housed Cornell Brothers and Jelke's milk processing plants became the Huntley Brewing Company following the end of prohibition. The plant on south Church Street produced Bel Boy, Indian Maid, and Copperhead beer. Although the company filed for bankruptcy in 1935, this advertisement is dated 1937. (Courtesy of Tom and Barb Conley.)

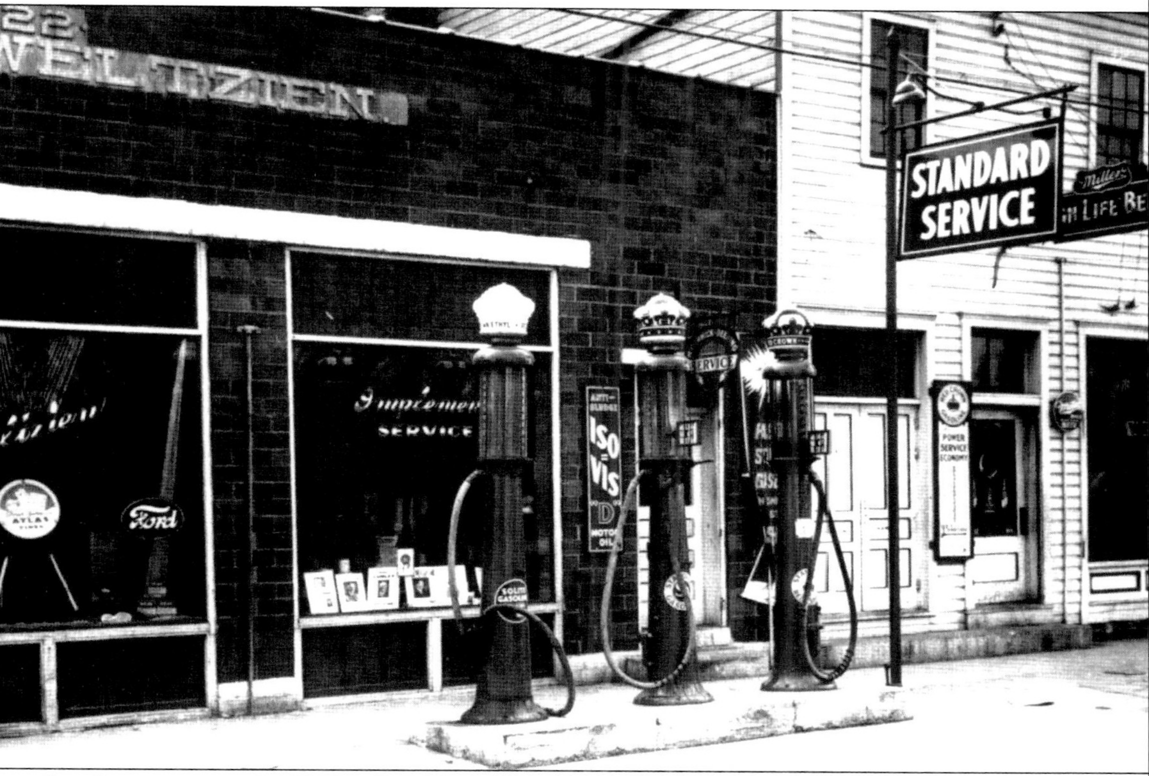

An election poster for Vincent Lumley's 1936 McHenry County state's attorney candidacy is seen in the window of the building across from the First Congregational Church. The L-shaped building, which fronts on Main and Church Streets, was built in 1922 by John F. Weltzien (1866–1949) for his Ford dealership and is still standing. Weltzien also sold Standard Oil products and McCormick-Deering farm implements and serviced the farm products. The sign on the facade showing the year and Weltzien's name were formed out of cement by Frank A. Seiler. The building to the right housed cousin Ed and Gertrude (Karsten) Weltzien's Well-Seen Restaurant and tavern. That building burned in 1939 or 1940. (Courtesy of Jim Weltzien.)

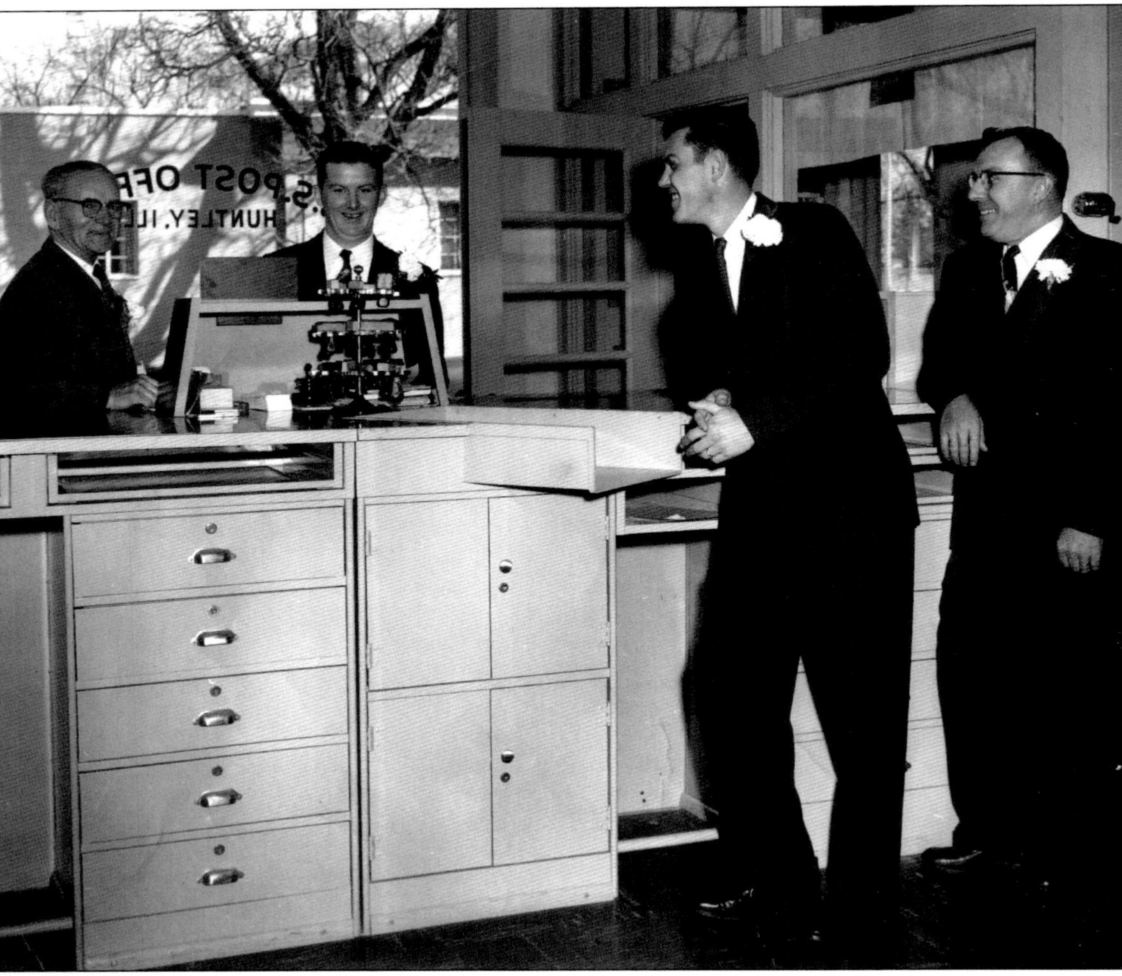

Huntley's first post office was established in 1851 with Stewart Cummings as first postmaster. Over the years, the post office was located wherever the appointed postmaster of the time happened to be in business. The first permanent post office was housed in the building at the southwest corner of Main and Woodstock Streets, known earlier as Sawyer and Kelley Mill. In 1957, Huntley's new post office on Woodstock Street was dedicated. On hand for the grand opening celebration, from left to right, are longtime rural carrier Charles Lazansky, postmaster Wayne Donahue, and clerks Dick Michelsen and Carl Walde. (Courtesy of Elgin Courier News.)

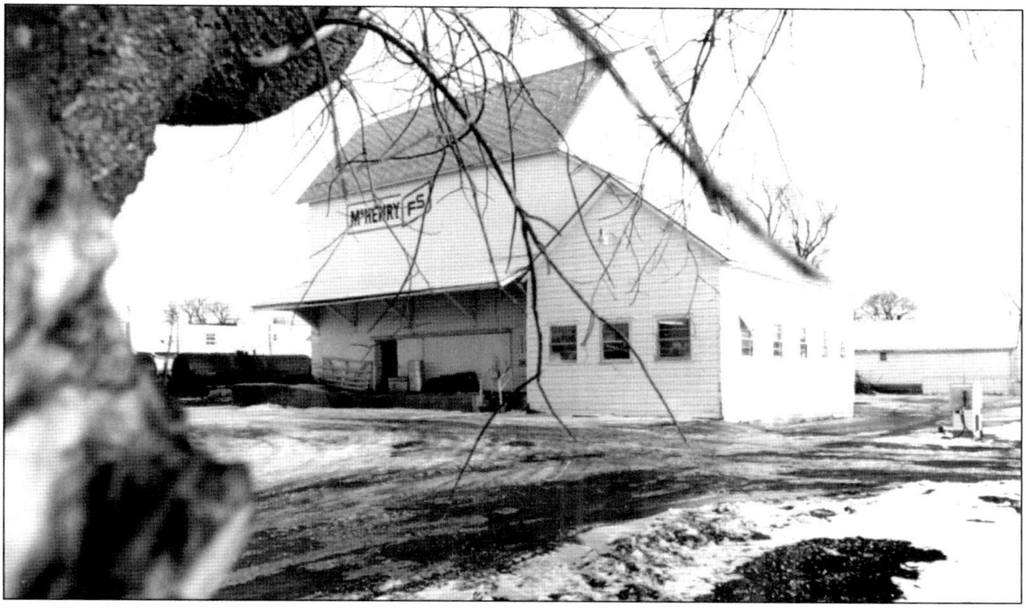

The McHenry Farm Service building stood on the sight of several former companies that had served the local farmers. The Cornell brothers had a milk processing plant at this location near the railroad tracks. Their building burned in 1907. In 1911, Enos Conley opened his feed, seed, and coal business at that spot. Conley was in business until 1960. McHenry Farm Service used the building until the 1990s. It has since been torn down. (Courtesy of Mary Beth Manning.)

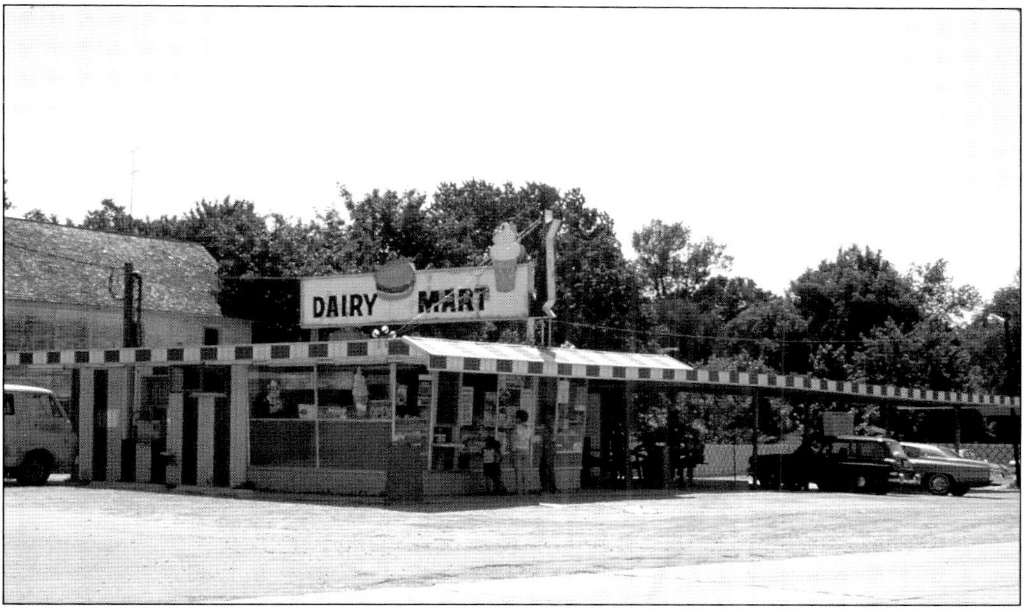

Visiting the Huntley Dairy Mart for soft-serve ice cream after a Little League baseball game or soccer match has been a tradition in the community for years. The business was opened in 1955 and has had a succession of owners, including Howard and Milly Ruth, Ruby and Helen Rehberg, Margene and Glen Mobley, and, most recently, Steve Grechis, who worked at the store as a teenager. This photograph was taken in 1976. (Courtesy of Gene and Norma Lindsey.)